IT'S ALL GOOD

A John Sinclair Reader

headpress

www.headpress.com

IT'S ALL GOOD
A John Sinclair Reader

Photographs by Leni Sinclair

AUTHOR'S NOTE

IT'S ALL GOOD collects twenty two poems and twenty two writings selected from a lifetime of work to mark my forty four years as an American poet and journalist. These poems and writings initially appeared in the following emanations:

[01] "John Sinclair" was written for the program booklet issued at BeatleCon, a massive Beatles and pop product exposition in suburban Detroit in May 1991.

[02] "friday the 13th"; [12] "everything happens to me"; [14] "in walked bud"; [16] "brilliant corners"; [28] "rhythm-a-ning"; [30] "my melancholy baby"; and [36] "monk's dream" are taken from my elongated jazz work in verse, *always know: a book of monk*.

[03] *Getting Out From Under* was written in 1965 in collaboration with Robin Eichele and published in *New University Thought*.

[04] "Consequences"; [06] "blues to you"; and [32] "Spiritual" are taken from *SONG OF PRAISE: Homage to John Coltrane*.

[05] "I Just Wanna Testify" was written in Detroit in the fall of 1978 and has never previously been published.

[07] *DKT/MC5: The Truest Possible Testimonial* was written for *Detroit Metro Times* in June 2004 in anticipation of the Detroit appearance by DKT/MC5 at the Majestic Theatre.

[08] "Ain't Nobody's Bizness"; [10] "The Screamers"; and [42] "Fat Boy" were recorded with Wayne Kramer & the Blues Scholars in Los Angeles in 1995 for the Alive Records album *Full Circle* and printed in a small collection of the same name by minimal press in Burlington VT in 1997.

IT'S ALL GOOD

[09] *The Wild One: The True Story of Iggy Pop* was written in Detroit in 1989 as a book review, but I can't remember who published it.

[11] *Sun Ra Visits Planet Earth* was commissioned by Michael Erlewine in his last days at allmusicguide online and published there in 1999. The Sun Ra interview was conducted in New York City in August 1966 and published in the *Warren Forest Sun*.

[13] *Art Ensemble of Chicago: Ancient to the Future* was written for the *Detroit Metro Times* in October 1988.

[15] *The Prophesy of Jack Kerouac* was first written as a book review of *Pomes All Sizes* for Dennis Formento at *Mesechabe* magazine in New Orleans in 1992 and expanded and revised in 2000 for publication in *Heartland Journal*.

[17] *Robert Lockwood Jr.: Blues from the Delta* was written for *Detroit Metro Times* in the summer of 1990.

[18] "21 Days in Jail"; [20] "Fattening Frogs For Snakes"; and [24] "We Just Change the Beat" are taken from my blues work in verse, *Fattening Frogs For Snakes: Delta Sound Suite*, published by Dennis Formento at Surregional Press in New Orleans in 2002.

[19] *Willie King: The Secret History of the Blues* was written in 2002 as liner notes for the Rooster Blues album *Living in a New World* by Willie King & the Liberators.

[21] *North Mississippi Hill Country Blues* was published by Tom Speed as a cover story for *[An] Honest Tune* magazine in Oxford, Mississippi in 2003.

[22] "Scuze Me While I Kiss the Sky" was commissioned by George Clinton in 1994 as the text for a recording by guitarist Ras Kente for the album *P-Funk Guitar Army* and subsequently printed as the frontispiece to the book *Voodoo Chile: An Illustrated History of Jimi Hendrix*.

[23] *The Sounds of New Orleans* was originally three sets of liner notes written for the albums *The Sounds of New Orleans, Volumes 1-2-3* that I helped produce for WWOZ Radio in New Orleans in 1994–95.

[25] *Walter "Wolfman" Washington: The Wolfman is at Your Door* was composed for Scott Barretta as a cover story for *Living Blues* magazine in 1998.

[26] "Thank You, Pretty Baby" was printed as an obituary for Allison Miner by *OffBeat* magazine in New Orleans in January 1996.

[27] *Irma Thomas: An Audience with the Soul Queen of New Orleans* was published by Cary Wolfson as a cover story for *Blues Access* magazine in the spring of 2000.

[29] *Wade in the Water* was published as a cover story in *Honest Tune* in 2006 > *Dr. John Comes Clean* was published in OffBeat in 1994.

A John Sinclair Reader

[31] *They Call Us Wild: The Mardi Gras Indians of New Orleans* was written for the *Detroit Sun* in 1976 and revised and expanded for publication by the Detroit Council of the Arts in *City Arts Quarterly* in 1988 and later in the first issue of *OffBeat* magazine in New Orleans.

[33] *Invitation to a Ghost Dance* was published in *Gambit Weekly* in New Orleans during JazzFest 1997.

[34] "If I Could Be with You" was published by the *Michigan Quarterly Review* at the University of Michigan circa 1989 and recorded with Ed Moss & the Society Jazz Orchestra in Cincinnati in January 1994 for the album of the same name issued by Schoolkids Records in Ann Arbor.

[35] *Hastings Street Grease: Detroit Blues is Alive* was written as liner notes for *Hastings Street Grease, Volume Two* issued in 1999 by Blue Suit Records.

[37] *Johnnie Bassett: Cadillac Bluesman from the Motor City* was composed as a cover story for *Living Blues* magazine in 1999.

[38] "My Buddy" was composed at Snug Harbor on Frenchmen Street in New Orleans after enjoying a brief visit with the spirit of my old friend Henry Normile at my table in the balcony overlooking the stage. Henry had been murdered in January 1979 at his apartment next door to his bar, Cobb's Corner, at Cass & Willis in Detroit, and I hadn't seen him since the funeral. I recorded the text with James Andrews & the Blues Scholars at the Howlin' Wolf club in New Orleans in 2000 and the recording was issued by SpyBoy Records on the album *Underground Issues*.

[39] *Bob Rudnick: Remembering the Righteous One* was written in October 1995 for Michael and Paige James at *Heartland Journal* in Chicago.

[40] "Hold Your Horn High" has been published on my website, www.johnsinclair.us, and recorded with the Motor City Blues Scholars for the album *DETROIT LIFE* issued by No Cover Records in November 2008.

[41][42] *Masters of War* was written for Jeremy Voas at *Detroit Metro Times* and published there in 2003 in tandem with the poem "Fat Boy" which had been recorded with Wayne Kramer and Charles Moore in 1996 for the Alive Records album *Full Circle* by John Sinclair & His Blues Scholars.

[43] *Moving Together* was written for Annie Nocenti in 2004 during the brief editorial reign of Richard Stratton at *High Times* and published in the Republican Convention issue.

[44] *It's All Good* was composed in November 1998 as the closing section of the *Viper Mad* suite premiered by the Blues Scholars at Melkweg in Amsterdam during the 1998 Cannabis Cup festivities. The text was revised and expanded and then recorded with Langefrans & Baas B for the Dutch album *Knockout* issued by the 420 Café in November 2002. After additional revision the text was published by Jeremy Voas in the *Detroit Metro Times* in 2003.

John Sinclair
Amsterdam
August 17 > September 27, 2008

THE BLUES OF JOHN SINCLAIR

By Mark Ritsema

IN THE early afternoon of a cold October's day in 2001 I pack my guitar and leave my hometown Rotterdam by train with destination Amsterdam. I feel slightly excited and nervous, for this evening John Sinclair and I will not only play for the first time together, our debut will also take place at the prestigious Crossing Border Festival. Among other guests on this three-day music and literature festival are Norman Mailer, Dave Eggers, Michael Franti & Spearhead and Echo & The Bunnymen.

But my nervousness is also caused by the fact that John and I have not rehearsed or even discussed what we are going to do during our coming half-hour appearance on stage. Poetry and guitar—so much we know, briefly communicated by telephone and e-mail, for John has arrived from the USA only this morning. But there will be time to talk it over and maybe rehearse some stuff at his hotel this afternoon before we check in at the festival.

I meet John in his hotel room a few hours later, just refreshing himself from a nap to kill the jetlag. He looks well, is in good spirits (as always) and happy to be back in Holland. These days John still lives in New Orleans and comes over to Holland once a year for a few weeks, mainly to be part of the annual Cannabis Cup events. We met three years earlier in Rotterdam where he was a prominent guest at an art manifestation about Detroit in the late sixties called *I Rip You, You Rip Me, Honey We're Going Down In History* (after Death Trip by Iggy & the Stooges).

I had written a preview of this weighty event for a local cultural magazine and participated as singer/guitarist in a Motor City tribute band. When we shook hands at a photography exhibition by his former wife Leni Sinclair (who was also brought in for the event) I told him I was interested in an interview. He agreed and this became a long and pleasant speaking session a few days later on a terrace outside a local cafe.

John—happily smoking a (Dutch quality) joint and downing espressos—was full of funny remarks while musing on his youth in Flint, Michigan where he spent his days glued to the radio that sent him jazz and rhythm & blues from the outer world; his discovery of Kerouac, Ginsberg, Burroughs and other beatniks who inspired him to become a writer and poet himself; the lessons in life he took from the Afro-American hipsters and hustlers in the backstreets of Flint in the early sixties, the figurehead of the psychedelic revolution in Detroit and America that he became in the late sixties which led to his unfortunate two and a half year imprisonment, and finally the Nixon-fueled aftermath, when it was all over and "time to get a haircut and a job".

But Sinclair never did get a job. Through the seventies and eighties in Ann Arbor and Detroit he worked with musicians and bands, produced radio shows, concerts, festivals and recordings, and contributed his writing to underground newspapers and music magazines. In the early eighties he returned to composing and performing his poetry and then left Detroit in 1991 for New Orleans, which in his opinion was the last bastion of genuine hipness and cool and easygoing people in America.

I had long run out of interview tape by the time we parted that afternoon. "'Free John Sinclair,'" John Lennon sang, but John Sinclair will not have himself barred anymore, by government nor hippie-dogmas,' I loudly opened the article that was published in the Dutch music connoisseurs magazine *Smilin' Ears* a few months later.

Back to Amsterdam 2001. We have seated ourselves in the lounge of the friendly hotel. We have become good friends through the years and have lots of stories and laughs to share. Since John is back in tolerant Amsterdam, for the first time this year he freely enjoys his beloved weed. The sweet, herbal smoke of his joint fills the lobby. He is high and relaxed and looking forward to our show tonight. More Americans, mainly visitors to the Cannabis Cup, stay in the hotel and come to shake the hand of the man who once was sentenced to ten years for the possession of two joints in their 'Land of the Free'.

My guitar is still in its case and there seems to be no hurry to get it out. Our reunion is celebrated and tonight is another story. I can't help but ask anyway: "So, what are we gonna play tonight, John?" John takes a deep drag and coughs. The heavy Amsterdam skunk seems to lower his impressive speaking voice even more when he simply replies: "We're gonna play some blues, Mark."

And we do. And it's all good!

"We're gonna play some blues." I guess I took a little music lesson there. Not that it made me start to practice B.B. King licks, but to trust the moment (and the poet)—to listen, to react and to play what you feel. After a successful *Crossing Borders* we've done countless shows as a duo all over Europe and recorded an album together in two nights: just playing some blues. We never rehearsed for a minute and hardly even make a set list before we go on stage (well, okay, we were forced to when we played in Sevilla and John's poems were translated into Spanish and projected on a screen behind us).

"We're gonna play some blues." To me this is John Sinclair in full—in the way he lives (free and careless but also intense and considerate) but even more in the way he writes. Whether he muses behind his loyal white laptop (his portable office) about the MC5 and Detroit or pays homage to Sonny Boy Williamson or Thelonious Monk, his prose, essays and poetry are always full of swing and rhythm, zestful, spontaneous and flavoured with humour. Accessible but deep and truthful. Like a bluesman he 'woke up this morning' and writes down what happens next or tells it like it is. 'No time for poetry but exactly what is,' as his lamented literary hero Jack Kerouac once put it in another way.

Since 2003 John has established himself in Amsterdam, amiably strolling by the old canals, meeting fellow hipsters of all ages and nationality, hosting his online music and talk radio shows for Radio Free Amsterdam, writing, holding office in coffee shops and freely smoking his weed. No bars, no boundaries, no borders: just playing some blues.

Rotterdam
April 2008

IT'S ALL GOOD
A John Sinclair Reader

This book is dedicated to my granddaughter
Beyonce Sinclair-Woodard

"JOHN SINCLAIR"

It ain't fair, John Sinclair
In the stir for breathing air.
Won't you care for John Sinclair?
In the stir for breathing air.
Let him be, set him free,
Let him be like you & me.

They gave him ten for two—
What else can the judges do?
Gotta, gotta, gotta, gotta, gotta,
Gotta, gotta, gotta, gotta, gotta, gotta, gotta,
Gotta, gotta, set him free.

—John Lennon
Northern Songs Ltd., 1971

THE TRUSTIES' visiting room at the State Prison of Southern Michigan at Jackson is a brutal place. Men are brought in from their cell blocks or farm assignments to spend a carefully guarded hour or two with wives, babies, older children, parents, friends or other loved ones—their only contact with the world from which they were forcibly removed upon incarceration. The ubiquitous prison guards (better known as "screws") keep close watch on all parties present to ensure that contraband is not passed, sexual liberties are not taken, extended caresses are not shared.

Some men are enjoying various types of business visits, anxiously awaited conversations with attorneys, business partners, government agents, reporters or investigators who offer some small glimmer of hope for better days ahead to these desperate inhabitants of the grim shadow world of penitentiary life.

It's early in December, 1971, and I'm sitting on the edge of my seat on the prisoner's side of one of the tables reserved for such visits, right leg wildly a-jiggle with twenty eight months' worth of pent-up energy, listening incredulously as Dennis Hayes delivers the latest of what have become almost daily reports by the disheveled young Ann Arbor attorney on developments in the ongoing battle to gain my freedom from a nine and a half to ten year prison sentence for possessing two joints of marijuana one December day five years before.

An all-out drive is on to spring me. My brief on appeal, an unprecedented challenge on several grounds to the constitutionality of Michigan's oppressive drug laws, has been heard two months previously in the Michigan Supreme

Court, and we're waiting for a decision.

The Michigan legislature is about to vote on a long-debated measure that would reclassify marijuana from a "narcotic" to a "controlled substance", making the "crime" of possessing a few joints subject to a maximum penalty of one year in jail. We've taken out a full page ad in the *Detroit Free Press*, undersigned by prominent citizens from all over the country, calling for my immediate release.

Even more urgently, a mammoth rally and concert—the latest and by far the largest of a long succession of rock & roll benefits staged regularly by my comrades in the White Panther Party (by now re-named the Rainbow People's Party) to help pay my legal expenses and keep up the steady stream of "Free John Sinclair" propaganda among our supporters and the public at large—has been scheduled for Friday, December 10 at the 14,000 seat Crisler Arena at the University of Michigan.

Every possible contact, no matter how remote, in the rock & roll and radical activist communities nationwide is being exhorted by our people to join the bill for this ultimate event, which has been designed to put irresistible pressure on the legislature to pass the new drug bill before its 1971 session is recessed for the holidays.

Old friends from the musical sector like Commander Cody & His Lost Planet Airmen, Archie Shepp & Roswell Rudd, Detroit's Contemporary Jazz Quintet, David Peel & The Lower East Side, and The Up (themselves members of the RPP) were committed to appear at Crisler Arena, along with poets Allen Ginsburg and Ed Sanders, Black Panther Party Chairman Bobby Seale, anti-war activists Rennie Davis and Dave Dellinger, radical Milwaukee priest Fr. James Groppi, Shiela Murphy from the Labor Defense Coalition in Detroit, Johnnie Tillmon of the National Welfare Rights Organization, and Jerry Rubin of the Yippies, who was planning to bring along his pal Phil Ochs, the great left wing folksinger.

Our central concern for this event was filling the arena with people—far more people than we'd ever turned out in one place before—in order to demonstrate what we now considered the enormous breadth and depth of popular support for a drastic reduction in the scope and severity of Michigan's draconian anti-marijuana laws (ten years for possession, a mandatory twenty year minimum sentence for selling or otherwise dispensing this benevolent herb) and for my immediate release from prison pending the disposition of my appeal.

A massive turnout was definitely called for, and anything less than a smash success at Crisler Arena would seriously undermine our efforts to persuade the media and the Legislature that public opinion was with us on this issue like never before.

My old friend Peter Andrews, the producer of the event and our inside man at the University of Michigan (he had been summoned from the rock & roll community to develop an Office of Major Events which would present official rock concerts at UM venues for the very first time), was particularly concerned about the attendance issue.

Peter and I had known each other since he was managing a band called SRC and I was working with the MC5; we had played many great concerts together at the Grande Ballroom in Detroit and at dancehalls and early regional rock festivals all over Michigan during 1967–69, including the legendary Saugatuck Pop Festival, the Detroit Rock & Roll Revival at the Michigan State fairgrounds, and a mammoth all-Detroit show at Olympia Stadium—then the home of the Detroit Red Wings and the place where both Elvis Presley and the Beatles had played—which drew 16,000 people in the spring of 1969 to an all day concert headlined by the MC5 and SRC.

Peter and the SRC, along with literally scores of other area bands and their managers, had contributed repeatedly to the Free John Sinclair campaign since I had been incarcerated in the summer of 1969, playing the countless benefits, rallies and free concerts organized by our people to build support for the cause and bring in money for legal and survival expenses.

Now Andrews had put his incipient career as UM's in-house concert promoter on the line, using his position to help us secure the use of the university's largest indoor facility for our most insanely ambitious effort to date, and the reports I had been receiving at Jackson indicated that he was growing increasingly nervous about our ability to secure enough top-of-the-line talent to fill Crisler Arena on December 10—a date which was growing disastrously closer every day with no true headliners yet under our sway.

Just a day or two before, Andrews had reviewed the list of projected participants proposed by my brother David, Chief of Staff for the RPP and, along with my wife Leni, my personal representative in all matters pertaining to my freedom as well as Party affairs.

Peter's lengthy experience as a concert promoter brought a frown to his face as he studied the scribbled line-up. There was no way this rag-tag assemblage of poets, political radicals, way-out jazz artists and small-time rockers would attract more than 1,000 people, let alone 14,000!

With less than a week to go before the big show, Andrews explained with a grimace, we were in serious trouble, and nothing short of a miracle of some sort would save the day. Lacking any serious headliners, he counseled, the only way we would avoid a serious public relations setback would be to drop our plans to use Crisler Arena and reschedule the event for a smaller venue—or cancel the whole thing at once.

This is where Hayes had left me at the end of our last visit, and I had lost a couple nights' sleep trying to figure out how this potential masterstroke would be salvaged before Andrews lost all patience and—reasonably enough, I was forced to conclude—decided to shut the project down rather than take the chance of having it cave in on top of him.

The indefatigable Dennis Hayes held out hope that our contacts across the country would soon be successful in enlisting the participation of sympathetic rock stars who were familiar with my case, but I was in a blue funk contemplating the consequences of a collapse and wouldn't stomach the slightest shred of phony optimism.

All was quickly being lost—without a powerful prod from the great unwashed public demanding my release, the Legislature would let their session lapse once again without bringing the drug reclassification bill to a decisive vote, and I'd languish helplessly in prison for another year before we'd get a chance like this again.

At this point I was quite literally at my wits' end. The long months of plotting and scheming to mount an effective campaign for my release, so close to paying off in a big way, were about to go down the drain with the rest of my hopes and aspirations.

We had decided early on that only the most relentless program of constantly increasing pressure on the media, the courts, the Legislature, and the general public would force a positive turn of events, and the "Free John Now" rally at Crisler Arena had seemed such a perfect stratagem. We would demonstrate the size and strength of our outlaw culture and use it against the forces that had meant to suppress it by locking up people like myself.

Instead of recanting and 'reforming' myself under the ultimate pressure of a long prison sentence, I would be freed by sticking to my principles, fighting back, and winning the support of thousands of hippies, activists, and liberals led by a cultural vanguard of poets, rock & roll bands, jazz musicians, psychedelic artists and underground journalists. It was like a sheet of White Panther Party propaganda come to life!

As a political prisoner, a radical cultural and political activist jailed and held without bond as a 'danger to society', I had been selected by the established order to be made an example of for the rest of my generation. Potential refugees from the straight and narrow who might have been tempted to join the revolution would certainly have to think twice, the authorities reasoned, now that they'd drawn the line.

Ten years for two joints! Why shit, nobody in their right mind would keep smoking marijuana, freaking to rock & roll, wearing jeans and long hair, throwing off the shackles of conventional morality and fighting against racism and the war in Vietnam after they saw what happened to that loud-mouth Sinclair. Get it straight, kids: you can't get away with that shit here in the USA!

Conversely, my entire public career to that point had been dedicated to the opposite proposition—that you could get away with defying the way things were supposed to be…and have a natural ball doing it. As a cultural activist on and around the Wayne State University campus in the mid sixties I had organized countless jazz and poetry events; established a large collective of weirdos with a base at the Artists' Workshop and a beatnik housing cooperative west of campus; published an endless stream of mimeographed poetry and jazz magazines, books and pamphlets; printed and passed out 'free poems' on the streets; wrote for and edited underground tabloids; started a Detroit chapter of LEMAR to demand the legalization of marijuana; suffered arrests for possessing and distributing marijuana; served six months in the Detroit House of Correction on the second bust, and came out of DeHoCo on August 5, 1966 to find an incipient mass movement of long-haired rock & roll dope smokers and acid heads about to burst upon the scene.

This seemed to provide proof that my friends and I were on the right track, and I quickly redoubled my commitment to causing trouble for the status quo by attempting to link up the early psychedelic literary/jazz vanguard—inspired by Jack Kerouac and Allen Ginsburg, Charlie Parker and Thelonious Monk, John Coltrane and Ornette Coleman, Charles Olson and William Burroughs, Malcolm X and Fidel Castro—with the rising tide of young would-be drop-outs weaned on the Beatles and the Rolling Stones, tuned in to Timothy Leary and Stanley Mouse and the Mothers of Invention, tripped out on marijuana and LSD, and already exploring the possibility and actual practice of living a life centered on the daily pursuit of "rock & roll, dope, and fucking in the streets".

During the three years between my release from DeHoCo and my incarceration in the state prison system on July 25, 1969, I blazed a trail of boundless energy across the skies of Detroit and southeastern Michigan to establish myself variously in the imaginations of my fellow citizens. To people my own age (I turned twenty five in 1966) and class (white, college graduate) as a demonstrably insane renegade from the American Dream; to our elders and authorities of every stripe as the garish embodiment of everything they were committed to eradicating from American life before their children, their very hopes and dreams, would be infected; and to the best and brightest of the coming generation between fifteen and twenty five as perhaps an interesting character with some wild ideas, a lot of nerve, a feverish vision of the way things could and should be in modern life, and a frenetic yet unshakable commitment to enacting that vision on as many fronts as would prove humanly possible.

Inspired by the writings and practice of the poet Ed Sanders to mount a "Total Assault on the Culture" and by the Black Panther Party to wage it "By Any Means Necessary", I wrote inflammatory screeds for scores of underground papers; mounted a serious constitutional challenge to the state's marijuana laws in response to a third bust in 1967; organized and promoted regular series of rock & roll benefits, free concerts and multimedia events throughout lower Michigan; appeared at schools, universities and in the media as a spokesman for the cultural revolution and the legalization of weed; cofounded the White Panther Party as a political vehicle through which white youth could openly express solidarity with the black liberation movement and the struggle of the Vietnamese people while smoking dope and dancing to rock & roll; and wrote, edited and published poems, books, magazines and pamphlets exhorting young people to take ever more direct action against the social structure they were coming to hate and fear.

But it was my association with the MC5 that cemented together all the disparate elements of my activity and enabled me to begin to build a mass base of support for my ideas. First, as a close friend of lead singer Rob Tyner and then as the band's manager, I worked closely with the MC5 to develop the band's musical and performance potential until, in the summer of 1968, everything fell into place and the MC5 began to emerge out of Detroit as the most exciting rock & roll band in the world.

What made them unique in the history of the music was their explosive fusion of basic rock & roll energy with space-age electronics, the wild abandon of postmodern jazz, the supersonic stagecraft of rhythm & blues, and a series of powerful, twin-guitar driven compositions carrying lyrics that spoke insistently to the widest concerns of the day—all delivered with big attitude and a belligerent, flamboyantly fearless stance against the established forces of law and order.

Kick Out The Jams, Motherfucker! / Come Together! / The Motor City Is Burning! / Human Being Lawnmower! / Call Me Animal! / Let Your Love Come Down! An MC5 performance circa 1968–69 was a demented amalgam of rock & roll dance, Pentecostal revival meeting, political rally on acid, and potential sex orgy…with almost all the participants still fully dressed. You came to see a band and went home a budding cultural revolutionary, ready to spread the word to people at your school or in your little town that there was finally an alternative to the square rat race concept they'd always been programmed to embrace.

Week after week we played in high school gymnasiums, teen clubs, community centers, psychedelic ballrooms, coffeehouses, churches, parks and fields—never in bars—but anywhere teenagers and the hipper college students would go, we would play for them and make more and more converts to our cause.

After a year of steady advance, including a record contract with Elektra Records and a first release—recorded live at Detroit's Grande Ballroom—which met with considerable national acclaim, the MC5 was poised to become an incendiary international sensation, a rocket shot straight through the heart of the music industry to explode in the minds of millions of potential followers and bring them into the burgeoning revolutionary ranks.

A dispute with Elektra Records over their refusal to defend record store clerks who had been arrested for selling the 5's album—coupled with their subsequent erasure of the album's liner notes and censorship of the recording itself—led to a parting of the ways after only six months of contractual bliss, but the band was quickly picked up by Jerry Wexler at Atlantic Records, given a better contract and a bigger advance, and rushed into GM Studios in Detroit to begin work on a second LP between tour dates.

Then my marijuana case—now two and a half years old and long delayed by pre-trial challenges to the constitutionality of the law itself—finally came up for trial in Detroit Recorder's Court. The 'dispensing' charge (I'd given two joints to an undercover policewoman in December 1966), which carried a mandatory twenty year minimum sentence, was dropped by the prosecution the day before the trial was to start; I was tried and convicted of possession of the same two joints, sentenced to nine and a half to ten years in prison, denied bond on appeal, and shipped off to Jackson for processing before being transported 600 miles in chains to Marquette Branch Prison in the Upper Peninsula several weeks later.

I served a year in Marquette and was sent back to Jackson as a 'disciplinary problem' as a result of my efforts to help a group of black inmates organize themselves to demand better educational and rehabilitative opportunities from the prison administration.

Meanwhile I'd also been charged by the federal government with conspiring to place an explosive device in the doorway of a clandestine CIA recruiting office just off the University of Michigan campus in September 1968.

The charge was lodged against me by Nixon's Justice Department in the fall of 1969 and served the government as an excuse to deny my repeated applications to be released on bond pending the outcome of my appeal. (My conviction was ultimately reversed and the marijuana laws declared unconstitutional by the Michigan Supreme Court in March 1972.)

Pre-trial hearings in what we termed the 'CIA Conspiracy' case began in September 1970 with William Kunstler, Leonard Weinglass and Detroit attorney Hugh M. 'Buck' Davis heading the defense effort. A motion to discover if any evidence against us had been obtained by means of illegal wiretaps led to a government admission that one of my codefendants, Larry 'Pun' Plamondon, had been overheard and recorded on a phone that had been tapped by the Justice

Department without a warrant in the interest of what they called 'national security'.

Federal District Judge Damon Keith agreed with us that the US Constitution expressly prohibited warrantless intrusions into citizens' privacy and ordered the government to turn over to the defense the logs of the disputed conversation or dismiss its charges against us.

John Mitchell's Justice Department refused to do either one and challenged Judge Keith's ruling by appeal to the Sixth US Court of Appeals in Cincinnati and, subsequently, to the US Supreme Court, where Keith was ultimately upheld by an 8-0 vote (newly appointed Justice William Renquist abstaining because he had been one of the drafters of the Justice Department's 'national security wiretap' program). The government then dismissed its case against us rather than reveal the target of its illegal wiretap.

Throughout my long struggle against the marijuana laws, the narcotics police, the courts, the prison administration and now the federal government, I had steadfastly refused to back down in any way and instead continued to confront the enemy at every turn.

My comrades in the Party and our friends throughout the community worked without rest to develop an ever-growing base of supporters, utilizing my case as an inarguable example of state repression of the cultural revolution and a natural rallying point for all of those opposed to such reprehensible activity.

Now the struggle was at a crucial point: we were on the offensive in a big way, public opinion was beginning to shift toward our position at last, and all we had to do was make the rally at Crisler Arena into a smashing success—14,000 people gathered in one place to demand freedom for John Sinclair!

The victory that had seemed so near was starting to drift inexorably out of our grasp, and I was in an irascible mood while I waited for Hayes to join me at the visiting room table for our meeting. I had been trying for two days to prepare myself for the worst, and I fully expected Hayes to tell me that the whole thing had been called off.

Yet the young attorney was wearing an almost maniacal grin on his face as he bounded toward our table, bubbling with an enthusiasm I couldn't bear to countenance in my depressed state. "What's the deal, Hayes?" I greeted him with a sneer, "and what the fuck are you grinning about, for chrissakes?"

I should be able to recall every word of what Hayes said, because it rocked me down to my feet, but all I can recall is the sense of utter incredulity which filled my being when I heard him say that John Lennon and Yoko Ono would be coming out with their pal Jerry Rubin for the rally on December 10. John Lennon? I couldn't believe my ears, and I turned on Hayes with barely suppressed rage.

"Don't bullshit me, you son-of-a-bitch! How can you do this to me? I'm strung out enough just being in this godforsaken place for the past two and a half years, and now you guys think you can just tell me anything to try to make me feel better.

"I'm not going for it for one minute, and I wish to hell you'd stick to what's going on with the concert instead of trying to lay this ridiculous fantasy trip on me. Don't fuck with my mind, you rat bastard, and tell me right now exactly how messed up things really are with this thing."

Hayes seemed to back up a few paces, his hands held palms out before his face as if to ward off an unanticipated blow from his frantic *pro bono* client. "No shit, man," he pleaded, "Jerry Rubin called to confirm it, and get this: Lennon's writing a song about you that he's gonna play at the rally! Rubin's already heard some of it at Lennon's place, and he was raving about how great it was.

"This is going to blow the whole thing wide open—there's no way they're gonna be able to keep you in here after Lennon comes out to Ann Arbor for the concert, man!"

This struck me as even more preposterous. I'd heard that Rubin had been hanging out with John and Yoko in New York City, showing them around the scene and introducing them, at their request, to movement people of every stripe. Word was that Lennon was about to make a move himself, and everyone was waiting breathlessly to see which way the popular ex-Beatle would go.

But come to Ann Arbor? To free John Sinclair? And write a song about my case to boot? Bullshit! I simply could not believe it, and I gave Hayes a pretty hard time, demanding some kind of proof of Lennon's intentions before I'd accept the news that everything was gonna be alright.

Hayes came back the next day with a tape. On the tape was the actual voice of John Lennon, sending revolutionary greetings and pledging his support in unequivocal terms. Then he sang some of the song: "It ain't fair, John Sinclair / In the stir for breathing air / Let him be, set him free / Let him be like you and me."

The little electrodes in my brain cracked and sizzled as it began to sink in: Lennon is really coming out to Ann Arbor to try to get me out of here! It's going to work! These bastards can't possibly keep me under lock and key after December 10! YIPPIE!!!

An announcement was authorized by the Lennon camp, and the Rainbow People's Party called a press conference to drop the bomb on an unsuspecting public. All 14,000 tickets, which I had insisted remain priced at $3.00, sold out within a matter of hours, and every television news show, radio station and newspaper in the state rushed to bring its audience every detail of the coming Lennon visitation.

Stevie Wonder called up and asked if he could bring his band out, at his own expense, to play at the rally. Bob Seger's management finally jettisoned its stand against the singer's participation in the event, and he came on board with his backing band, old friends David Teegardin and Skip VanWinkle.

Once-skeptical hippies and apolitical Beatles fans all over Michigan were knitting their brows trying to figure out how to get tickets to the show, while radio station WABX-FM laid plans to broadcast the entire event live from Crisler Arena.

Channel 56, Public Television in Detroit, wanted to videotape the concert for a later broadcast, and New York called to say that Lennon would be bringing his personal film and recording crew with him to document the proceedings for a possible film of the affair.

Everything was falling irresistibly into place, and my spirits—caged for so long in a prison cell—were soaring beyond measure. I didn't know exactly how soon my nightmare would be over, but now it was going to be just a simple matter of time—and not very much more of it at that!

On December 9 the other shoe fell when the Michigan state legislature brought the drug reclassification bill to a vote—and passed it! Under the new legislation, possession of marijuana would be reduced to a misdemeanor with a maximum one year sentence; convictions for sales of marijuana would bring a four year max; and the new law would take effect on April 1, 1972.

Lennon had put the key in the lock, and the legislators were turning it. My attorneys renewed my petition for bond on appeal, a necessary technicality, and soon I'd be a free man at last!

The rally was held on December 10, a Friday night, and I tossed and turned in my bunk while pressing my ear to the little portable radio in my hand to hear the WABX broadcast from Crisler Arena through the static and distance which separated me from the people who were trying to get me out of prison.

Following an emotion-drenched weekend in the Lily Farm barracks, where I had been stationed in the trusty division at Jackson after twenty seven months of hell in a cell, I was called out to the visiting room to meet a triumphant Dennis Hayes.

This time I offered no resistance when he told me my brother was on his way up to the state capitol at Lansing to post a $2,500 appeal bond, and I'd be out by nightfall—on my way home to my wife, my baby daughters (Sunny, four and a half, and Celia, almost two), my wonderful parents, my beloved political comrades at the RPP commune, my many friends in the rock & roll community, and my thousands of ecstatic supporters.

The hours dragged by a minute at a time as I returned to the barracks and began packing up my meager possessions. Nightfall came and I was still waiting for the word. Finally the phone rang in the barracks and I heard a guard call out those magic words: "Sinclair, get your shit, you're going home!"

I was driven up to the big prison walls and escorted into the reception area for a final round of formalities before the front gates opened and I staggered out into the arms of my wife and family.

Peter Andrews was waiting outside the prison compound to whisk me away in an impeccable Bentley limousine, the same car that'd been used to transport the Lennons from the airport to Ann Arbor and back over the weekend, and I worked my way slowly to the Bentley through a small army of friends and comrades, laughing and crying hysterically in the throes of my new-found freedom.

A television news reporter thrust a microphone in my face to ask me that most inane of all questions: "How do you feel now, Mr Sinclair? And what's your position on marijuana now that you've been released?"

"I wanna go home and smoke some joints, man!" I roared—and that's exactly what I did:

Lots of 'em!

Detroit
May 1, 1991

#51

"friday the 13th"

for Mike Liebler

any day
can be the lucky one,
or the one with your number

written all over it, 123
507 in the poet's case,
walking out

the front door
of the penitentiary,
8:30 p.m.

14 years ago today,
2 times 7 years the cycle
of struggle, to make it through

in one piece, on the yard
or in these streets, "anyone
who can pick up a frying pan

owns death," burroughs said,
& sometime in new york city
coming home from the recording studio,

walking up to his front door,
john lennon with a gun
stuck in his face,

oh,
oh, sweet giant of song,
with heart of huge dimension

& eyes deep in the sky,
there has to be a day
when each of us must pass

beyond this tedious sphere,
to enter some wondrous place
of which we do not know

IT'S ALL GOOD

whether we're ready or not,
some other place or space
out of time

where no punk with a weapon
will ever press you again
or blow off your face

out of the depths
of his madness, no one
will hold us

against our will
in a cell with bars in front
& back, 6 feet by 4 feet

by 8 feet high,
no one will take us
out of our natural lives

& send us away from here
by means of some murderous fantasy
in which we are denied

 everything we have lived for—
oh please let us die
at the end of our own time

& not before, free
in our world of strife,
let us have life

as long as we can
& please, let there be men
like monk & john lennon

to share of their hearts
& light up our ways
as long as we may live

Detroit,
friday, december 13 > december 30, 1985

GETTING OUT FROM UNDER

The Detroit Artists' Workshop Society

By Robin Eichele & John Sinclair

DETROIT, DESPITE all its pretensions, has been artistically 'dead' for longer than most people here want to admit. Young artists of all disciplines—music, poetry, painting, photography, filmmaking—have made it a necessary point in the past generation or two to get out of Detroit as soon as possible for the vital centers of US *kulchur*—New York, San Francisco, even Chicago—because the Detroit milieu is if anything anti-artistic.

Detroit has really been nowhere, as the saying goes: one halfway decent theatre, one museum, a decaying jazz scene, no community of poets, painters, writers, anything.

A group of young Detroit artists—at first primarily poets and musicians, most of us students at Wayne State University—got together in the late summer of 1964 and decided to do something to make Detroit a viable and vital place to live and work.

A number of us, having found Detroit an inhabitable urban environment with little of the intense pressure of New York City or the residual hangers-on of former centers of activity like San Francisco and Chicago, had made various efforts to provide a focal point for Detroit artistic activity in the past: poet George Tysh's Touchstone was a storefront gallery and meeting place that failed to survive due to lack of strong support, and more recently Tysh and painter Carl Shurer operated the Red Door Gallery, a center of avant garde film showings, exhibitions of paintings, and general hanging out that ceased operation with Shurer's departure for Greece in June 1964.

The people who had been active in these ventures formed the nucleus of a new group, the Artists Workshop Society, a totally cooperative organization designed and structured to draw upon the resources of every participating individual in order to perpetuate itself—and promote community thinking on an artistic and personal level—through its own cohesive community nature.

Two artists who had not been around to take part in the previous activity met in June of 1964 and immediately began looking for ways to draw the generally dispersed artistic community back together into an effective, working group. Charles Moore, a musician, and John Sinclair, a poet and writer involved in the Detroit jazz scene, were at first concerned with providing a place for musicians to rehearse and present formal concerts of the new jazz music.

As we talked to more and more people about our plan, we found a large (although rather cynical) interest, and our original conception of a Detroit Artists Workshop grew broader as more of our friends and associates offered ideas and support for its implementation.

On the November 1, 1964 the Society presented the first in what has become a series of weekly Sunday afternoon events, which integrate jazz, poetry readings, and exhibitions of graphic art and are presented with no admission charge to interested members of the community.

Moore's group, the Detroit Contemporary 5, donated its time and talent for free concerts, the readings were done by Workshop members and supporters, and Detroit photographers and artists displayed their work—all for the benefit of the community rather than financial remuneration.

The group wanted more than this surface unity, however: our goal was (and is) to pull together the active and potential artists in the Detroit area into a working, cooperative community of human beings that would offer to each individual an open, supportive, artistic environment.

Having become thoroughly disenchanted with the established methods of 'dealing with' art, we determined to create our own human milieu by working as independently as possible within the economic framework the established order left us.

We saw Detroit as essentially virgin ground—there was everything to be done, the raw material was at hand, and we started working to exploit the situation in the best interests of every artistically-oriented individual in the community.

With the physical forces in operation, a spiritual focal point quickly evolved. The Sunday programs began to draw upwards of 100 people weekly, almost wholly from the peripheral student-beatnik-artist community that already loosely existed. No outside advertising was done—in the first place, we had no money for an advertising budget, in the second, we had seen too many times what havoc the average 'dilettante' intellectual could wreak.

The people in the immediate vicinity were informed of the Workshop's doings by mimeographed flyers announcing each week's program, passed out by members to their friends in the area. The Workshop had come into being, after all, as an emergency measure to help salvage the salvageable; 'outsiders', e.g. entertainment seekers and culture vultures, would have defeated the group's purposes.

The charter members began passing around copies of the Society's 'manifesto' and urging our friends to join. As the group gained more support and became assured of its continuing existence, new programs were instituted.

Cooperative self-education classes in jazz history and music appreciation, practical filmmaking, and contemporary poetry were organized and taught by Workshop members as a supplement the University's meager programs in these areas and as a means of educating members in the community in the artistic disciplines in which they were interested.

Like the Sunday programs, the classes were designed and implemented by the artists themselves; Sinclair and Moore, who were working in jazz as individuals, combined their forces in the jazz class; Larry Weiner and Robin Eichele, both of whom were actively engaged in the process of making independent films, taught their class the basics of filming and editing; and Sinclair, Eichele and Tysh, all working poets who had done a great deal of independent study of contemporary poetry, shared what they had learned through their study and their work with younger, less informed poets and serious readers.

Weekly business meetings were held at first, giving each member the opportunity to help direct the organization. As the organization grew, the meetings became less necessary, and members were assigned tasks on an informal basis, the emphasis being on getting jobs done rather than on forming non-functionary committees and other bureaucratic encumbrances.

Soon the Artists Workshop Press was organized to mimeograph weekly bulletins and other propaganda, with the ultimate goal (soon to be realized) of printing books of poetry and prose by Workshop members for national and local distribution.

Benefits for independent poetry magazines and presses were staged at the Workshop, and a number of the finest small independent literary magazines were obtained for sale to members of the community because the bookstores in the Detroit area didn't stock them.

A film-screening group started bringing in avant garde films by contemporary American filmmakers who had no popular economic support. Another jazz group, the Workshop Arts Quintet, was formed by Workshop member Pierre Rochon specifically because the Workshop gave its members a place to rehearse and play under optimum performance conditions—e.g., an intensely attentive audience, no musically-ignorant clubowner dictating the music to be played etc.

And a series of Friday night readings from the 'New American Poetry'—the vital body of non-academic work that has had to make its own audience in the face of total opposition and even suppression by the establishment hacks—was begun by Workshop members in order to expose more young poets and readers to the work they should have been getting all along.

We are operating on what is truly a grassroots level—dealing with people who still can be saved—and the success, however large or small, of such a venture depends entirely on personal, individual, immediate direct action in the radical sense of cutting to the root of the problem and working from there.

We will work with anyone, any group, any persons who demonstrate through their actions that they are ready to take whatever measures necessary to try to establish, in our small but not insignificant way, a human environment in which artists and other people can live and work to their fullest capabilities.

We have come from nowhere—powerless, no money, with only our personal visions and energies to keep us working at what we believe is useful—and we have made a dent in the huge mountain of ignorance and greed looming high before us in the dark.

We at the Artists Workshop believe that if enough of us are willing to start at the bottom, recognize the walls that our general society has put up for us, stop beating our heads against these walls, organize, and GET TO WORK, we may avert the "total disaster now on tracks".

We don't claim to have the 'only way', or the 'true way'—these labels are not relevant—but we do have *a* way, and we are following it. And we do mean business.

Detroit
Spring 1965

A MANIFESTO
November 1, 1964

WHY A community of artists? One of the most important things to young, formative artists is having a group of one's peers (in the best sense of the word, taking into consideration one's advanced level of consciousness &c), that one can be a part of, can talk to, work with, work out ideas, &c and can give crucial support.

Modern society has succeeded to a frightening degree in alienating artists from one other (and of course from people in general; or at least *vice versa*) and atomizing what could be a vital, active community into a group of lone, defensive, hung-up people who are afraid to talk to and/or work with anyone but themselves and (maybe) three or four friends.

A community of artists means that a group of highly conscious people have resolved their individual ego problems and can help each other in very real ways—by giving support, stimulation &c. Artists working alone are cutting themselves off (tho not consciously I'm sure) from sources of inspiration and influence that can help them immeasurably in their work.

The lone artists have no one to listen to their work (LeRoi Jones: "how you sound"), no one to offer criticism, ideas &c that would bring their work into sharper focus with itself. They stumble along, hung up in their own egos & their own work, no perspective, they can only listen to the generations before them & those who are getting exposure now (if they know how & where to find them) to get inspiration & perspective—solitary, at best an artificial situation.

Hard to get as excited, as completely involved in one's work by oneself; when you can talk about it with/to others who are trying to do the same thing as yourself (i.e., create some art [read: beauty] "out of the garbage of their lives" [viz. LeRoi Jones] and communicate it to others) you can achieve and maintain the state of consciousness Henry James called "perception at the pitch of passion." And who better to communicate to than those few people who are operating at the same level of awareness and involvement as oneself?

Poetry (or any art) does not need to be "sullen" (*solus:* alone) any more. We are now in a period of expanded consciousness in all the arts, the most immediately important aspect of which is the transcendence of what is understood as the "ego" (in the accepted—the worst—sense of that word).

Left alone, without any real criticism (i.e., "constructive" criticism from those who are involved in the same thing you are, not from dilettantes & culture vultures, 'art lovers' &c), the artist's peculiar ego swells, he becomes deadened to his mistakes, he after a while can't bear real criticism, he's defensive, gets more atomized, separated, alone, can't talk to anyone, everyone else is crazy: becomes (alas!) the old "romantic" figure, misunderstood, one man against the world—no good. NOW is the time to find out what's wrong with your work, NOW, at least get an inkling of what other real people will think of it, how it communicates, &c.

So: what we want is a place for artists—musicians, painters, poets, writers, filmmakers—who are committed to their art and to the concept of community involvement to meet and work with one another in an open, warm, loving, supportive environment—what they don't get in the "real" world—a place for people to come together as equals in a community venture whose success depends solely upon those involved with it.

To this end we have acquired a "studio" workshop which will be maintained (rent, electricity, heat) by the artists themselves, through individual subscriptions of $5.00 each (i.e. initial investment—the pledge will be adjusted, on a monthly basis, and probably downward, as the Workshop program is totally implemented and we have a concrete figure for maintenance costs.) This method of supporting the Artists Workshop is necessary, we feel, because:

1. Each member of the Workshop is to assume an equal responsibility in the project's success;

2. Members have to go into their already near-empty pockets, thus the project cannot be treated lightly;

3. We feel that any commercial means of support, at least (& especially) in the beginning, would tend to create an artificial community hung together on money, rather than a genuine community built on mutual need and mutual support and interest;

4. No "outside" pressures, hangups, interferences;

5. The Workshop ideal can be maintained, i.e. there will be no pressure on artists to produce work that would result in commercial success, rather than integrity and aesthetic honesty, as its ultimate purpose.

We do believe, however, that commercial ventures will come into being as logical and desirable outgrowths of the Workshop as it has been conceived and as it is now operating. For example, we can see in the future a coffeeshop where musicians would present their work; a gallery for painters and other graphic artists to exhibit their work; a small printing and/or publishing concern through which poets & writers could introduce their work; an operating film society that would enable local filmmakers to produce and possibly market cinematic ideas.

Other individual projects that are being planned as part of the Workshop's total program:

1. Lectures on modern music, painting, poetry and film, by the artists themselves, that would serve to introduce & enlighten an often-puzzled public to the artists' aims, purposes, & finished work;

2. Free jazz concerts and workshops, featuring in particular the work of Detroit's musical 'avant garde,' with commentary on their work by the musicians themselves and by enlightened critics & students of the music

3. Interpretive poetry readings, with background and explanatory commentary by the poets

4. Screenings of films by Detroit experimenters and by independent filmmakers from New York and San Francisco who are involved in what has been called the "New American Cinema," and whose work is not readily available, via commercial theatres, to its eager audience.

5. All these will be "free," non-commercial affairs that are planned, programmed, & produced by the artists themselves.

We sincerely believe that our Artists Workshop Society can and will succeed: The time is over-ripe, the people are ready to convert their ideals into real action, there is no real reason why we can't make it.

We need all the support we can get, especially your spiritual support and blessing; we are trying to establish ties with the isolated groups of artists that exist in this country and throughout the universe, and we sincerely wish to cooperate with anyone who will let us. Please help.

DETROIT ARTISTS WORKSHOP SOCIETY

John Sinclair, Robin Eichele, Charles Moore,

George Tysh, Larry Weiner, Danny Spencer,

James Semark, Richard Tobias, Gayle Pearl,

Allister McKenzie, Ellen Phelan, Paul Sedan,

Bill Reid, David Homicz, Joe Mulkey, Bob Marsh

"Consequences"

after John Coltrane

[04]

The music moves inside my self,
I mean I feel saxophones inside my meat, a force in-
spiring that meat
to sing pure electricity. Flashes. Scream,

Move out from the wall
of your self. Out from there,
Now, or you stay there. What you thought
that man was screaming, that he wanted
to get inside you. "You," again, like some stupid
broken record.

          The music moves inside,
& stays there. A part of what you are. & NOT
"from." But the song of meat energy
burning to come through you. *In charge.* & that energy
makes its way. Yes, shapes it, & is in charge. *In,*
goddamnit, IN the meat,
and of it. Yes,

yes, yes. A
firming it. And where you can go
to find that one place, I mean
it is the meat. And the song
that moves that self,
& shapes it, ah, ah,

        well yes it does

Detroit
December 20, 1966

32

"I JUST WANNA TESTIFY"

"Renaissance? Re-nascence?
But what do you DO?"
        George Tysh, Detroit 1964

I CAME TO DETROIT in 1964 for the same reason young men have always abandoned the boondocks for the big city: that's where the action was, and I was desperate to be in the middle of it.

By the time I left Detroit four years later, I was in the middle of much more action than I could possibly handle, and I had to split town before it all caught up with me.

But even that wasn't enough, and within a year the long blue arm of the Detroit Narcotics Squad had reached out into Ann Arbor and pulled me back into a Motor City courtroom. I was convicted of possessing two joints of marijuana and sentenced to ten years in prison—without appeal bond or parole.

My last coherent memory of the spring of 1968 in Detroit revolves around the assassination of Martin Luther King and the three-day "preventive curfew" called by Detroit police to ensure the maintenance of law and order in the nation's fifth largest city, a massive urban jungle still wholly torn by the worst rioting in the history of these States just the summer before.

All citizens were ordered off the streets at 8:00 p.m., leaving the city entirely to the 5,000-man Detroit Police Department all through the night. The communal headquarters of any number of small groups of known activists, black and white, were kept under twenty four hour surveillance. The most notorious of this select group were treated to sadistic displays of police harassment by officers operating without restraint or fear of censure.

Nothing was happening but the police. They had everything covered, and if you moved after dark you were snatched up and taken to jail without fail. If you stayed inside they came in after you, kicking down the doors and ransacking everything in sight.

Where they knew the occupants were armed for self-defense they moved with more caution: police cars would cruise up and down the streets outside such houses, issuing threats over their loudspeakers and shining their supercharged spotlights into the windows, returning every half hour or so to repeat their vicious tricks until you were afraid to go to sleep.

Detroit was Police City, baby, and you never forgot it—not for a minute. Civil war raged across the city, an ice-cold war between whites and blacks in the

33

political arena which was from time to time illuminated by the ferocious flames of actual street warfare.

The over ninety per cent white Detroit Police Department operated openly and quite proudly as the last line of defense against the 'savage niggers' who were taking over the white folk's town. Backed to the hilt by the big money of industry and finance and its guardians in city hall, the front-line troops of the DPD were charged with the awesome, almost impossible responsibility of keeping the blacks and their white renegade allies firmly in line at all times.

Brutal excess was literally the order of the day, and the whole city suffered under a vibe so intense and evil that it hit you smack in the face as soon as you stepped out into the street.

When I came back to Detroit in 1974 it was a very different city. The once-ubiquitous police squad cars were now few and far between, and when you saw one cruising slowly down a side street in the central city it was likely to contain two black officers, a black and a white, or even a male and a female officer, most of them looking well under thirty and offering a strangely subdued face to the increasingly black world around them.

The endless streets of Detroit, once filthier than you would care to imagine, had taken on a whole new identity, a clean mien which rose to a sparkle in the city's many intact neighborhoods and dropped to a dull shine in even the most desolate areas of town.

The rebuilding of downtown Detroit had begun, with the skeletal towers of the fabled Renaissance Center already redefining the skyline, and the decrepit old Motor City was fairly humming with a brand new dynamism—nothing tangible, really, except as spirit life is tangible to those who are ready for it, but definitely alive and in the very air.

The war which had ripped apart the basic fabric of life in Detroit was over, at least for the time being, and while the police still bristled it was clear that their day as the saviors of Detroit's uniquely American system of apartheid was over too.

Not that they had failed, exactly, but more like they had never had a snowball's chance in hell, to coin a phrase. Inexorable historical forces moving beyond the modest range of their intelligence had already determined the outcome of their desperate *kampf* against the African American population, and the fatal blow came when then Police Commissioner John "Black Jack" Nichols lost an extremely close decision in the mayoral race of November 1973.

Emerging victorious from the bitter electoral contest for control of the city was Detroit's first black Mayor: a lifelong labor activist, floor leader of the

Michigan State Senate, Democratic National Committeeman, former commie agitator—and my main man—the Honorable Coleman Alexander Young.

"KEEP YOUR EYE on the money," Coleman is telling me as we sit discussing his first four years in the Mayor's office. Out the window, long heavy ore boats trudge their way down the Detroit River to Henry Ford's River Rouge facility, site of many bloody UAW organizing battles in the not so distant past. The $337 million Renaissance Center, now completed and already hustling with activity, shimmers in the afternoon sunlight just a stone's throw up the riverfront.

"These rich guys aren't putting millions of dollars into downtown Detroit because they think it's good for people," the Mayor says. "They're gonna make a ton of money out of this venture, and Ford's people are already buying up whole blocks of land all over the downtown area so they'll be able to make out even better in succeeding stages of redevelopment.

"Hell, if I had any damn money I'd be doing the same damn thing myself, but you know as well as I do that there isn't enough capital in the black business community to rebuild a damn city block, let alone the whole city.

"So if we want to do anything at all, we have to work along with the money guys and get them to see, as they have in fact begun to realize, that our interests are the same as regards the future of the city.

"They have to deal with it because it's the center of the economic life of the whole damn region, and we have an interest which is quite clear because this is where we live, this is the place where we are going to begin to develop the kind of city we want to live in.

"We don't have anything else, you see, and that's exactly why this partnership means so much to the citizens of Detroit. We need the construction, we need the jobs, the tax revenues, and right now especially we need the visible, tangible signs of commitment to the future of the city that the Renaissance Center represents."

Coleman leans back in the Mayor's chair and lets the suppressed chuckle that seems to be always just under the surface of his conversation, no matter how serious the subject, escape its temporary prison.

Coleman Young is a man who loves to laugh, an earthy, supremely cultured product of the streets of Detroit's old Black Bottom who has outlasted his lifelong opponents to become, at the age of fifty nine, not only the Mayor of the city he grew up in as a ghetto youth and radical union organizer, but the best damn Mayor in the history of Detroit.

Coleman has his hands on the levers of political power now, and it is with tremendous relish that he moves those levers this way and that to make things happen the way he's wished they'd happen his entire life.

With everything beginning to turn up roses after four impossibly hard years in office, Coleman is clearly savoring the sweet smell of political success, and nothing is more satisfying to the Mayor than having turned Detroit's fifty year economic tailspin upside down.

"Let 'em look at that $337 million worth of mirrors over there and say that Detroit is dying. No way, man. We've got this thing turned around now, and the doom-sayers and doubters who've done their best to destroy Detroit are just talking to each other these days.

"Anybody who isn't totally blind can see what's happening here, and they're all gonna start creeping back into the city to try to get their hands on some of the action. But things are very different now, and they're gonna have to deal with a whole different set of people—folks they wouldn't've given the time of day to ten years ago."

NO ONE is in a better position to know just how much things have changed in Detroit since Coleman Young's election than the Mayor himself, who reminded his constituency during the first mayoral contest that he had "come up on the other end of the nightstick" from his opponent, the reigning Chief of Police.

And not just on the streets, either, but in the head-knocking union organizing battles of the thirties and forties, where Coleman was one of a very small number of black labor activists in the United States.

"There was a barbershop in my neighborhood where a bunch of union organizers used to come. This was in the thirties, while I was in high school. I'd sit around and listen to these guys argue union politics—all kinds of social ideologies, and I knew them all: Marxists, Trotskyists, Social Democrats. . .

"This was a period of people being thrown out of their homes and the workers moving them back in. I've seen groups of workers invade welfare offices and pass out shoes and clothing where there was too much red tape. There were soup kitchens around, and a lot of turmoil and excitement, which I got caught up in.

"I was in a college prep program at Eastern High School and was entitled to a scholarship at the University of Michigan but got screwed out of it by being black, even though I was number two in the class.

"So I entered an apprenticeship program for skilled trades at Ford's, as an electrician. There were two of us—I came out of the course with 100 on all the goddamn tests. The other guy was white, with a sixty eight average, but his father happened to be a foreman, there was only one job to be had, and I don't have to tell you any more.

"So I found myself in the motor building and became active in the union movement, which at that time was underground at Ford's. They had thugs, fighters, murderers and outright gangsters as 'security men' at the plant, who dressed plain like workers and infiltrated the workers' organizations.

"I wasn't as cool as some of the old-timers and talked a little bit too much to the wrong people—the agents didn't wear badges, so you couldn't tell who they were.

"When my activities in the union became known to the company, they put a big goon on me, on the machine right across from me on the assembly line. He called me a black son of a bitch, or a nigger, some name to provoke a fight, and he started to cross the conveyor line between us.

"I hadn't been raised in the ghetto for nothing, man. I had a steel bar maybe an inch in diameter used to unjam the machinery, and just laid it across his head. He fell into the conveyor full of sharp metal shavings and got dumped into a bucket car. They fired me for fighting, and from then on I became a union organizer.

"I was involved in the Ford Rouge Plant strike in May of '41, which forced Ford's to recognize and negotiate with the UAW for the first time, and then I went to work for a couple of civil rights organizations.

"I spent some time at the post office—five months and twenty nine days, to be exact—and edited the union newspaper until I was fired. See, I made the mistake of calling this supervisor a Hitler, and that of course was my ass.

"When I came out of the post office I joined a local civil rights coalition that was fighting to integrate the new Sojourner Truth housing projects in the northeast end of town. The racists down there, many of them not so long off the boat from Warsaw or Krakow, were opposing having blacks move into that area of the city.

"There was a real lynch atmosphere—in fact the President, FDR, ended up having to send in 1,750 troops before blacks could move in—but we eventually won that fight, where probably for the first time in the civil rights movement we introduced the union tactics of mass protest and picketing.

"This strike ushered in a new militancy, the recognition that you had to do more than kiss ass and negotiate behind closed doors.

"Then I was drafted into the Army, where we forced open the Officers' Club to blacks and were arrested and put in the brig for a while.

"Coming out, the post office union I helped organize—public workers—put me on the payroll as an international rep. So I proceeded to help organize Detroit city employees—the same guys who are giving me trouble now.

"In 1947 I was elected Director of Organization of the Wayne County CIO, at the time the highest elected position of any black labor figure. The whole idea of a black caucus emerged there.

"In '48 I split with the union and the Democratic Party because I went to work for Henry Wallace's third-party campaign. Wallace was the first candidate in the history of the nation who went into the Deep South, together with Paul Robeson, and defied the Jim Crow segregation laws. Now that was something in 1948.

"I was a pretty hungry guy after losing the next CIO election due to supporting Henry Wallace, so I went back to my original skill for a while—dry cleaning, spotting, etc.—my father's trade.

"In 1951 I helped found the National Negro Labor Council, an association of black caucuses in the union movement across the country.

"We had two main thrusts: to fight for the promotion of black leadership within the unions, and to fight against job discrimination against blacks.

"We eventually cracked the UAW, and on the economic front we finally forced Sears to hire blacks for jobs beyond janitor.

"We were picketing, believe it or not, for the right to be served in downtown Detroit, and even on 12th Street. That's how recent this change has been. Well, of course all this activity was regarded as dangerously subversive, and in February of 1952 I was called up before the House UnAmerican Activities Committee [HUAC].

"This was during the height of McCarthyism, when they were going into different cities and literally terrorizing people. The mere mention of somebody's name by some damn stool pigeon was enough to get them fired, and in some cases physically harmed.

"I've forgotten the name of the chairman of the damn thing—he was from Alabama, and we did a little research on him. We found out that about eighty five per cent of his district was black, but black people weren't allowed to vote. And he's gonna lecture me about 'un-American activities'. I said, "I ain't gonna take this shit," and I did not.

"That was the beginning of the end. We beat the HUAC attack back, but soon after the NNLC became a victim of the Subversive Activities Control Board, which we called SCAB.

"We were declared a subversive activity. They said the NNLC was a Communist organization and that Coleman Young, who heads the organization, is one of the leading Communists in the United States. "He takes orders directly from Moscow," and all that bullshit.

"Well, somebody in Congress inserted the whole goddamn report into the Congressional Record, with no proof or anything, and every time I run for office somebody brings up that damn 'official record'. We tried to answer the charges, but it cost us $35,000–$40,000 just to draw up a brief for the first hearing, and it broke the organization.

"So we dissolved the NNLC in 1954, burned all our membership records, and

I went out into the streets to try to find some work, which was difficult as hell since I was on the blacklist.

"I went back to Ford's and got fired on the ninetieth day of my 'probation' period. I went to Dodge Main in Hamtrack and got a job in the foundry, where they put all the blacks then, but a superintendent recognized me on my way to the foundry and ordered me removed from the plant.

"I worked odd jobs around town after that, between 1955 and 1960, when I reentered politics by running as a delegate to the state constitutional convention.

"Then I was elected to the Michigan Senate in 1964, where I fought against racial discrimination in the Detroit Police Department and the State Police, authored the Detroit school decentralization bill, and pushed for low-income housing and a steeply graduated state income tax, which I'm still trying to get through.

"We got the state's Open Housing Act passed, and I pushed very early for abortion law reform, police review boards, consumer protection legislation, and a drastic revision of the state's ridiculous marijuana laws.

"Still, the city of Detroit meant a great deal to me, and I left the Senate in 1973 to run for Mayor because I felt the time was right to successfully challenge the all-white Detroit Police Officers Association leadership and the incipient police-state situation that had forced Detroit into utter social and economic stagnation.

"The DPOA [the police union] gained political control of the city in 1969, when Sheriff Roman Gribbs squeaked by Richard Austin, the first major black candidate for Mayor who is now Michigan Secretary of State.

"They put out a statement that the DPOA was going to run and elect its own candidate, that they were in effect going to take over the city and run it the way they wanted to. These are the people who constantly refer to the black citizens of the city, in their newsletter, as 'jungle bunnies'.

"Gribbs managed to run the city straight downhill for four years, and then the DPOA announced that it was going to run the damn police chief this time.

"That was the last straw for me, and I set out to beat Nichols so we could get this city turned around and start back on the right track again."

TURNING DETROIT AROUND was the slogan Coleman adopted for his first two years in office, and only a Detroiter can fully appreciate the enormity of the task characterized by those three words.

By 1973 Detroit was a ruined city, a bombed-out shell of a great metropolis which had been progressively stripped of its resources and then abandoned by literally hundreds of thousands of white citizens for the promise of the racially pure suburbs.

With the white exodus went the bulk of the city's tax base, thousands of jobs, and hundreds of small businesses, leaving Detroit with some seventy miles of abandoned storefronts.

To accommodate the suburban flight, monstrous freeways were built, sixty five miles of super highways which were dug through some of the city's oldest and most vital neighborhoods in order to provide the white racists with a quick clear path in and out of the downtown business district.

Whole sections of the city, encompassing hundreds of square blocks, were written off as 'bad risks' by the banks and insurance companies, which refused loans and coverage to homeowners and small business people throughout the central city based solely on their geographical location.

The riots of 1967 finished off what the automobile industry, the banks and the slum lords had started and furnished the fleeing whites with another compelling reason to relocate quickly.

Housing and business property damaged in the riots—the most severe in the nation's history—was left to rot indefinitely, and the boundless chaos of the aftermath of the 'disturbance' set the stage for a more subtle, yet no less devastating cataclysm: the wholesale destruction of dozens of remaining neighborhoods by an unholy conspiracy of corrupt HUD officials, white real estate profiteers, and a complacent, incompetent city administration.

Their scheme involved selling homes, many of them in fatal disrepair, to poor black people without the means to make the house payments each month.

Since the federal government was underwriting the mortgages on these houses through the Department of Housing and Urban Development (HUD), the inevitable foreclosures by the real estate speculators after three or four months of occupancy were rewarded with payment in full by the government.

The houses were then deeded to HUD, which was by the time of Coleman Young's inauguration the proud possessor of some 14,000 abandoned homes and 4,000 vacant lots within the Detroit city limits.

The overwhelming complex of urban problems inherited by the city's first black administration represented the culmination of a long process of deterioration and decay in Detroit that can be traced back to the beginnings of the automobile industry, early in the twentieth century.

The rapid acceleration of industrialization during the first two decades of the century drew hundreds of thousands of European immigrants to the Motor City, raising the city's population from 300,000 in 1900 to a cool million in 1920, with another quarter of a million citizens already resettled in the city's expanding suburbs.

By 1950 the Detroit area boasted a city population of 2.1 million people, plus another million suburbanites, and the decline of the city itself was well underway.

Ten years later Detroit had shrunk to a million and a half residents, and the suburbs had posted a staggering 1.1 million increase, finally surpassing the city for good.

Within this polyglot populace could be counted an increasing number of African Americans: 150,000 by 1940, 300,000 by 1950, close to half a million by 1960, 700,000 by the mid seventies.

As the black population increased and more and more whites fled the city proper, the racial balance began to tip to the African American side: 16.2% in 1950, 33% in 1960, 50% by 1975. Yet only the political strength of the black community grew in proportion to its numbers, while social and economic gains by blacks were worse than pitiful.

The Motown Record Corporation, for example, a Detroit-based, black-owned company which left the city in 1972 to seek greater economic opportunities in the west coast entertainment industry, is presently the nation's most successful black business with a yearly gross of $50 million—a sum which represents just five days' net proceeds for General Motors, another Detroit-based company which posted $1.1 billion in profits for the second three months of 1977 to set a new corporate earnings record for these States.

Motown, however successful, is far from typical. Most black enterprise, in Detroit and across the nation, is far less profitable, and nowhere has black capital managed to make even the smallest dent in the structure of white American business.

Progress for blacks within the industrial workforce has been even less hopeful, with African Americans remaining in the lowest paid unskilled positions and barred from advancement opportunities by virtue of their complexions.

Let's take some statistics at random from, say, 1963. That year, up to 60% of the workers in some Detroit-area factories were African Americans, but only half of 1% of all skilled workers were black.

At GM, where blacks comprised 23% of the workforce, there were but sixty seven skilled blacks out of 11,125 GM craftsmen. At Chrysler, where 26% of the workforce was black, only twenty four of 7,425 skilled workers, ten of 3,000 clerical workers, and zero out of 1,890 engineers were black. At Ford's, with a 40% black labor force, only 250 of 7,000 skilled workers were African Americans.

More specifically, of tool-and-die workers 1.5% were black; of structural steel workers, 0.5%; of printing craftsmen, 0.9%; of carpenters, 0.2%; of electricians, 2.1%; of machinists and job-setters, 5.2%.

And being trained as apprentices to move up into the skilled trades were fewer blacks than in 1950.

But those blacks who had skilled jobs—or any jobs at all—were extremely lucky members of their community, where fully 40% of the African American population was unemployed. This figure included 67% of all black men in their late teens and roughly 50% of all black men in their early twenties.

A third of the black population of Detroit enjoyed an income of less than $3,000 a year, and 83%—or five persons out of six—earned less than the median income of whites.

Looking to the public sector, less than 5% of Detroit fire fighters were black, and of 455 African American residents of Detroit who applied to join the police department in 1962, only two were finally accepted.

Of FHA loans granted to Detroiters, a hearty 1% was approved for blacks. In the schools, only 8% of black youths in 1963 could be said to attend integrated schools, and 72% of black children attended schools which were 90% to 100% black.

I CAME TO DETROIT in 1964 as a refugee from white American society attracted to this teeming center of African American culture. Detroit was the birthplace of the Nation of Islam and the hotbed of bebop, the place where you could hear jazz all night long and cop weed or pills whenever you wanted to.

The plight of black Americans was known to me from the street level, as I had had the honor of spending a number of my formative years in Flint, Michigan under the direct tutelage of some of the fastest young hipsters on the set, intense young men and women who held Malcolm X and Miles Davis in equal esteem and who introduced me to the wonders of daily marijuana use as a means for dealing more creatively with the terrors of life in white America.

Regular trips to the jazz mecca of Detroit had been a central component of the hip curriculum, and my private research had led me to conclude that the Motor City was definitely the place to continue my studies on a permanent basis.

Within weeks of my arrival I had found my place as a beatnik organizer and producer of poetry readings, jazz concerts, underground journals and related cultural adventures with an interracial group of students, poets, musicians, painters, filmmakers, diggers, dope fiends and political activists of many descriptions.

My contacts in the urban underground provided me with one of the only regular bags of reefer in the Cultural Center district of Detroit, and I was able to support my artistic activities with the earnings from my modest marijuana business—until I was so very rudely interrupted by the plain clothes goons of the Detroit Narcotics Squad in October 1964.

I pled guilty to possession of less than an ounce of weed, paid a fine and was sentenced to two years probation in Detroit Recorder's Court.

Nine months later I picked up another marijuana beef and found myself back in court for the second time. Faced with a mandatory minimum twenty year prison term for sale of half an ounce of marijuana, I was forced to cop another plea and throw myself on the mercy of the court—not a very pleasant prospect in those primitive years of modern American jurisprudence.

My attorney solicited letters to the judge from prominent citizens, educators, published poets and writers, and political figures who would come to the defense of a dope-selling beatnik poet.

Chief among the proponents of my right to remain on the streets was none other than State Senator Coleman A. Young, a prominent Democrat from Detroit and a person who knew me not from Adam.

Cleaving strictly to the principle that weedheads had no business in jail, Senator Young urged Judge Gerald W. Groat to release me from the bonds of the legal system and return me to my community, where I was—in the Senator's humble opinion—making a positive contribution to the cultural life of the city.

The judge turned him down, and I was sentenced to six months in the Detroit House of Correction. When I returned home, in August 1966, the Narcotics Squad immediately assigned an undercover team to infiltrate the Artists' Workshop, my center of operations across the John C. Lodge Freeway from Wayne State University, and I was busted again in January 1967—this time for giving two joints to an undercover policewoman who had signed up for a poetry workshop I was conducting at the time.

A challenge to the constitutionality of the Michigan marijuana laws was quickly mounted, and while I fought the case in the state's appellate courts on a pre-trial basis for two and a half years, I gained great local notoriety as a popular marijuana advocate, left wing activist, organizer of rock & roll festivals and benefits, manager of the MC5 and media strategist for the White Panthers, an anarchist gang of LSD-crazed hippies who swore public allegiance to the Black Panther Party and the international Communist revolution.

By the time my case came to trial in July 1969—on the same day two Americans walked on the moon for the first time in human history—I was so hot that my probation officer had ordered me to stop reporting to him at the Recorder's Court building. My very presence in the building, or so he told it, caused the police to go apeshit, and it was partially on my parole officer's advice that I finally split town to resettle fifty miles west in Ann Arbor, home of the University of Michigan.

I was eventually found guilty by a Recorder's Court jury of possessing two joints and sentenced to ten years in prison without appeal bond or possibility of parole, then dragged out of court and shipped off to Michigan's Upper Peninsula penitentiary, situated on the shores of Lake Superior, 600 miles north of Detroit.

A series of organizing activities among African American convicts at Marquette led to my transfer to Jackson, "the world's largest walled prison", where I spent many months in administrative segregation—a polite name for what is known to prisoners throughout the world as "the hole".

Meanwhile my family, friends and political supporters were organizing a massive defense campaign on my behalf, enlisting as many public figures as they could get to endorse a left wing marijuana maniac who persisted in making more trouble than he could handle.

Lobbying efforts in favor of a comprehensive reform of the state's archaic marijuana statutes were undertaken as part of that campaign, and our principal advocate in the Michigan Senate was none other than Coleman A. Young, now Floor Leader of the Democratic majority and one of the major political powers in the state.

Another black senator from the Detroit area, Basil Brown, played a leading role in the freedom effort on my behalf, and both men helped us organize state House and Senate support for my legal challenge to the weed laws, which was then inching its way toward the Michigan Supreme Court.

I was released from prison in December 1971 after John Lennon, Stevie Wonder, Bob Seger, Commander Cody, Phil Ochs, Archie Shepp, Allen Ginsburg, Bobby Seale and a wildly improbable collection of musicians and movement activists joined with 15,000 marijuana law reform advocates in Ann Arbor's Crisler Arena to demand my freedom.

I went home to Ann Arbor, where my sprawling commune had fled in 1968 to escape the Detroit police, and spent the next two or three years operating simultaneously as a community organizer and music business entrepreneur, plotting the election of third party radicals to the Ann Arbor City Council, managing bands, making radio programs and co-producing the Ann Arbor blues & jazz festivals.

A severe back injury in the fall of 1973, followed by the death of my beloved father and a total emotional collapse six months later, led me to consider drastically altering what had become for me a very dangerous lifestyle. And the relentless quest for the next meal, which forced me to fall back on my music business skills to support my family, finally led me straight back into the Motor City to manage a new downtown nightclub.

There, in the now-defunct Shelby Hotel, I spent many happy months in the Depression years of 1974–75 reacquainting myself with my many Detroit friends and the myriad delights of life in the urban night.

In my absence, I soon discovered, the Detroit of the late sixties, the incipient police state which had seemed eternally dedicated to total control of the streets and their African American inhabitants, had undergone a radical change.

Coleman Young was now the Mayor of Detroit, fighting mightily to implement his campaign demand that the police be absolutely responsible—and equally responsive—to the community which paid their wages.

Foremost was Coleman's insistence that the DPD be transformed into a 50-50 black-white and male-female service force with roots in the neighborhoods and its feet on the streets. The first of fifty police mini-stations were being opened, forcing officers out of their menacing squad cars and into storefront offices situated in the city's many decaying business strips.

But it was more than just changing the mission and the composition of the police force that was happening in Coleman Young's Detroit. The Mayor had campaigned under the general slogan of *Turning Detroit Around*, and it was apparent as early as his inaugural address that he intended to carry out his promise as swiftly and as thoroughly as possible.

Business and community leaders were being mobilized into task forces to deal with questions of economic development, unemployment, repairing the damage of the HUD housing scandals, and rebuilding the city in every way.

Coleman made a personal commitment to restore Belle Isle, the city's gorgeous island park which had been allowed to deteriorate by previous administrations because of increasing black use, to the tune of $10 million, and he pledged to revitalize nightlife and the entertainment industry in what had been, until the seventies, an important national center of black performing and recording activity.

Above all, the city's first black Mayor was concerned to blaze new trails in race relations.

"The first problem that we must face as citizens of this great city—the first fact that we must look squarely in the eye—is that this city has too long been polarized," the Mayor declared, addressing the city for the first time since his election.

"We can no longer afford that luxury of hatred and racial division. What is good for the black people of this city is good for the white people of this city.

"What is good for the rich people of this city is good for the poor people in this city. What is good for those who live in the suburbs is good for those of us who live in the central city.

"It is clear that we have a community of interest. The suburbs cannot live without the city. The white population of this city cannot live while its black people suffer discrimination and poverty.

"And so I dedicate myself, with the help of the City Council, and more basically with your help, toward beginning now to attack the economic deterioration of our city—to move forward.

"There is also a problem with crime, which is not unrelated to poverty and unemployment, and so I say we must attack both of these problems vigorously at the same time.

"I issue open warning now to all dope pushers, to all rip-off artists, to all muggers: it's time to leave Detroit.

"Hit Eight Mile Road. And I don't give a damn if they are black or white, if they wear Superfly suits or blue uniforms with silver badges.

"HIT THE ROAD.

"Ladies and gentlemen," the Mayor concluded his inaugural remarks, "the time for rhetoric is past. The time for working is here.

"The time for moving ahead is upon us. Let's move forward together."

MOVING DETROIT FORWARD, Mayor Young's new slogan, had traditionally meant moving white Detroiters to the suburbs and leaving the city to rot around its increasingly black population.

Henry Ford himself had started this process back in 1914 with the unveiling of his mammoth new automobile assembly plantation in Highland Park, located just outside the Detroit city limits and just beyond the city's taxing authority.

The smart money for the next sixty years took the same course: move the industry outside the city into little suburban municipalities that can be closely controlled, and then invest the profits in housing and shopping center developments for use by white workers and managerial personnel.

Use the city itself as a dumping ground for the least desirable workers and the permanently unemployed while continuing to exploit its services and other resources without remuneration.

Get the federal government to underwrite the cost of freeway construction and urban demolition in the city and of suburban housing and commercial development in the suburbs, with all the FHA mortgage loans going to a ninety eight per cent white constituency.

Then blame the remaining residents of the city for its downfall, like the vampire blaming the victim for its lack of blood.

The *Detroit Master Plan*, first proposed in 1946 by Mayor Jeffries (a freeway namesake of today) and adopted by Common Council in 1951, institutionalized this process and accelerated its effects.

A chain of Detroit Mayors, unbroken until Coleman Young, unfailingly contributed to the unfolding of the Master Plan, cooperating with the suburban developers and their federal sponsors in tearing up the neighborhoods and laying down the long strips of freeways which carried the suburban workers and their $4 billion in annual earnings out of the city at the end of each working day.

The cycle of degradation and decay set off by the adoption of the *Detroit Master Plan* was self-reinforcing. The destruction of acres of homes and businesses to build freeways and abortive urban renewal projects not only cost the city millions of dollars in lost tax revenues but literally undermined neighborhood after neighborhood across the city.

The deteriorating school system, another victim of the disappearing tax base, forced class after class of graduating youngsters to enter the workforce almost totally unprepared to compete for decent jobs, while the constant attrition of unskilled positions in industry pushed more and more Detroiters into lives of unyielding unemployment, welfare and crime.

The banks and financial institutions did their bit by red-lining 'undesirable' areas of town and refusing loans to builders and business people who wanted to invest in the black-dominated inner city.

Washington made some feeble attempts to attack the problem in the sixties, under Kennedy and Johnson, but the riot of 1967 and the ascension of Nixon soon after brought all such programs to a grinding halt.

Daniel Moynihan's vile doctrine of "benign neglect" realized its apotheosis in Detroit during the Nixon-Ford regime, and the sum of their efforts could be seen in every decrepit street and devastated neighborhood in the Motor City.

The general strategy seemed to be to let the city finally collapse into bankruptcy, reorganize its assets under a regional system of government controlled by the white suburban majority, and lock the black residents of the central city forever into place as a squalid underclass minority.

Then the whites could move back into town, tear down everything left standing, and rebuild the city in their own image, pushing the blacks and other politically disenfranchised residents of the central city out into the decaying ring of aging suburbs no longer suitable for white habitation.

Central to this strategy was a steady stream of anti-black invective which held the victims accountable for the disastrous social effects of the Master Plan.

The ruined buildings, the garbage-strewn streets, the miles of deserted storefronts, the loss of essential city services, the exodus of industry and home-owners to the lily white suburbs—all of these are charged to the hated blacks, as if they had engineered the collapse of one of the nation's major industrial and commercial centers.

But it was in fact the bankers and industrialists, the barons of the automobile business and their stooges in city hall who had destroyed a dynamic American city in less than twenty five years. And now they hovered, vulture-like, on the suburban horizon, sharpening their claws and waiting to swoop in for the kill.

Soon the city would be theirs to reorganize at will, and a whole new crop of superprofits stood to be reaped from land speculation, housing and commercial construction, and the redevelopment of industry within the city.

IN THE FACE OF twenty five years of failure Coleman Young thrust forth a new approach to urban planning which would guarantee the city a different future than his predecessors had proposed.

His first substantive act as Mayor of Detroit was to commission a new *Detroit Master Plan*, a comprehensive prospectus for urban economic revitalization which was soon published in part as *Moving Detroit Forward*, a spectacular 162 page document designed to pry billions of dollars out of the federal bureaucracy for the rebuilding of Detroit.

A brilllant piece of bottom-line social planning, *Moving Detroit Forward* carefully analyzed the city's heartbreaking economic problems and cautiously offered "a five year plan for restoring Detroit's ability to compete successfully for the massive amounts of private investment needed to rebuild the City. . .

"It is a plan for Federal participation, along with other public and private partners, in an investment program which targets limited dollar resources on development projects that will return healthy dividends and provide significant capital appreciation."

Official efforts at revitalization of the city dated back to the post-war period. Indeed, the Master Plan of 1946–51 had ostensibly been meant to turn the city around, and the extensive Federal urban renewal, housing and anti-poverty programs of the JFK-LBJ years were supposed to have corrected the deficiencies of the Eisenhower period.

But none had presented a comprehensive solution to the urban situation, and each shoddy piece of patchwork only served finally to exacerbate the problem beyond reason.

Since the riot of 1967 only one major redevelopment project had seen the light of day: the gigantic riverfront hotel-office complex called Renaissance Center, initiated by Henry Ford II and underwritten by fifty one major Detroit-area corporations in what many Detroiters regarded as a grand but essentially futile public relations gesture designed to cover their final retreat from the city.

But by 1974 the RenCen too was stalled by sky-rocketing energy and construction costs, a colossal victim of the new Depression which had struck Detroit with particular weight and force. The eerie uncompleted towers of the Renaissance Center stood in stark relief against the downtown skyline, threatening to serve as the city's tombstone unless Hank the Deuce and his

Renaissance Partners could raise another $100 million to keep construction on the big baby in progress.

Coleman saw the RenCen as the centerpiece of his own master plan and worked feverishly with Ford, GM Chairman Richard Gerstenberg and other corporate bigwigs to secure its existence as the cornerstone of a revitalized Detroit.

By the end of his first year in office he could claim with cautious pride, beginning a painfully succinct evaluation of the state of the city, "When unemployment lines are long, the sound of steamshovels—and the pounding of jackhammers on high steel—is sweet music. Rising on that river is a whole new center that could be the future of the City of Detroit."

The smart money still snickered and called it "Coleman's Folly", and they laughed out loud when the Mayor took Henry Ford, Governor Milliken, Senator Robert Griffin and a mind-boggling "leadership coalition" of top Detroit bankers, industrialists, city planners, politicians and community activists to present the *Moving Detroit Forward* package to President Ford in Washington, DC.

Coleman's proposal called for the creation of thousands of federally-funded jobs and training opportunities, the tearing down of blighted neighborhoods and commercial strips, and the rebuilding of city facilities, commercial centers, industrial parks and public housing.

The President's response was generally cold and noncommittal, but there was enough real meat in the conspicuously business-oriented package that the dogs of benign neglect would have to bite at some of it.

The Republicans and their big-business buddies in Detroit had expected a list of "nonnegotiable demands" presented by a bunch of crazy niggers in fatigue outfits, or at best a hastily-sketched laundry list of impossible urban desires which would try the patience of a Hubert Horatio Humphrey.

Instead they were given a hardheaded action plan for urban redevelopment which welcomed them as partners in progress—as long as they came up with some of the big money needed to get the show on the road.

All the while the Mayor was putting together his program and its essential support in Washington and Detroit, the city itself was falling down around his ears.

Detroit was a Depression town, hit hardest of all American cities by the national economic downturn, and it faced the very real possibility of municipal bankruptcy.

A $40 million deficit was forecast for the end of the 1975–76 fiscal year, with an additional $100 million shortfall projected for the following year, and borrowing was out of the question.

Essential services had to be cut drastically—"right into the marrow", as

49

Coleman put it—and within two short years the city workforce had been cut by twenty one per cent. This included nearly 1,000 police officers, who were laid off at the beginning of the worst Motor City summer since the thirties.

Whole city departments were slashed out of existence, major cultural institutions were shut down, and the city squeezed every possible penny out of the pitiful pile of dollars it had to work with.

If the federal funding was going to come, it would take at least two years, and all the Mayor could do was try to keep the lights on long enough for help to arrive from DC.

Conditions were ridiculous. To quote from *Moving Detroit Forward*, "Adult unemployment had reached 25%, 60% of Detroit youth were jobless, and a total of 136,000 Detroiters were out of work and on the streets.

"Detroit led the nation in every category of urban misery—unemployment, heroin addiction, HUD mortgage defaults, neighborhood decay and repeated school millage defeats."

Yet in the middle of this urban inferno the Mayor was determined to put every one of his non-economic programs into action.

Reorganization of the police department, affirmative action throughout city government, cleaning up the streets and alleys, assembling packages of abandoned HUD homes and vacant lots for neighborhood redevelopment, opening police mini-stations, integrating the top command of the fire department, opening up new areas of city employment for women and minorities, and generally starting to generate a whole new spirit in the city—the Mayor was determined to let nothing stop him from achieving these and other progressive social goals.

He staked his reputation and his future as an elected official on the successful implementation of these "people programs", and gradually—very gradually—he began to make them work.

Nothing was harder than dealing with the police. Coleman had made police reform a basic tenet of his platform, reasoning that economic revitalization would be impossible with the black population held squirming under the thumb of a white army of occupation.

Removing the brutal police presence and replacing it with community-oriented male and female officers who lived in the city and had a stake in its neighborhoods was the only sure recipe for racial harmony, and racial harmony was a prerequisite for economic recovery.

Once the police were put back in their proper place, the city could move smoothly ahead with unity of purpose and will.

The Detroit Police Officers Association and the virtually all-white top command of the DPD, however, shared no such interest in racial unity.

Their power base had grown spectacularly with the rising rate of friction between the races, finally allowing them to install a police Mayor—Roman S. Gribbs—and then run their own Chief against Coleman Young, whose margin of success had been frighteningly small.

For years the police had utterly had their own way with local politicians and the populace. Their wages had more than doubled—from $9,000 to $19,000 a year—within ten years after the riot, and they ran the streets like rampaging grunts in Saigon during the late conflict.

Police officers operated prostitution rings and blind pigs, peddled heroin they ripped off from dope dealers, pushed people around at will and shot 'jungle bunnies' like fish in a barrel. Their power had just barely been bested in the November election, and they began to dig in for a long and grueling battle for military control of the city.

When the Mayor initiated affirmative action to achieve 50-50 integration of the force, promoting black officers over whites with higher test scores to make up for the long years when blacks were denied access to the command ranks, the DPOA took the city to court.

When he insisted on enforcing the city's long-standing residency rule, requiring police and other city employees to reside within the city limits rather than driving in like mercenaries from the suburbs, the DPOA filed another suit.

When the Mayor demanded the integration of women into the force on the same basis as male officers, building toward an eventual 50-50 parity within the department on all levels, only a federal court order enabled the Mayor to begin to carry out his plan.

The two sides were headed straight for a showdown, and the ultimate budget crunch of 1976 touched off the fuse to the fireworks just before the 4th of July.

THE PONDEROUS CIVIC EVENTS of Detroit's Bicentennial Summer are forever burned into my brain. I will never forget the feeling I had every day for six months that year, waiting for the Mayor's body to turn up on the bottom of the Detroit River, his feet encased in a pair of concrete kicks.

A sense of impending doom permeated the very air as the police made their big move, cheered on from the sidelines by the two Detroit dailies and a whole gaggle of goofy television news performers.

I was covering the contest for the *Detroit Sun*, an alternative tabloid for which I had been working since the fall of 1975 as Arts Editor and then Editor-in-Chief.

My tenure as editorial director began on July 1, 1976, the day the Mayor announced that he was laying off almost 1,000 police officers as part of a new, crippling round of budget cuts that began the 1976–77 fiscal year.

Anticipating the layoffs, hundreds of police had refused to report for duty the weekend before, leaving hundreds of thousands of Detroit and Windsor residents who had gathered downtown for the annual Freedom Festival" fireworks display bereft of police protection.

A couple of teenage gangs from the teeming east side slums took advantage of the widely publicized walkout—quaintly termed "blue flu" by the cop-loving media—to carry out a series of organized raids on the downtown celebrants. People were assaulted, purses were snatched, random violence was visited on white suburbanites without relief.

The coppers crowed with glee and predicted a city-wide gang takeover of the streets if all the laid-off officers weren't called immediately back to work.

Carrying their resistance one step further, hundreds of policemen had scheduled their vacations in such a manner that the city's sixteen precincts were left with skeleton crews during the hottest months of the year.

Those officers who remained on duty seemed to cower inside their armored outposts, venturing into the streets only periodically to check on the progress of the 'crime wave' their absence had generated as the restless young gangsters realized they could get away with murder.

A group of east side thugs broke into a downtown jewelry store in broad daylight and went unapprehended. Teenage toughs terrorized entire neighborhoods, scrawling their B-movie monikers—Errol Flynns (spelled Earl Flinns), Black Killers (or B.K.'s), the Chene Gang, the Corleones (spelled Coney Oneys)—all over every available surface.

The tension built visibly through July and the first half of August. The relatively scattered acts of actual violence around the city were played like pitched battles in a fire war by the local media, with every racist newspaper and television geek in town competing to set new records in bad taste.

To make things even more exciting, the top command of the DPD was locked in a life and death power struggle.

Chief Phillip A. Tannian, a white former FBI agent whom Mayor Gribbs had picked to replace John Nichols during the 1973 mayoral campaign, was carrying on a running battle with his Executive Deputy Chief, a black career officer named Frank Blount who had been appointed by Mayor Young as the highest ranking African American policeman in Detroit history.

Tannian had allies in the press who rallied to his defense, using the Tannian-Blount confrontation as another brickbat in their mounting assault on the Mayor.

The shit hit the fan for real the night of August 15, 1976 when a small army of consolidated east side gang members made a vicious raid on a racially mixed concert audience at downtown Cobo Hall.

The young thugs entered the Average White Band/Kool & the Gang show in groups of twos and threes and, once inside, used pre-arranged signals to deploy their forces against the stunned concert-goers.

Young men and women were knocked down and robbed while a band of fifty or so armed police officers gathered outside the hall and decided that they didn't have enough men to attempt to stop the trouble inside. So they left the area altogether, permitting the thugs to run wild outside Cobo Hall as well.

At least two young suburban women were raped before they could get to the safety of their cars, and thousands of citizens were terrified out of their skulls.

The weird, irresponsible behavior of the police was hard to figure out until the papers came out the next morning with the news that the Mayor was out of town on a short vacation when the trouble jumped off.

This revelation sent waves of self-righteous shock through the vulturistic local media, as if the Mayor had planned to be out of the way when some terrible catastrophe occurred.

The chorus of cries for Coleman's hide grew louder and more hideous each day, while out in the precincts the white cops and their command officers chuckled softly to themselves and slowly spun the cylinders of their pistols, thinking "nigger death, nigger death", all day long.

The police strategy was working. By withholding protection from the citizens and letting the petty criminals run free in the streets, then handing the flame to their friends in the media and watching them torch the racist imagination of the suburbs, the DPOA had Coleman on the run.

If they had any chance of defeating the Mayor in the 1977 elections, now just a year away, they had to knock him down immediately and spend the next twelve months trampling his face into the dirt.

But the Cobo Hall Massacre and the howling outcry for more law and order which followed presented the Mayor with a two-edged sword, and he promptly snatched it out of the hands of his attackers and swung it masterfully against the DPOA.

Accusing the police of incompetence and lack of commitment, Coleman took personal responsibility for the safety of the streets and promised to make whatever changes were necessary to get things back in line.

A 10:00p.m. juvenile curfew was slapped on the city, forcing the teenage toughs off the streets, and such measures helped reclaim for the Mayor the shaken confidence of the black community and shattered the temporary DPOA/news media propaganda victory.

Black citizens began looking for ways to work with the police to combat crime and gang terrorism, and the police were under direct orders to respond.

Then the other shoe dropped, all the way from Washington, as the leftover

Nixonites in the Ford Administration jumped into the Detroit fray by way of the local Drug Enforcement Agency outpost.

Executive Deputy Chief Frank Blount and several top-ranking police and city officials—possibly including Mayor Young himself, his cousin Claud Young, and other members of his immediate family—were under investigation by a DEA grand jury for suspected narcotics trafficking and other crimes too hideous to mention.

An efficient information pipeline was established between the DEA office and the newspapers so that their readers were treated daily to the most lurid charges of official corruption and wrong-doing, all focusing directly on the Mayor as the shadowy kingpin of crime behind this complex anti-social conspiracy.

The *News* and the *Free Press* outdid each other daily in their ugly, unprincipled attack on the Mayor's black ass. Their venomous stories changed drastically from day to day as each set of supposed facts leaked by the feds was proved to be a fabrication or a smear, but they never failed to mention each and every principal's connection with Coleman A. Young.

Now Coleman was seriously on the ropes. His political enemies around town could almost be seen circling overhead like buzzards, ready to claw him apart at the slightest show of weakness.

The DEA business had come at the worst possible time, just as the Mayor was planning a sweeping shake-up of the DPD's top ranks, and Blount had been his well known choice as Tannian's replacement.

No matter that there was no substance nor shadow of truth to the DEA charges against Blount and the other city officials, but the cloud of suspicion cast over nearly all the top black command officers in the department made it impossible to know which way to move until the heat cooled down.

The pressure mounted. Finally, after almost two full months in the spotlight, the DEA probe fizzled out completely, producing not one indictment nor official claim of wrongdoing by Blount or any of the other rumored principals in the phony scandal.

Then Coleman made his move, ousting Tannian and installing William Hart as the city's first black police chief. James Bannon, a popular white career officer who had been banished to the precincts by Tannian, was appointed Hart's deputy, and the department was finally in the hands of professional police administrators who held themselves directly accountable to the Mayor.

Almost simultaneously, a largely unheralded internal police union election within the DPOA saw a moderate slate defeat the hard-line anti-Young forces which had led the charge against the Mayor ever since his election.

The new slate, which had even included a black candidate for office, pledged to pipe down and try to work with the city administration to achieve the police union's goals instead of constantly sniping at the Mayor.

This stroke of good fortune, coupled with the new DPD command team and the defeat of the DEA attack, broke the back of the anti-Young opposition—not just within the police force, but all over town.

The Mayor was back in the saddle, and there seemed to be no way to head him off. He administered the *coup de grace* to his foes by honoring a DPOA invitation to address the union ranks at the installation of the new slate of officers out in suburban Southfield, laughing and joking with his former tormentors to the eternal chagrin of the buzzard brigade.

Three weeks later the heavens opened up and truly began to smile on Coleman A. Young.

First, President Ford made a last minute pre-election commitment to a $600 million mass transit package for Detroit, a sum which was to be granted on the condition that the city secure an equal amount of privately financed redevelopment activity for the area to be served by the mass transit system.

Other small grants, in the works for the past two years, finally began to flow into Detroit, providing funds for two downtown malls, the renovation of four neighborhood shopping centers and a number of ethnic business areas (Greektown, Chinatown), and the first $5 million toward construction of a 20,000 seat riverfront sports and entertainment complex which the Mayor had designated one of the cornerstones of downtown economic revitalization—and which had initially been slated to be built in the suburbs.

President Ford had vetoed these grants, but he had been overridden by Congress. Then suddenly Gerald R. Ford was on his way out, and Coleman Young's good buddy James Earl Carter was preparing to move into the White House.

Coleman, a Democratic National Committee member (and now Vice-Chairman of the Democratic Party), had been one of Carter's earliest and most outspoken supporters, coming to his rescue during the 'ethnic purity' hassle and leading the charge against the popular Mormon Mo Udall in Michigan's Democratic primary.

More importantly, Coleman had been one of the first prominent blacks in the nation, as well as one of the first major urban spokesmen, to come out without reservation for Carter early in the campaign.

The mayor's activities on behalf of "The Peanut", as Coleman fondly referred to the Georgian during the race, extended into organized labor circles as well, where UAW chiefs Leonard Woodcock and Doug Fraser, both long time Young intimates, gave Carter another early boost.

Carter's election was the turning point for the Detroit Renaissance. Several top Young staffers were picked for important government posts in Washington, and the streamlined Detroit city administration was laboring to grease the slides for the incoming cargo of federal dollars.

The $2.6 billion *Moving Detroit Forward* plan was redone for the Carter Cabinet to give its fullest consideration, and an updated group of top-line Detroiters was assembled for the obligatory trip to DC to present the proposal—only this time the red carpet was rolled out for the Mayor of the Motor City and his leadership delegation, and everybody came back home with great big smiles on their faces.

MONDAY, JANUARY 31, 1977: The Mayor rises to deliver his State of the City address to a packed City Council chambers. Applause.

"Thank you for the opportunity to report this year to the Council on the state of our city—and to ask for your continued commitment to the renaissance of Detroit.

"It doesn't take too many fingers to count our triumphs in recent years, and we will suffer new setbacks in the months to come.

"Nevertheless, we have seen—and beaten—the worst. Detroit, I believe, is on the threshold of a physical and moral recovery. . .

"Nearly a billion dollars in new federal monies have already been committed to Detroit as a result of this administration's efforts in Washington. It is already at work—and it is only the beginning.

"We had to establish a new relationship with the federal government to replace one that had complete and callous disregard for the Detroits of this nation—whether the President was from San Clemente, or from Grand Rapids.

"It sometimes seemed that moving Pharaoh would be easier. But slowly, slowly, the changes have come. . .

"Today we face new threats to our hopes for renewal. The speculators and red liners, like vultures, have come to roost in the wreckage left behind—and now we must fight them, too.

"But last year HUD was working against us. This year we have HUD's attention. The local and regional HUD leadership has got to either move—or be removed. Next year, by God, HUD will be working for us.

"In 1914, on the eve of World War I, Detroit officials submitted a plan calling for rapid transit lines on Woodward and Gratiot Avenues. It was the first of fifteen separate transit proposals over the next three generations—and every single one was turned down.

"This year we got it. . . . This year, after sixty three years of waiting, we can begin. Six hundred million dollars, the largest single federal grant ever made to Detroit or Michigan, will begin to flow this year.

"This year, it will be different."

IT IS SIX MONTHS LATER. The mayor is addressing a packed house in a Cobo Hall auditorium, making his formal announcement for re-election. The theme: *We're not going back to 1973.*

Mayor Young: "A struggling city has come from its knees to be closer together than it's ever been. There's a new spirit in this city. You can feel it—you can touch it.

"Detroit's image is changing nationally. But the image begins with you. If you believe you are nothing, then you are nothing.

"Our sometimes backward and ill-informed media are now talking positively about our city because you are positive.

"I'm proud to have been the mayor of what I believe to be the greatest city in the world for the past four years.

"I said when I ran for this office that I knew the way to Lansing and Washington and knew what to do when I got there. And I think I've proved it. So I'm going to run on my record.

"But some of my opponents are running on the promise to end affirmative action and the city's residency requirement. I've got news for them—I'm not going to let anybody take us back to 1973.

"This is 1977, and we ain't goin' back!"

The crowd roared with glee. Coleman, always at his very best when addressing the working populace, was off and running for his second term. Placards carrying the Mayor's photo posed majestically against the Renaissance Center waved wildly in the air, introducing the incumbent's no-nonsense campaign slogan: *THE FUTURE IS NOW.*

His opponents were a sorry lot. Three challengers had distinguished themselves in the field of ten only because they were able to raise enough money to make their crackpot views known throughout the city.

Otherwise the mayoral hopefuls were entirely out of Coleman's league, and they could only flail about at phony 'lifestyle' issues while offering nothing in the way of a comprehensive program for urban survival, regeneration and growth.

The re-election campaign itself was a virtual masterpiece of political strategy. Using his incumbency as a bludgeon and playing always to his own strength, which is something to behold, Coleman first tied up all the significant political money and support in town and then sat back for a few months to let some long-ripening plums fall softly to the ground.

First the Renaissance Center opened the season with a spectacular April 15 unveiling. Work began on the Washington Boulevard and Woodward Avenue malls downtown and in the outlying commercial areas marked for redevelopment.

Belle Isle unveiled the beautifully restored Scott Fountain and reflecting pool which previous administrations had allowed to deteriorate.

More of the ugly buildings abandoned by HUD mortgage defaulters seemed to be coming down every day, and all over town the city hummed with new, constructive activity.

Almost every week another federal grant request was honored by the Carter administration in Washington, and Detroiters had something good to look forward to for the first time in many years.

Nobody could tell the bulk of people in the streets that Coleman A. Young wasn't the best damn Mayor Detroit had ever had, and nothing was going to stop them from putting their man back in office for another four years.

After that the city would be straightened out for good, and the promise of fresh new political leadership was especially strong.

The prominent young attorney Kenneth V. Cockrel, a former radical firebrand and one of the most visionary of all Detroiters, would place high in the race for City Council, making him the early front-runner in the 1981 mayoral contest and an exciting bright hope for the city's future.

Other experienced activists, from union men Jim Watts and Malcolm Dade to Jim Ingram, Dan Aldridge and Larry Nevels, were gaining valuable political leadership experience in the city administration itself, working to help implement the Mayor's programs and running his re-election campaign.

Coleman himself feels particularly good about the future.

"I'm a great believer that peoples' needs produce leaders—I don't follow the theory that history is a recounting of the deeds of great men.

"I think great crises produce leaders—and that leaders wlll emerge from the type of situations they have to confront.

"I think that we have developed today a greater potential crop of young leadership than we've had at any time in the past—people who are more and more militant, and who do not slink from radical change, which I feel is necessary.

"I don't think it'd be a disaster if something happened to me or about a hundred other guys I can think of. It'd be a disaster for me—but that's for history."

LAST WILL AND TESTAMENT: When I first came to Detroit in 1964 I scoured the city for people who believed a Renaissance was possible. There weren't many of us then, and our voices were usually drowned out by the sound of police sirens cutting through the night air. When we were heard, people usually laughed at what we had to say about the possibilities for a future for the city we loved.

But the cultural and political explosions of the late sixties shattered forever the reality of those times, and the last few years have seen a slow but steady regrouping of many of the most creative young minds in town.

The survivors of the civil rights movement, the Black Liberation struggle, the New Left confrontations, the jazz underground, the Motown studios, the myriad university scenes, the artists' lofts, the labor movement, the alternative press—all were beginning to come together in the New Detroit, heralding an urban renaissance which combined visionary political leadership with economic revitalization and an exciting cultural reawakening.

"But what do you DO?" had been our slogan in the early sixties, in a time when movement had seemed almost impossible and the path was blocked by a lot of people who had a big interest in keeping anything vital and real from happening in Detroit.

Now the city had literally been turned around, and people with visionary ideas and energy were being recruited into city government, where they could actually make things happen.

The visions of re-nascence which had seemed to lay buried in the underground were returning to light up the entire city, and the Mayor had hooked up the big money which could make it all happen.

The big shots could share in the profits from redevelopment and growth, but they would do it according to a new set of rules held firmly in the clutch of Mayor Coleman A. Young.

The city needed their money just like it needed the combined resources of all its citizens to keep Detroit turned around and moving forward. Soon Detroit would be a wonderful place to live. It would never return to the past.

I came back to Detroit with my family in 1975 to stay. I love it here; I've never felt so much at home in my life. The city has a spiritual quality and a dynamism which fit my metabolism like nothing I've ever experienced, and I feel like I'm home for good.

Last year, on the fifth anniversary of my release from prison, I went into Wayne County Circuit Court to get my name changed, and I took a name which had come to me in a dream: Omowale, Yoruba for "the son who has returned".

I'm proud to live in a city which has chosen Coleman Young as its Mayor, and each day I am more impressed by his performance in office.

Downtown Detroit once held a very special terror for me as the seat of the police and the courts; now it's the place where everything interesting is beginning to happen again, and I spend a lot of time on the set, checking it out.

One night late last spring, shortly after the Renaissance Center had been thrown open to the wondering throngs, a friend and I were strolling through the lobby around midnight and had stopped to admire a scale model of future riverfront developments on display there when a hand tapped my shoulder.

"How'ya doin', man?" a voice said in my ear, then moved swiftly toward the door to the street outside.

I turned and spied the Mayor, chuckling and waving back at me as he slipped into the city limo.

Taken somewhat aback, I uttered the first words that came to mind:
"My man!"
And that he is.

Detroit
Fall 1978

"blues to you"

for danny spencer

[06]

we wanted them to love us,
as a first term. to know that we knew,
& would tell them with our eyes,
& our pumping feet. would sit & stare

at the bandstand
or at each other, & grin. or get up from the chair
& walk smack into a pole
after 45 minutes of elvin jones. john coltrane

was a hero beyond legend, i mean
he was right there in front of us, right there
where we could see him, & know for ever
the whole thing was real.

        or sit for days, literally days,
& play the records through our meat, & dream
of touching them, the musicians,
as they walked off the stand, & moved past us,

smiling, toward some secret place
we would never go. & loved them always
for a simple nod, as if we were really real.
we needed them to speak to us

of pure revolution. to put down their saxophones
& spout pure poetry, or our lives
weren't shit. were gobs of dream
splattered against the world.

        oh we were young
& made of america. it made us
what we were. & are. &, if we are lucky,
we will live through it all. yes, & the music

will ring in our ears. & we will hear it,
& it will bring us through. we will wake up
singing
        of a world of our own. a world

where they will love us, just as if
(& only if)
we are as real
        as they are

Detroit, January 3, 1967 /
New Orleans, December 22, 1993

DKT/MC5

The Truest Possible Testimonial

IT'S BEEN MORE than ten years since Wayne Kramer, Michael Davis and Dennis Thompson took the stage together in Detroit at Rob Tyner's memorial concert at the State Theatre, and more than thirty years since they lurched their way through their final performance as members of the MC5 at the Grande Ballroom on New Year's Eve 1972.

Thirty years is a long time in anyone's life, especially when most of those years are spent in lives mired in frustration, poverty and despair. But once in a while a small miracle occurs, and all of a sudden everything is right back on the beam, and the future opens up on a brand new note, and everybody who's managed to survive is right back center stage where they belong.

So, when Davis, Kramer and Thompson return to Detroit "in celebration of the MC5" at the Majestic Theatre on June 10, the disaster years will melt away and they'll begin to enjoy a new day in the sun, bringing the noise from the glory years and illuminating the dismal present with the power of the music created by the MC5. It's an amazing thing, but when you hear it and see it, you'll know what all the shouting was about.

MC5 singer Rob Tyner and guitarist Fred "Sonic" Smith have left us, of course, and it's difficult to imagine the 5's music without them. But the essence of the MC5 was in its songs and the high-energy methodology the band developed to deliver them, and those are the core elements brought back to life by the DKT/ MC5 celebration band. (DKT stands for Davis, Kramer and Thompson.)

"We've gone to great lengths with all the promoters to make it clear that it's not an MC5 reunion," Kramer says. "It would be wrong to call it that, because Fred Smith and Rob Tyner have passed on. They can no longer be with us, but we're still here, and these shows are a celebration of the music of the MC5 and the work of Fred Smith and Rob Tyner. It would be an insult to their memory and to the fans to pretend that this is an MC5 reunion."

While it's impossible for anyone to take their place, Royal Oak native Marshall Crenshaw will fill in on second guitar, and singers Mark Arm (Mudhoney) and Evan Dando (ex-Lemonheads) will share the lead vocal duties. But it's Davis, Kramer and Thompson who know how it's supposed to go, and they haven't lost a step since the days of yore. Kicking out the jams is still the order of the day, and they'll be up there doing it without reservation.

"I don't feel like we're from the deep, dark past," Davis says with a chuckle. "What we're bringing to the stage is just as urgent and relevant as it ever was, and not out of step with 2004. We might've recorded this stuff last year—and, in fact, we did!"

"The MC5 was hard-chargin' and all out. There were no reservations," Kramer reminds us. "The MC5 was visceral—all sweat and muscle and the whole concept of high energy. It's a real thing. It's not just a theory. It's a way of life and a way to play music. It's wonderful to share it."

Yet the spirit of celebration is tempered by a simmering conflict. The Detroit show and the band's subsequent world tour are unfolding in the midst of a protracted battle over distribution of *MC5: A True Testimonial*, a critically acclaimed documentary film about the band.

Lawyers are involved.

IN THE INTEREST of full disclosure, as we say in the journalism racket, a caveat is in order. While this writer may be seen wearing several hats during the unfolding of the MC5 story, I'm here today principally as a professional journalist attempting to negotiate the twists and turns of a fascinating tale and tell it the best I can.

I first met the MC5 in August 1966, the day after I was released from the Detroit House of Correction after a six month sentence for possession of marijuana. They played at the Artists Workshop party celebrating my release.

I saw them perform at the Michigan State Fair a month later, and I was there when they played at the opening of the legendary Grande Ballroom in October.

I loved their music, missed few opportunities to hear them play, and gradually became close friends with Robin Tyner, the band's lead singer and chief theorist.

A year after I met them, I would also become the band's manager.

Somehow, over the years, a popular myth evolved by a succession of reactionary rock journalists came to hold that the MC5 had been a bunch of innocent suburban rock boys who were corrupted, bamboozled and manipulated by their left wing radical manager (that would be me) into fronting for his bankrupt revolutionary politics.

But the fact is that Tyner was himself a radical firebrand and a charismatic frontman who sang fervent pleas from the stage urging people to rise against the government and to reject the constraints and constrictions of mainstream culture and its human being lawnmower of a system.

Let me put it as simply as I can: I was probably even more deeply influenced by Tyner's thought and practice than he was by my own, and—with the possible exception of Thompson—so was the rest of the band.

Tyner was our leader in thought and action, plain and simple. I was a poet, music journalist, underground newspaper writer and director of the Detroit Artists Workshop when I met the MC5.

Tyner and I found that we shared a common outlook on what was wrong with our country. Our views matured and developed as a result of what was happening in the exact world we lived in, and we grew into radicalism together.

For the next year I attended virtually every performance by the band and spent many long nights scheming with Tyner over endless joints and periodic acid trips, attempting to find a way to make some kind of positive change in the world around us.

By September 1967 I had somehow assumed the duties of full-time manager of the MC5—not by contract or oral agreement, but almost by osmosis—and by the fall of '68 had secured for them a recording contract with Elektra Records.

We cut the first MC5 album live at the Grande Ballroom on October 30–31, 1968, dates declared by the Oracle Ramus—Jesse Crawford, the 5's road manager and stage MC—as the beginning of the First Year of Zenta.

The next day we announced the formation of the White Panther Party as an organization of fiercely resistant white youths committed to the principles and practice of the Black Panther Party for Self-Defense. The founding members of the WPP included this writer, Pun Plamondon, Crawford, Tyner, Kramer, Smith, Davis and Thompson.

I served as the band's manager until Crawford, Bob "Righteous" Rudnick and myself were abruptly and summarily discharged in mid June 1969.

Others had convinced the band members that ideological advocacy would impede possible commercial success, and they went for the old-time okey-doke with a greedy passion.

A month later I was convicted in Detroit Recorders Court of possessing two joints of marijuana and sentenced to up to ten years in prison.

I spent the next twenty nine months in Marquette and Jackson prisons before I was released on appeal bond in December 1971.

My conviction was overturned on appeal by the Michigan Supreme Court in March 1972, and the state's marijuana laws were declared unconstitutional on several of the grounds raised in my appeal.

By the time I was released from prison late in 1971, the MC5 was well along its protracted slide from the musical and commercial peaks the band had reached in 1970 to its painful and ignominious demise in the final minutes of 1972.

A succession of ineffectual managers and two failed albums for Atlantic Records—exacerbated by the destructive drug habits developed by several members of the band—led inexorably to the utter disintegration of the once-mighty ensemble from the Motor City, and the MC5 was soon consigned to the dustbin of rock & roll history.

BUT, OH, IN ITS HEYDAY the MC5 was truly a wondrous thing to behold, and above and beyond everything else was the power and beauty of an MC5 performance. Holding nothing back, the 5 pounded and pulsated with unbelievable energy and incredible stagecraft.

Though the MC5 itself had little commercial impact, millions upon untold millions of dollars have been made since by reducing and narrow-casting the musical concepts, maniacal stage antics, defiant attitude and blazing guitaristics perfected by Kramer and Smith and their brothers in the MC5 between 1965 and 1972.

The MC5's go-for-the throat audio onslaught and over-the-top theatrics—though utterly stripped of their social context and creative intelligence—live on in the legions of heavy metal huffers who've repackaged the sound and fury of the 5 and gleefully sold it to successive generations of rebellious teenagers without a cause.

The band's reckless advocacy of recreational drug use and its all out, gob-of-spit-in-the-face-of-god-and-art defiance of authority and social convention likewise inspired the punk rock movement and whatever has succeeded it. But the 5's focus on musical invention, rhythmic thrust and social change was replaced by the embrace of a musically inept, socially sleazy pseudo-anarchism lacking comparable intelligence or emotive force.

The MC5 also pioneered combining jazz and rock to make a new musical form infused with unbridled energy and improvisational freedom, equating the imaginative explorations conducted by John Coltrane, Archie Shepp, Pharaoh Sanders, Cecil Taylor and Sun Ra with their own irrepressible urge to take the music to a higher level of emotional and intellective registration. But their music bears little relation to the lame brand of 'fusion jazz' that rose to popularity in the wake of the 5's demise.

Even the MC5's fearless commitment to radical social causes and their incessant fundraising for community organizations, political prisoners, victims of the dope police and other outcasts helped create the template for socially-conscious popular musicians who would allow their art to be utilized to raise millions of dollars for worthy recipients who were otherwise without hope or support.

But all that is now just so much water under the bridge. There has been no MC5 for more than thirty years, and there will never be another time like that—nor another MC5 to illuminate it.

What remains is the music made by the MC5, and the way they played it. To celebrate the MC5 in 2004 by applying the principles of kinetic engagement with the music to its performance makes a beautiful tribute to what the Motor City 5 was all about.

FOR YEARS the idea of an MC5 reunion has been a particularly abhorrent concept. The band was indelibly stamped with the heat of the moment of its time, and it seemed ludicrous to think that its members could shake off all the negativism and distrust that led to its disintegration.

When Kramer, Davis, Thompson and Smith got together in 1991 to honor Rob Tyner, however, the music they made together was anything but ludicrous—the surviving members hit hard and deep, their fabled attack still fully intact.

But no one seemed to have any intention to make it more than a one-time thing, and even if they had, there were no market forces that would make a reunion tour economically feasible.

So the MC5 survivors went their separate ways again: Kramer back to Nashville, where he was working as a finish carpenter and cabinet-maker; Davis to his ranch in Arizona and his musical assignments with a series of hard-edged young Southwestern rock bands; and Thompson to his home in suburban Detroit and his duties in the work-a-day world, from which he would emerge from time to time to essay various attempts at making music in public again.

Kramer, in fact, had pretty much given up on the music scene after spending the late 1970s and early eighties trying to revive his career. Released from federal prison after serving almost three years on a cocaine conviction, he settled in New York City and did some lightweight touring with a band called Kramer's Creamers, formed Gang War with guitarist Johnny Thunders, toured and recorded with Detroit's all-star Was (Not Was) revue, then devoted several years to developing an underground gangster-rock musical, *The Last Words of Dutch Schultz*, with lyricist Mick Farren and a dedicated cast of musicians, singers and actors.

Kramer found paying work outside the music world as a carpenter and showcased *Dutch Schultz* at a succession of small venues in the city on the side, but his efforts met with little success. So he finally packed it in and moved all the way south to Key West, where his musical opportunities were severely limited to the occasional bar band gig.

This situation proved so unsatisfying that he decided to abandon his quest for meaningful musical expression and concentrate on his woodworking skills.

But the reunion with his former bandmates in Detroit made Kramer start thinking about playing music again, and he got his chance when the owner of a Nashville recording studio where he was installing some cabinetry realized who this contractor really was and offered to trade him studio time in exchange for some additional carpentry work.

Kramer recruited a rhythm section and cut some tunes, then took the tapes to Los Angeles in a bid to get them released. Bret Gurewitz at Epitaph Records, a member of the band Bad Religion, confessed that Kramer was one of his musical heroes and offered him a multiple-record deal with a cash advance sufficient to cover his living costs while he recut the tunes with a supporting cast drawn from the ranks of other Epitaph acts.

Kramer decided to resettle in Los Angeles to try to make the most of this unexpected opportunity, which resulted in four albums for Epitaph and the resumption of touring in support of their release.

The label's promotional efforts and the concomitant growth of the worldwide web spawned considerable new interest in Kramer and his history with the MC5, but Epitaph was unable to garner enough radio play or adequate sales to advance his career, and Kramer soon found himself back at square one without a record contract.

IN THE middle of all this commotion Kramer was called back to the Motor City to mourn the untimely demise of his old comrade-in-arms, Fred Smith, who died in 1994. In recovery from years of drug and alcohol abuse, Kramer was moved to attempt to make things right with remaining MC5 bandmates Michael Davis and Dennis Thompson.

There was a lot of unpleasant history to overcome, but it became increasingly important to Kramer that they put the past behind them and celebrate—while there was still time—the positive things they had done together.

Then another minor miracle took place: a team of first-time moviemakers from Chicago contacted Kramer, Davis and Thompson about making a feature film that would document the story of the MC5.

Operating as Future/Now Films, director David Thomas and producer Laurel Legler struck deals with Davis and Thompson with respect to their participation in the project. The filmmakers would form a company with the surviving MC5 members and representatives of the estates of Tyner and Smith, providing for any net profits the film made to be split among the members of the company.

Future/Now envisioned Kramer as the film's central on-screen informant and interpreter of the MC5 story, while Kramer also saw himself as music supervisor for the film and producer of the soundtrack album.

Kramer and his manager, Margaret Saadi, were organizing their own production company, MuscleTone Records, and wanted to secure the right to produce and release the soundtrack on their label.

In return, Kramer would cooperate fully with the film production, perform as directed in several shoots for the film, and personally instruct his music publisher, Warner/Chappell, to provide to Future/Now a gratis license for the use of his compositions in the movie.

Kramer and Saadi worked closely with Future/Now for the next four years as the film went into production, the producers sought financing and distribution, and the MC5 story slowly unfolded itself onto film.

"We became so involved in the creation of this film," Saadi says, "because we thought it was a great story which needed to be told and because we had an agreement that there was a job for Wayne."

Saadi and Kramer introduced Future/Now to Warner/Chappell, helped set up filmed interviews with Jon Landau, Danny Fields and this writer, and vouched for the fledgling film production company with potential lenders and distributors.

Completed in 2002, *MC5: A True Testimonial* follows the rise and fall of the MC5 from its origins as a teenage band in Lincoln Park to its phenomenal local success as the kingpin of the Detroit rock & roll scene; its daring appearance as the only band to show up during the 1968 Democratic Convention to play at the Festival of Life in Chicago; its emergence as a touring act with a Top Thirty album on Elektra; its unique experience as co-founders and propagandists for the White Panther Party; its defection from the WPP and ensuing pursuit of conventional success in the music industry; its failure to gain popular acceptance or significant record sales, and its messy disintegration and dissolution in 1972.

David Thomas turns in a fine job in his directorial debut, marshalling the many disparate elements of the MC5 story into a coherent, well-paced exposition of the band's explosive impact and denouement.

Most impressive is his deft editing of the archival performance footage— shot sans sound in the sixties with 16mm Bolex and Super 8 cameras by Leni Sinclair (full disclosure: this writer's ex-wife)—to recorded performances of such MC5 staples as Kick Out The Jams, Looking At You, High School and Shakin' Street.

The performance footage, most of it previously unseen, is tightly interwoven with intimate interviews, government surveillance film shot at the Festival of Life, still photographs and images of the musicians from childhood to the present, and a powerful soundtrack pulsating with the triumphal yet under-acknowledged music of the MC5.

MC5: A True Testimonial had its international premiere in November 2002 at the International Documentary Film Festival in Amsterdam. The film was then shown at the Raindance Film Festival in London, the Goteborg Film Festival in Sweden and the Toronto International Film Festival, drawing enthusiastic audiences and widespread critical acclaim.

GOING INTO 2003, everything seemed to be clicking right along. A new round of screenings would include the San Francisco International Film Festival,

Tribeca Film Festival in New York City and the Melbourne International Film Festival in Australia, and the filmmakers turned their attention to landing a DVD deal and signing with an agency to arrange commercial theatrical screenings for the movie.

But that's exactly when the shit hit the proverbial fan. Kramer had been a little edgy since 2001, when Future/Now screened a twenty minute sequence from *A True Testimonial* that had been edited and soundtracked by director Thomas without Kramer's participation.

More importantly, there was the matter of the absence of a written agreement between the parties with respect to Kramer's services. Also undocumented was Kramer's purported share in the ownership of the film and how he would be compensated for services rendered to the project.

In 2000, Future/Now had incorporated an entity called Zenta (a name they lifted from its originators without permission nor request) LLC to own the film and distribute the net proceeds among its members, who were to include the investors as well as the three living bandmates; Tyner's widow, Becky Derminer, and the estate of Fred Smith.

Membership in the corporation was contingent upon its members signing the Zenta LLC operating agreement, including an attached 'publicity release', a waiver which delivered all appropriate rights to the corporation for its use in commercial exploitation of the completed film.

All the pertinent parties signed except Kramer, whose deal was somewhat more complex. He and Future/Now had exchanged contract drafts without resolving their respective issues, and Kramer was particularly adamant in his rejection of a stipulation that would have granted the filmmakers "the absolute and irrevocable right" to use Kramer's name and likeness "for any purpose whatsoever, including but not limited to" the film.

"They want to own everything about me forever," Kramer has written.

Kramer signed and returned the Zenta LLC operating agreement in June 2002, but not the attached 'publicity release'. Instead he says he submitted language of his own which granted the use of his name and likeness "in connection with the promotion, distribution, and exhibition of the Film".

Kramer also sought written confirmation that MuscleTone Records would have the "exclusive right to produce, manufacture, promote, and distribute ... audio products ... as the Film's soundtrack", reserving for MuscleTone final approval of the musical program, packaging and promotion of the album.

Though still not accepted into membership by Zenta LLC, Kramer joined his bandmates in August 2002 in approving the issuance by their publisher, Warner/Chappel Music, of a gratis one year music license that allowed Future/Now to screen the film at festivals in order to attract distributors.

"We didn't want to stand in their way," Kramer writes on his website. "We wanted them to sell their movie. We hoped that they would do the right thing."

WHILE KRAMER AND SAADI tried to resolve their differences with Future/Now so *A True Testimonial* could achieve commercial release, another thorny rights issue emerged from an entirely unanticipated direction.

In Europe, Levi Strauss had issued an MC5 t-shirt in its Vintage Clothing collection and announced a complete line of casual shirts, jackets and other apparel that would "celebrate" the "revolutionary spirit" of the MC5 with designs using the band's logo and the likenesses of its members.

Levi Strauss had licensed MC5 designs from artist Gary Grimshaw and photos of the band from Leni Sinclair, then secured to Levi's satisfaction the rights to the MC5 name, logo and likeness through the agency of Rob Tyner's widow, Becky Derminer.

The whole deal cost Levi's a trifling amount (less than five figures), and the textile manufacturer suddenly seemed to be the proud and fully licensed 'owners' of the MC5 legacy.

Shocked by this new development, Kramer and Saadi thought first of a lawsuit, but decided on a course that could turn the situation to the advantage of the band while avoiding a court battle.

When they contacted the Levi Strauss office in London, they had a bold plan in hand, and found themselves talking to people at Slice, the company's public relations firm, who were more than a little receptive.

MuscleTone's concept was simple: since Levi's was "celebrating" the MC5, why not stage a musical celebration at a London venue that would bring together Kramer, Davis and Thompson with an array of sympathetic guest musicians and singers for an intimate, one-time, invitation-only concert—and film and record the event for release as a DVD.

They would call it *A Celebration of the MC5*, and Levi's would foot the bills as part of the promotion for the MC5 Vintage Clothing line.

Slice's Alec Samways signed on to the project and became co-executive producer of the celebration documentary with Saadi. As the plans for the project began to take shape, MuscleTone invited Future/Now Films to participate in the projected four-camera shoot, help with production of the film and DVD release, and also to screen *MC5: A True Testimonial* at the concert, scheduled to take place in March 2003 at the 100 Club.

But Future/Now, still operating without a signed agreement with Kramer, refused to participate, and rejected Levi's invitation to show its film at the London concert. From this point on they seem to have regarded Kramer and

Saadi—and, by extension, Davis and Thompson, both very much a part of the London project—as adversaries. The whole Future/Now project began to steer a very perilous course.

THERE IS a certain cruel irony at work here: Three men in their fifties who had been bitterly estranged for twenty years are reunited in a creative context to make a film about their long-defunct band and the incredible music they made together.

They begin to heal their wounds and build a new basis of artistic cooperation and trust by working together on the movie.

They get cut out of what might have been a major licensing deal with Levi's yet manage to emerge smelling like roses, the heroes of a hot-ticket London concert celebrating their music that will be documented for release on DVD.

But the people who brought them back together to make *A True Testimonial* now seem to regard them as some sort of Frankenstein's monster that's grown out of control and come to pit the movie of the MC5 against the lives of the surviving band members.

So the two projects centered on the history and music of the MC5 rolled ahead on separate tracks.

A Celebration of the MC5 was staged under Levi's sponsorship to wild acclaim. Davis, Kramer and Thompson brought the 5's music back to life in a series of rehearsals and were joined onstage for the concert by guest rockers Lemmy Kilmister of Motorhead, Nicke Royale of The Hellacopters, Ian Astbury of The Cult, Dave Vanian of The Damned and singer Kate O'Brien, plus imported former Detroiters Dr Charles Moore on trumpet and Ralph "Buzzy" Jones on tenor saxophone.

The set list for the show included MC5 favorites Lookin' At You, Gotta Keep Moving, Skunk (Sonically Speaking), Rocket Reducer No. 62, Tonight, High School and, of course, Kick Out The Jams.

The sound was hot and fresh, the stage remained in frenetic motion, and the crowd went crazy. The British music press responded with equal fervor.

"After all, the MC5 created the blueprint for all that's cool in modern rock 'n' roll," *New Musical Express* enthused. "They rip the 100 Club to shreds with a force-50 gale of everything you love about rock 'n' roll."

"You only get to see so many truly legendary gigs," *Mojo* magazine summed up, "and tonight was definitely one."

The concert's success also inspired the production of a thirty minute MC5 documentary hosted by *Mojo*'s Andrew Male and Zane Lowe of BBC Radio 1 that focused on the 100 Club show.

Once the program aired on UK Channel 4, MuscleTone licensed the production for inclusion in *Sonic Revolution: A Celebration of the MC5*, the DVD that documents the concert with sixty scintillating minutes of performance footage.

By the end of 2003, MuscleTone had fully cleared all the music for the celebration DVD and licensed it to Image Entertainment and its affiliates for worldwide release on July 6, 2004.

To make things even rosier, concert promoters all over the world, excited by the reports from London, had begun to agitate for the chance to hear and present *A Celebration of the MC5* on their own stages.

Before they knew it, Kramer and Saadi had cobbled together a string of dates that would take the show all over North America, Australia, Japan and Europe this summer. Detroit is the second stop.

MEANWHILE, *A True Testimonial* was careening along on a contradictory course: Future/Now had built the film's enthusiastic reception by festival audiences and film critics into a deal with Avatar to book the movie into commercial theatres, plus a DVD distribution agreement with Private Music, a division of BMG.

But Future/Now still had not concluded a working arrangement with Kramer for the right to use his name and likeness or his compositions.

Future/Now's limited license to exhibit the film at festivals expired at the end of the summer of 2003, and Warner/Chappell informed Future/Now that the publishing house would not be able to grant them synchronization rights to the MC5 compositions until the filmmakers had worked out their issues with Kramer.

A screening scheduled for October 30 at the Detroit Institute of Arts—the film's first ticketed theatrical exhibition—was allowed to proceed under a special dispensation from Warner/Chappell, but final clearance would be withheld pending Kramer's authorization to proceed.

Despite this serious setback, Future/Now closed its deal with Private Music and accepted an advance, apparently maintaining that its licensing problems would be resolved by the projected release date, which had been set for May 6, 2004.

On the theatrical front, Avatar was arranging commercial bookings for the film in New York City, Chicago, San Francisco, New Orleans, Detroit, Ann Arbor and other cities for the spring and summer of 2004.

Evidently convinced that Kramer would not cooperate, Future/Now and Becky Derminer teamed up to file a motion in Los Angeles on February 27,

2004, to reopen Kramer's Chapter 7 bankruptcy case from 1999.

Future/Now claimed that Kramer had "entered into several agreements [in 1996 that] gave FN Films personality rights, and entitled and authorized FN Films to use all music and recordings in which [Kramer] held an interest."

Future/Now claimed further that "Under the agreements FN Films paid all of [Kramer's] expenses in connection with various shoots and interviews, and agreed to give [Kramer] … membership interests in [Zenta LLC]."

Yet, eight years after all these deals purportedly were struck, no written agreement had been executed, and Kramer filed papers with the bankruptcy court denying that he had any income coming from *MC5: A True Testimonial*.

"Future/Now Films and their attorneys have asserted for many years now that there is no agreement," Kramer states in his filing with the court.

"I have since been denied membership in Zenta LLC because I have refused to give my story away for no compensation whatsoever. There is no income stream for me related to their film."

Producer Laurel Legler, whose nine-year film project languishes in limbo, counters: "I disagree with everything that comes out of Wayne Kramer's mouth, because he doesn't tell the truth.

"We never reneged on agreements with Wayne Kramer. We tried to give him everything he wanted."

An equally exasperated Kramer says: "They have as yet made no concrete offer to solve their problem. We have lots of solutions for their problem, but it's not up to us to fix it. And I find it amusing that their story keeps changing. They can't keep their lies straight.

"No one's more disappointed than I am. I worked hard on that movie, and I always anticipated that they would do what we had agreed upon."

KRAMER WAS FURIOUS about the court action, which he considered an attempt to pressure him into signing over the rights to his music, his image and his personal story, and decided to bring the torturous negotiations to an end.

In court papers, Kramer contended that the motion had been filed in an "attempt to scare, harass, and intimidate Mr Kramer… [but] Mr Kramer will not support the Film Project".

A week later Davis and Thompson declared their solidarity with Kramer by means of a letter from their attorney, Jay W. MacIntosh, to Future/Now. Dated March 4, 2004, MacIntosh's letter says:

"Please be advised that my clients Michael Davis and Dennis Tomich (aka Dennis Thompson) do not support the release of, licensing of, screening of, and/or sale of the film 'MC5: A True Testimonial' until all issues have been resolved between the film company and MC5 band member and songwriter Wayne Kramer, and documentation of such has been provided to my office.

"Please note that this statement supersedes any statements previously made by myself or anyone else on behalf of Mr Davis and/or Mr Tomich. Any failure to recognize this shall be considered willful misrepresentation."

The next day Kramer attorney Edward Saadi (Margaret's brother) wrote to Future/Now's lawyer to say that Kramer would do nothing "to assist Future/Now in its effort to obtain [the] license" from Warner/Chappell.

He demanded that Future/Now "immediately and permanently" refrain from using Kramer's image and pay Kramer any money already generated from merchandising, box office receipts and other sources.

Warner/Chappell followed with a cease-and-desist letter barring further distribution of the film and mandating the cancellation of current and future commercial screenings. Private Music had distributed advance copies of the *True Testimonial* DVD for media review, but the company was forced to announce that the film's release had been delayed.

Thompson says he believes Future/Now "made some errors in judgment. They essentially were showing a film without a license". He hopes all the wrangling can be resolved.

"We're all getting a little tired of hearing about it. Once it gets to the lawyers, who knows what's going to happen?' Thompson says, adding, "I don't wish them [Future/Now] any ill will whatsoever.

"But I support Wayne Kramer. Wayne and I have come a long way toward making amendments to ourselves as human beings. This is about the music and the band.

"Future/Now is not MC5. We can create that spirit onstage. It's always this political cloud following us. There's always this black hole."

Rob Tyner's widow, Becky Derminer, is confident that *A True Testimonial* will eventually see theatrical and DVD release. "The film is a beautiful piece of art," she says. "This movie's going to come out. It's too beautiful to be hidden in a closet."

Derminer says she won't be attending the show at the Majestic.

SO THERE IT SITS, the one vehicle disabled and fuming on the shoulder of the road, the other wheeling its way to the starting line with a full tank of gas and a precision crew at the controls.

Of course, MC5 fans the world over hope that *A True Testimonial* will eventually hit the screen and DVD racks, but those of us in the Motor City and the other stops on the DKT/MC5 tour won't have to wait any longer to see how Wayne Kramer, Michael Davis, Dennis Thompson and their friends are celebrating the legacy of the MC5 on stage right now.

"It's great to get back together with Wayne and Michael and to be able to do this, and be able to bring this music to people who have never been able to hear it," Thompson says.

"The bottom line is we've got a world tour coming up. We had great rehearsals out in LA. We rehearsed some thirty five or odd songs, so we'll be capable of playing any and all of the MC5 songs going all the way back to the beginning.

"This is about growth. This is about the MC5 attitude, the MC5 energy and spirit in 2004. This is not really the MC5. It's really a celebration of the MC5's music. If anyone is capable of playing this stuff, it's Wayne, Michael and me."

Kramer concludes: "It's like uncorking some kind of nuclear device or something. This shit rocks hard, and we're having big fun doing this.

"It's one of those times when you can say that it doesn't get any better."

New Orleanss
June 8, 2004

75

"ain't nobody's bizness"

for henry normile, bradley jones, & bob "righteous" rudnick

we have a right to our bad habits
& if we want to blow our minds
or fuck up our lives, shoot dope
or smoke cocaine,

if we want to eat too much meat,
sit around all day & watch t.v.,
stay up all night listening to music
by charlie parker & screamin' jay hawkins,

if we want to walk around naked,
fuck our eyes out,
eat some pussy or suck a cock,
take it up the ass, get our nuts off

700 times a day,
lay around & drink whiskey,
bet on games, shoot dice,
sell some pussy on the street,

if we want to gamble in casinos
or spend our money in a whorehouse,
give the president a blow job
in his big chair in the white house,

walk around the streets
with all our belongings in little bags,
sleep in doorways,
piss in the gutter,

if we want to sleep away the day
& never answer the telephone,
take every meal in restaurants & bars
& never exercise—

& if it comes to the end
of the line for us, we have every right
to blow our motherfucking brains out
or jump off the bridge

or take ourselves away from here
any way we might want to— then baby please,
we got a right to our bad habits
& it ain't nobody bizness if we do

harmonie park
detroit
august 6 & 10, 1988 /
august 9, 1990 /

new orleans
august 1998

THE WILD ONE
THE TRUE STORY OF IGGY POP

By Per Nilsen & Dorothy Sherman (Omnibus Books)

ANN ARBOR'S OWN Iggy Pop, the shamanistic pioneer of postmodern pop music who can reasonably be dubbed the father of punk rock by virtue of his slash-and-burn, search and destroy theatrics and thunderous, aggressively minimal musical attack as leader of The Stooges (1967–74), has cut a uniquely compelling figure in the pantheon of rock legends and demi-gods for more than twenty years now.

Although the Ypsilanti-born Jim Osterberg—he got the "Iggy" as the drummer in a teen band called the Iguanas, and his colleagues in the Stooges added the "Pop"—has never enjoyed a hit record of his own nor the concomitant mass audience produced by regular radio airplay, his career has sustained an ever-growing cult following that remains fascinated by the Ig's impassioned commitment to his own twisted aesthetic and his violent disdain for commercial success.

Iggy's early recordings with The Stooges—their eponymous debut album on Elektra (1969), *Fun House* (1970), *Raw Power* (1973), *Metallic KO* (live at the Michigan Palace, Detroit, February 1974)—bristle and pound with an energy and a point of view previously unknown in pop music.

Not a 'rock & roll band' in any existing sense of the term except for their instrumentation and attitude—as Iggy told Anne Wehrer, "We couldn't possibly play our way through a Chuck Berry tune"—The Stooges were assembled by a twenty year old Jim Osterberg to "try to do something as different as possible from anything going on at the time".

While the Ig had developed a local reputation as an accomplished rock and then, with the Prime Movers, blues drummer, he decided to pursue an innovative, defiantly iconoclastic musical direction after spending eight months in Chicago playing with blues bands—J.B. Hutto, Big Walter Horton, Johnny Young—in all the south-side joints and crashing in Bob Koester's basement at the Jazz Record Mart.

When he peeped the reality of the blues idiom, that it was a form developed by African American musicians to express with great accuracy the everyday content of their lives, he reached a startling conclusion:

"When I found that out, I knew I had to come home and make my own music… I've got to take what I've learned here and apply it to my own experience…

"I wanted to make songs about how we were living in the Midwest. What was this life about? Basically, it was no fun and nothing to do. So I wrote about that."

Bypassing completely the sizable pool of competent, locally established rock & roll musicians, Iggy selected a pair of aspiring but basically unskilled brothers— Ron and Scott Asheton, from the west side of Ann Arbor—and proceeded to communicate his concept to them through months of doing "nothing but talk bullshit" and then several more months of rehearsing the kind of music Iggy had been trying to tell them about.

The Ig taught Scott Asheton the fundamentals of drumming and even designed a bizarre drum set for him out of a pair of fifty five gallon oil drums "which I got from a junkyard". Ron Asheton dealt with the huge droning bass sound Iggy was looking to hear, and the Ig featured himself on organ, electric piano, or "this sort of wild Hawaiian guitar with a pickup that I invented, which meant that I made two sounds at one time, like an airplane".

This early Stooges configuration stood up in practice until the night Iggy saw The Doors play the U-M Homecoming dance at Yost Field House in late 1966, where, as Per Nilsen puts it, "Jim Morrison had proved to Iggy that you could do virtually anything on the stage and get away with it. Iggy saw a completely loaded Jim Morrison roll around the stage and do gorilla imitations."

Osterberg says it right out to Dorothy Sherman: "It was after I saw Jim Morrison that I decided I'd be a singer, no matter how much I laughed, cried or died."

But what he meant by "singer" was something very different from any role models extant—Iggy acted out the imagery embodied in weird little tunes like I'm Sick and Asthma Attack, improvising wildly with sounds and incredible movements in front of "this thunderous, racey music, which would drone on and on, varying the themes...like jazz gone wild. It was very North African, a very tribal sound: very electronic".

The band was first called the Psychedelic Stooges, and as Iggy told Dorothy Sherman, the name was "a sort of tribute" to the Three Stooges: "We loved the one-for-all/all-for-one of the Three Stooges, and the violence in their image. We loved violence as a comedy.

"Besides sounding right, 'stooge' also had different levels of meaning: is calling yourself a 'stooge' a self-insult?"

The Stooges revealed their mind-blowing version of contemporary music to an invited group of friends at the Ann Arbor house of their original manager, Ron Richardson, on Halloween night 1967.

Four months later, on March 3, 1968, the Psychedelic Stooges made their public debut opening for Blood, Sweat & Tears (!) on a Sunday night at the Grande Ballroom in Detroit.

Blood, Sweat & Tears, on their first tour, had nixed the MC5 as an opening act for their Detroit date, but fate dealt them an even crueler hand that night as the Stooges totally destroyed the "completely amazed" crowd with their raw, throbbing, primitive electronic wall of sound and the specter of Iggy Osterberg dancing disjointedly out in front of the band, his face painted white and his menacing, eerily intoned vocal chants alternating with instrumental breaks on theremin, amplified vacuum cleaner, and his home-made Hawaiian guitar.

"People just didn't know what to think about us," Ron Asheton recalled for Dorothy Sherman. "We had our own instruments. For example, we poured water in a blender and put a mike on top of it. We got this really weird bubbling water sound which we put through the PA. And Iggy danced on a washboard with his golf shoes!"

The Psychedelic Stooges played several carefully selected dates in Detroit, Ann Arbor and outstate Michigan over the next six months, often on bills with the MC5, never failing to shock and astound audiences who had come to see a rock & roll band and ended up witnessing an indelibly unique and strangely moving performance experience which was almost completely different every time out.

By the end of September 1968 the Stooges had been signed by Danny Fields to a major recording contract with Elektra Records, in tandem with their pals the MC5, and soon unleashed their blasphemous sound and fury on the world at large.

The rest, as they say, is history, and you'll find the whole strange story recounted calmly, date by date and performance by performance, in Per Nilsen and Dorothy Sherman's excellent new biography, *The Wild One: The True Story of Iggy Pop* .

Dorothy, a Detroit native, conducted the thorough, well-pointed interviews for the book, and Nilsen wrote the text, and designed and typeset the generously illustrated package for publication in England last year.

An American edition with a new cover and even more photographs was issued at the end of 1988, making this impressively researched, clearly written report available to the Ig's many fanatical followers here in the States.

If you're one of them, check out *The Wild One* for yourself—like its illustrious subject, it's definitely the real thing!

Detroit
1989

"The Screamers"

for Kenny Schooner

stagger down overgrown sidewalks
of memory. giving hand &
giggling. (Earth Angel, how I long

for you. where you been, all these
years. Johnny Ace, with a hole
in his head. where you gwine,

Ivory Joe? or those stupid white
imitations, the Crewcuts, jive Pat
Boone, stealin' their songs. Sh-

Boom. Two Hearts. Chuck Berry,
Jimmy Reed. "I walk 47 miles
of barb wire. I use a cobra snake

for a neck tie. I got a bran/new house
by the road side, made from
rattle snake hide." Oh you really really

send me, baby,
you got to go for me or I'll
beat yo ass. who

do you love. (weird lullabies. "broken
hearts." long long &
lonely nights. for your

precious love, I wd have drank
gasoline, & all I wanted
was a little water. where I came from,

mysterious ofays of the imagination. why you aren't here
with me, old gang, beer

drinkers, bull
shitters. where
did you go?

Detroit
March 16, 1965
after LeRoi Jones

81

SUN RA VISITS PLANET EARTH

"People say I'm Herman Blount, but I don't know him. That's an imaginary person, he never existed. I have a sister and brother named Blount, but their father died 10 years before I arrived on the planet. He's not my father. If I tried to do anything with the name Sonny Blount, I couldn't... I'm not terrestial, I'm a celestial being."

—Sun Ra, *from John Diliberto's liner notes
to* Sound Sun Pleasure *(Evidence ECD-22014)*

THE AFRICAN AMERICAN musical genius known as Sun Ra was a delightfully unique individual whose startlingly innovative Arkestra and provocative persona generated considerable myth and controversy during most of the second half of the twentieth century.

The legendary pianist, composer, band leader, performance artist, musical pioneer and space philosopher was born Herman Blount around 1915 in Birmingham, Alabama and was known to family and friends as "Sonny".

He attended Alabama A&M and played with bands around the South before settling in Chicago after World War II, where he worked at the Club DeLisa as second pianist and arranger with the Fletcher Henderson Orchestra during 1947–49.

By the turn of the 1950s Sonny Blount was writing music for the shows, rehearsing the chorus line, and leading the relief band at the Club DeLisa two nights a week.

He formed his own trio to back up vocalists, instrumentalists, and floorshows in local nightspots, soon landing a regular gig at Budland supporting visiting stars like Sarah Vaughan, Johnny 'Guitar' Watson, LaVerne Baker, Dakota Staton and comedian George Kirby.

At this point the pianist began his long association with Chicago philosopher/businessman Alton Abraham, a pragmatic mystic who would become his mentor, personal manager, booking agent, recording supervisor and business partner for the next quarter of a century.

With Abraham's guidance Herman "Sonny" Blount took the name "Le Sun Ra" and began to reveal an elaborate, unprecedented cosmic philosophy through his compositions, song titles, poetry, wild costumery, and an innovative, ever-expanding musical ensemble first called the Solar Arkestra.

The Arkestra, billed as playing "Music from tomorrow's world-Magic Music of the spheres," began its spectacular forty five year lifespan in 1952 in the form

82

of a six-piece jazz combo organized to showcase Sun Ra's original compositions, arrangements and multimedia performance concepts.

There are photos of the Herman Blount Octet in Chicago in the mid fifties, identified as Pat Patrick (alto and baritone sax), John Gilmore (tenor sax), Dave Young (trumpet), Julian Priester (trombone), Richard Evans (bass), Bob Barry (drums), Jimmy Herndon (percussion) and Herman Blount (piano, leader).

With Abraham as its booking agent, early editions of the band worked five nights a week at Budland in the Pershing Hotel and played the Sunday dances at Robert's Show Club on South Parkway.

The Arkestra became a featured attraction at the Compass Club on the far north side, alternating with a local comedy troupe that included Mike Nichols, Elaine May and Mort Sahl, and also worked steadily at the Wander Inn on Cottage Grove on the south side.

The band attracted young musicians from DuSable High School who had studied with Captain Walter Dyett in the tradition of noted DuSable alumni like Nat 'King' Cole, Redd Foxx, Gene Ammons, Dorothy Donegan, Johnny Griffin and Joseph Jarman.

Visiting musicians were drawn to the provocative music and disciplined camaraderie of the Arkestra, and both Sonny Rollins and John Coltrane played and studied with the band in Chicago during the early and mid fifties.

Historically, Sun Ra's compositions and arrangements followed the advances made in the 1940s by Tadd Dameron and Jimmy Mundy and were contemporaneous with the early experimental writing of Charles Mingus and George Russell.

Instrumentally, the Arkestra was an extension of the popular "little big-band" format of the late forties and early fifties, utilizing trumpet, trombone, two or three saxophones, piano, bass, and drums.

The Arkestra rehearsed at Pat Patrick's house five days a week at noon, experimenting with the radical instrumental combinations and advanced musical concepts devised by its leader.

Sometimes two basses (one double bass, one electric), two drummers, two baritone saxophones and other odd pairings were effected; often tympani, bells, and other then-exotic percussion instruments were used to add new colors to the band's distinctive sound.

Other early musical innovations included Sun Ra's pioneering use of electric piano, Solovox, Clavioline, Hammond organ, Farfisa organ and electric bass; rich arco double-bass passages; group chanting; a saxophone section which doubled on flute, oboe, bassoon, bass clarinet and percussion instruments; and a massed percussion choir throbbing with African and Afro-Cuban polyrhythms.

Sun Ra's avant garde compositions introduced a "space key" where players were instructed to improvise without regard for conventional tonal centers; modal pieces with no fixed harmonic structure; superimposition of one chord over another; and songs played in multiple keys.

His works wove a musical tapestry of unusual rhythms and colors, swinging like crazy at will or moving entirely out of regular time to project a musical environment evocative of outer space.

Sun Ra's use of futuristic keyboards and unusual instrumental voicings goes back to his earliest recordings. He accompanied violinist Stuff Smith in 1953–54 with an ensemble comprising tenor saxophone, trumpet, two basses, drums, percussion and his own Solovox keyboard.

The ensemble then expanded to include three trumpets, six or seven reeds, two or three drummers, electric and acoustic bassists, an assortment of vocalists and an ever-increasing arsenal of electronic keyboard instruments.

The Arkestra's stage presentation was equally advanced: its members wore fezzes over green shirts and rust-colored pants, then graduated to futuristic Afro-space costumes featuring colorful sequin-studded robe-like garments and makeshift space helmets equipped with flashing lights like men in a mine shaft.

Among the many noted musicians who served in the Arkestra during its residency in Chicago (1952–61) were reedmen Marshall Allen, James Spaulding, Charles Davis and James Scales; trumpeters Hobart Dotson, Phil Cohran, George Hudson, Art Hoyle, Dave Young, Lucious Randolph and Walter Strickland; trombonists Julian Priester and Nate Pryor; bassists Ronnie Boykins, Wilburn Green (electric), Vic Sproles and Richard Evans; drummers William Cochran, Jim Herndon, Robert Barry, Edward Skinner and Nimrod Hunt; and vocalists Hatty Randolph and Clyde Williams.

Sun Ra's musical concepts and extra-musical concerns profoundly influenced an entire generation of Chicago musicians who became active in pianist/ composer Muhal Richard Abrams' Experimental Orchestra and later in the Association for the Advancement of Creative Musicians (AACM), as well as experimental jazz artists elsewhere like John Coltrane, Sonny Rollins, Pharaoh Sanders, Cecil Taylor and Marion Brown.

Organizationally, with long-time partner Alton Abraham, Sun Ra also had a deep and lasting effect on the self-determination movement in jazz. He established his own music publishing company, Enterplanetary Koncepts; his own production company, Infinity Inc.; and his own Saturn Records imprint which issued a series of iconoclastic LPs beginning around 1964.

Recorded in Chicago during the 1950s and packaged in crude space-age cover designs, these albums came bearing titles like *Sun Ra Visits Planet Earth*, *We Travel the Spaceways*, *Supersonic Jazz* and *Secrets of the Sun*, boldly presenting the idiosyncratic compositional creations of Sun Ra delivered with exceptional musicianship by the Solar Arkestra.

While he would go on to record for and lease masters to a variety of labels, including Transition, Savoy, ESP-Disk, Delmark, Blue Thumb and ABC/ Impulse, Ra continued to issue albums on Saturn Records all his life so that as much of his music as possible could be documented and made available to his small but fanatical public.

In 1961 the Arkestra left Chicago to play at the World's Fair in Montreal and then traveled down to New York City, where they became stranded after their vehicle broke down.

Some of the members drifted back to Chicago under their own power, but Sun Ra and his core contingent—John Gilmore, Marshall Allen, Pat Patrick, Ronnie Boykins, Clifford Jarvis and James Jackson—settled into a small apartment at 48 East 3rd Street and quickly became a vital part of the city's burgeoning avant garde jazz community.

In New York City between 1961–72, the Arkestra veterans were joined by a host of New York-based musicians including reedmen Ronnie Cummings, Marion Brown, Pharoah Sanders, Eloe Omoe and many others; trumpeters Kwame Hadi, Walter Miller, Clifford Thornton, Manny Smith and Ahktal Ebah; trombonists Ali Hassan, Teddy Nance, Kiane Zawadi (Bernard McKinney) and Bernard Pettaway; bassists Alejandro Blake and John Ore; percussionists Tommy Hunter, Lex Humphries, William Brister, Robert Cummings, Roger Blank and C. Scoby Stroman; and the great vocalist June Tyson.

After a fertile decade at the center of creative activity in New York City, the Arkestra moved en masse to Philadelphia, where Marshall Allen's father had offered the band a large house at 3848 Morton Avenue.

The City of Brotherly Love served as their base for the next twenty years as Sun Ra continued to develop the Arkestra's musical vocabulary and spectacular presentation style.

By this time the Arkestra was universally recognized as the premiere avant garde big band in jazz. Like Duke Ellington, Sun Ra had developed the Arkestra as a means of realizing his unique compositional concepts and created works built around the musical personalities of its members.

As a band leader, Ra always demanded a high level of musical and orchestral discipline as a means to unprecedented freedom of expression and achieved these goals through long hours of daily rehearsals.

These musical workouts were augmented by endless lectures on every topic under the sun until, somehow, Ra would manage to nail everything to the cosmic framework of his interplanetary vision.

In Philadelphia Sun Ra expanded the Arkestra's repertoire to include classical jazz pieces from the 1920s and thirties by Jelly Roll Morton, Fletcher Henderson,

Don Redman, Coleman Hawkins, Duke Ellington, Jimmy Lunceford and others, plus compelling arrangements of pop standards associated with the jazz idiom like Stardust, Deep Purple and Over The Rainbow.

These traditional elements were woven into the fabric of the Arkestra's seamless five hour public performances, presented in a stunning array of rhythms and colors featuring Ra's boldly conceived original works, anthemic space music compositions, wild group improvisations, throbbing multi-rhythmic orgies in percussion, June Tyson's other-worldly vocal performances, teams of energetic dancers, and compelling expositions of Ra's space philosophy set to music and chanted verse.

Almost invariably, at some point in the performance, the entire Arkestra would leave the stage to chant and snake-dance (or as we say in New Orleans, "second-line") through the audience.

Over the course of its existence the Arkestra operated under several banners— Sun Ra & His Solar Arkestra, Space Arkestra, Solar-Myth Arkestra, Astro-Infinity Arkestra, Intergalactic Discipline Arkestra, Astro Intergalactic Infinity Arkestra— according to the particular musico-philosophical goals Ra had established for each discrete series of performances or recordings to be undertaken.

During the late seventies and throughout the eighties, after Sun Ra had broadened the Arkestra's musical palette, he would bill the band as the Omniverse Arkestra and, when they started touring regularly, as the Omniverse Jet-Set Arkestra.

There was nothing like seeing and hearing Sun Ra & his fabulous Arkestra in the full flight of performance. To witness his space philosophy in action as interpreted by the carefully trained Arkestra was sure to provide aesthetic thrills beyond measure.

There was only one Sun Ra, and the world lost one of the most colorful and beloved figures in twentieth-century creative music when the celebrated pianist, composer, and band leader left Planet Earth on Sunday, May 30, 1993.

SUN RA: THE CLASSIC RECORDINGS
1955–1970

THE RECORDED OUTPUT of Sun Ra and his Arkestra is almost beyond measure. Beginning in 1953, when Sun Ra and Alton Abraham determined to document the Arkestra's music through a series of self-financed recording sessions, and continuing almost until the composer's death in 1993, Sun Ra recorded hundreds of his compositions with the Arkestra and saw to their release with the establishment of his own record company, El Saturn Records.

Sun Ra made his first real breakthrough with the record-buying public in 1972 as a result of his triumphant appearance at the Ann Arbor Blues & Jazz Festival (available on CD from Alive/Total Energy Records) and the release of his brilliant *Space Is The Place* suite on the pop music label Blue Thumb Records (now available on CD as MCA/Impulse IMPD-249).

Soon Impulse Records had rushed into print an entire series of albums licensed from Ra and Alton Abraham, and the Arkestra went on to enjoy a long and amazingly productive recording career with scores of LPs and CDs issued by a dazzling variety of record labels all over the world.

While his recordings from 1972–92 enjoyed an ever-widening currency among adventurous listeners, the vast majority of Sun Ra's early works were available only on the tiny El Saturn label operated by Alton Abraham from P.O. Box 7124, Chicago 6, Illinois.

Indeed, except for the occasional outside session—for Transition Records in 1957, Savoy in 1961, and ESP-Disk in 1965–66—El Saturn Records would be the principal outlet for the music of Sun Ra & the Arkestra for its first twenty years.

Packaged with bizarre hand-drawn cover art and often adorned with Sun Ra's poems and mystical writings, the El Saturn LPs presented the musical creations and visionary philosophy of the great composer and band leader and were passed almost from hand to hand among the Arkestra's family, friends and followers who were fortunate enough to get their hands on a maddeningly elusive copy.

Listening to the El Saturn recordings, now available on a remarkable Evidence Records series of fifteen CDs of music recorded by Ra and Abraham between 1955 and 1970, provides the opportunity to trace the development of Sun Ra's incredible musical genius and its manifestation through performance by his exquisitely disciplined ensemble.

From its origins in Chicago to its emergence in New York City ten years later as a completely unique jazz orchestra dedicated to exploring the new frontiers in music mapped out by its leader, the Arkestra can be heard negotiating its difficult course through Ra's constantly expanding musical universe and making hours and hours of delightful, challenging music in the process.

With the assistance of Alton Abraham, Sun Ra began making rough recordings of his Arkestra as early as 1953. These first efforts, backing violinist Stuff Smith on a Sun Ra arrangement of Deep Purple, can be heard on *Sound Sun Pleasure* (Evidence ECD-22014).

A set of five standard tunes arranged by Ra (also on the *Sound Sun Pleasure* CD) was recorded in 1955 by an ensemble which included saxophonist John Gilmore, Art Hoyle on trumpet, Victor Sproles and Ronnie Boykins on basses, and drummer Robert Barry.

The Arkestra began recording in earnest by 1956, cutting original compositions like New Horizons (on *We Travel The Spaceways/Bad and Beautiful*, Evidence ECD-22038), Saturn and Two Tones (on *Sun Ra Visits Planet Earth/Interstellar Low Ways*, Evidence ECD-22039), and a set of Ra creations titled Medicine For A Nightmare, A Call For All Demons and Demon's Lullaby (on *Angels and Demons at Play/The Nubians of Plutonia*, Evidence ECD-22066).

Fledging producer Tom Wilson signed the Arkestra for two LP sessions for his Transition label in 1957. Only the first was released, as *Jazz by Sun Ra* (now available as *Sun Song*, Delmark DD-411), with the composer taking this opportunity to spring full-blown onto the world stage with a comprehensive program of imaginative original works for orchestra and an accompanying pamphlet which laid out his space philosophy in poetry, prose and photos.

The recordings from the two Transition album sessions in 1957 (the second, unissued Transition date is available as *Sound of Joy*, Delmark DD-414) unleashed the oblique but hard-swinging mid fifties sound of Sun Ra & the Arkestra in all its glory, introducing compositions titled Brainville, Lullaby For Realville, Future, Sun Song, Planet Earth, Ankh, Saturn and El Is A Sound Of Joy, and adding Dave Young (trumpet), Julian Priester (trombone), Pat Patrick and Charles Davis (saxophones), William Cochran (drums) and Jim Herndon (tympani and timbales) to the core group of Ra, Gilmore, Hoyle, and Sproles.

By 1958 the Arkestra had expanded to ten or eleven pieces, five of them saxophones: John Gilmore, Pat Patrick, Charles Davis, James Spaulding and Marshall Allen. With Hobart Dotson on trumpet, Julian Priester on trombone, and Boykins and Cochrane in the rhythm section, the Arkestra recorded a program of provocative Sun Ra compositions including Enlightenment, Ancient Aiethopia, Hours After, Horoscope and Images, which would be issued some years later as *Jazz In Silhouette: Images and Forecasts of Tomorrow* (El Saturn LP 205, now available on CD as Evidence ECD-22012).

Ra and Abraham continued to document the composer's work with the Arkestra in Chicago with sessions held between 1958 and 1960 which captured Sun Ra themes like Interplanetary Music, Tapestry From An Asteroid, Space Loneliness, Tiny Pyramids, Between Two Worlds, Music From The World Tomorrow, Plutonian Nights, Nubia, Africa and Watusa, a staple of the Arkestra's repertoire for years to come.

The Arkestra's last days in Chicago in 1960–61 produced recordings of compositions like Space Mates, Lights Of A Satellite, Distant Stars, The Others In Their World, and Rocket Number 9 Take Off For The Planet Venus, another piece that would stay in the Arkestra's repertoire for many years (and probably heard to best advantage on the Blue Thumb *Space is the Place* album). This ensemble featured three trumpets, trombone, and only two saxophones.

In 1961 Sun Ra and the Arkestra resettled in New York City and brought their wildly original music, space-age philosophy, fierce musical discipline and communal economic organization into the center of the city's creative music community.

Many visionary young players—including Marion Brown, Pharoah Sanders, Lex Humphries, Roger Blank and Ali Hassan—soon sought them out in order to study, rehearse and perform with the Arkestra.

In New York Sun Ra first organized a 1961 session at the Choreographers Workshop with core members John Gilmore, Marshall Allen, Pat Patrick and Ronnie Boykins, joined by drummer Tommy "Bugs" Hunter, to record a program of standards and originals (Ankh, Searchlight Blues) later released as the El Saturn LP *Bad and Beautiful* and now on the Evidence CD *We Travel the Spaceways/Bad and Beautiful* (ECD-22038).

Ra also crossed paths again with producer Tom Wilson, now out of college and making a series of provocative albums by John Coltrane & Cecil Taylor, Charles Mingus, Bill Evans and others for labels like United Artists and Savoy.

Wilson got the Arkestra a date with Savoy in October 1961 and delivered *The Futuristic Sounds of Sun Ra* (on CD as Savoy Jazz SV-0213), a program of compositions like Where Is Tomorrow, Looking Outward and Space Jazz Reverie performed by the core group plus New Yorkers Kiane Zawadi and one-time Thelonious Monk drummer Willie Jones.

Between 1961 and 1963 the Arkestra recorded several New York City sessions at their own expense, realizing new Sun Ra compositions like We Travel The Spaceways, Calling Planet Earth, When Sun Comes Out, Voice Of Space, Cluster Of Galaxies, Solar Drums, Lights On A Satellite and Infinity Of The Universe," now available on the Evidence Records CDs titled *When Sun Comes Out* (ECD-22068) and *Cosmic Tones for Mental Therapy/Art Forms of Dimensions Tomorrow* (ECD-22036).

During this fertile period the Arkestra continued to grow in scope, proficiency and number as Sun Ra's master plan began to take visible shape.

By now the reed section had doubled, with Danny Davis, Robert Cummings, and James Jackson joining Gilmore, Allen, and Patrick; drummers Lex Humphries, Clifford Jarvis, Tommy Hunter and C. Scoby Strohman were on board; Clifford Thornton, Walter Miller and Manny Smith came in on trumpets, along with trombonists Teddy Nance, Bernard Pettaway and Ali Hassan, and former Monk bassist John Ore.

Sun Ra and the Arkestra also became involved in the avant garde jazz movement that would produce the Jazz Composers Guild—an alliance of radical composers including Carla Bley, Ornette Coleman, Don Cherry, Roswell Rudd, Bill Dixon, Paul Bley and others who proposed to form a producers' cooperative to record and issue their own album productions—and, in the fall of 1964, mounted the October Revolution in Jazz, a series of self-produced concerts showcasing the original music of Guild members and their ensembles which brought their music to the attention of the somewhat hidebound modern jazz community.

By this time Sun Ra and Alton Abraham had decided to begin to exploit the vast catalog of master recordings they had assembled over the past ten years by launching their own El Saturn Records label. The initial El Saturn releases—*Fate in a Pleasant Mood, Interstellar Low Ways, Supersonic Jazz, Jazz in Silhouette, Sun Ra Visits Planet Earth*—were mostly drawn from recordings made in Chicago, but soon Sun Ra's startling new compositional concepts and arrangements would be revealed in a series of contemporaneous releases which clearly established the composer at the forefront of modern music.

The major works Other Planes Of There (1964), at twenty two minutes, and The Magic City (1965), at over twenty seven minutes of ceaseless invention, introduced Sun Ra's extended form and all-encompassing vision to stunning effect with music which had simply never been heard before.

The Arkestra reached a slightly larger audience with its three albums for Bernard Stollman's ESP-Disk label in 1965–66. *The Heliocentric Worlds of Sun Ra*, Volumes 1 & 2 (ESP-Disk 1014 and 1017), with the extended works Cosmic Chaos and The Sun Myth, are in a class with The Magic City, and the live recording, *Nothing Is* (ESP-Disk 1045), presents the Arkestra in all its splendor as it appeared on stage, featuring vocal chants on Sun Ra And His Band From Outer Space, Theme Of The Stargazers and Next Stop Mars and unbridled improvisational passages by Arkestra saxophone mainstays John Gilmore, Marshall Allen and Pat Patrick throughout.

While their ESP-disc releases attracted the attention of the jazz press and a small coterie of avant garde jazz enthusiasts, the demand for any kind of jazz recordings—let alone the most advanced manifestations of the idiom—continued its steep decline in the wake of the rock revolution and its utter dominance of the popular music marketplace.

But Sun Ra continued to maintain a strong presence among his dedicated listener base by issuing a continuous stream of El Saturn releases offering music recorded between 1956 and 1970, including *Art Forms of Dimensions Tomorrow, The Lady with the Golden Stockings, Angels and Demons at Play, Cosmic Tones for Mental Therapy, We Travel the Spaceways, Atlantis, Sound Sun Pleasure* and *My Brother the Wind*.

EL SATURN RECORDS

NOTE: Since the lowest numbered El Saturn LP release here (LP 202) includes material recorded by the Arkestra in New York City in 1963, it seems apparent that the label issued its first releases in New York City in 1964.

LP 202	*Fate in a Pleasant Mood* (Chicago 1960/NYC 1963) (ECD-22068)
LP 203	*Interstellar Low Ways* (Chicago 1960) (ECD-22039)
LP 204	[?] *Supersonic Jazz* (ECD-22015)
LP 205	*Jazz in Silhouette* (Chicago 1958) (ECD-22012)
LP 206	*Other Planes of There* (NYC 1964) (ECD-22037)
LP 207	*Sun Ra Visits Planet Earth* (Chicago 1956–58) (ECD-22039)
LP 403	*The Magic City* (NYC 1965) (ECD-22069)
LP 404	*Art Forms of Dimensions Tomorrow* (NYC 1963) (ECD-22036)
LP 405	[?]
LP 406	*The Lady with the Golden Stockings* (The Nubians of Plutonia) (Chicago 1958–59) (ECD-22066)
LP 407	*Angels and Demons at Play* (Chicago 1956) (ECD-22066)
LP 408	*Cosmic Tones for Mental Therapy* (NYC 1961) (ECD-22036)
LP 409	*We Travel the Spaceways* (Chicago 1956) (ECD-22038)
LP 507	*Atlantis* (NYC 1967–69) (ECD-22067)
LP 512	*Sound Sun Pleasure* (Chicago 1958–60) (ECD-22014)
LP 523	*My Brother the Wind* (NYC 1969–70) (ECD-22040)
LP 532	*Bad and Beautiful* (Chicago 1960) (ECD-22038)
LP 2066	*When Sun Comes Out* (NYC 1963) (ECD-22068)

EVIDENCE RECORDS: EL SATURN ON CD

ECD-22011	*Holiday for Soul Dance*
ECD-22012	*Jazz in Silhouette*
ECD-22013	*Monorails and Satellites*
ECD-22014	*Sound Sun Pleasure!!*
ECD-22015	*Super-Sonic Jazz*
ECD-22036	*Cosmic Tones for Mental Therapy/Art Forms of Dimensions Tomorrow*
ECD-22037	*Other Planes of There*

ECD-22038	*We Travel the Spaceways/Bad and Beautiful*
ECD-22039	*Sun Ra Visits Planet Earth/Interstellar Low Ways*
ECD-22040	*My Brother the Wind Vol. II*
ECD-22066	*Angels and Demons at Play/The Nubians of Plutonia*
ECD-22067	*Atlantis*
ECD-22068	*Fate in a Pleasant Mood/When Sun Comes Out*
ECD-22069	*The Magic City*
ECD-22070	*Space is the Place* (film soundtrack, 1972)
ECD-22164	*Sun Ra: The Singles* (1954–82)

SUN RA MEMORIES

MY FIRST REAL EXPOSURE to the music and legend of Sun Ra came in the fall of 1964, when drummer Roger Blank passed through Detroit with a jazz trio I can't remember the name of.

We put him up for a few days in our stronghold at the Detroit Artists Workshop Cooperative Housing Project, and I watched Roger open his suitcase and pull out what were obviously his most prized possessions: two weird LPs on the El Saturn label with garish outer space art on the covers and names like *Supersonic Jazz* and *Jazz in Silhouette*.

I had read about the avant garde Chicago pianist and band leader in *downbeat* and other jazz magazines, but his music was still so far underground that few people outside the band's immediate orbit had ever heard it.

By this time the apocryphal *Jazz by Sun Ra* album on Transition Records was long out of print, and only *The Futuristic Sounds of Sun Ra* (Savoy, 1961) was currently available.

I knew the Arkestra had moved to New York City and taken the creative music community by storm, but its music was still pretty much only a thing of legend and not something you could put on your turntable and listen to at will.

Blank regaled us with tales of Sun Ra and his fantastic Arkestra—how they all lived together in a tiny apartment at 48 East 3rd Street on the lower east side of New York City, where at least a dozen grown men crammed into a three-room pad and rose each day for the mandatory noon rehearsal.

They might go for months without an actual gig, working religiously on mastering the uniquely imaginative compositions and arrangements created for them by their leader with no hope of more than a musical reward.

By 1964 Sun Ra and his long-time partner in Chicago, Alton Abraham, had launched their own label, El Saturn Records, but the fledgling company seemed to distribute its products strictly on a hand-to-hand basis.

Seeing two of them now, popping out of Roger Blank's suitcase in Detroit, sent thrills coursing throughout my being—they were so rare it was like the answer to a prayer.

Soon Sun Ra would release two startling albums—*The Heliocentric Worlds of Sun Ra*, Volumes 1 & 2—on the new avant garde jazz label ESP-disc, which finally brought his music to the attention of the jazz world at large.

On a trip to New York City in the fall of 1966 after I'd been released from a six month prison sentence at the Detroit House of Correction, I made a pilgrimage to 48 East 3rd and spent some time with Sun Ra and the Arkestra, even managing to interview the enigmatic composer for our underground paper in Detroit, the *Warren-Forest Sun*.

One evening I showed up at the pad with my tiny Opel sedan just in time to serve as the major transport for the Arkestra's gig that night at the Jazz Arts Society of New Jersey in Newark, where they ended up playing for just about as many people as were in the band—about fifteen.

In the spring of 1967 I arranged for the Arkestra to make its first Detroit appearance at the Community Arts Auditorium on the Wayne State University campus, a 600 seat venue. They shared the bill with the MC5 and the Magic Veil Light Show and played to maybe 100 people.

The gate receipts were so miniscule that one of the members of our Detroit commune, Emil Bacilla, ended up driving the Arkestra back to New York City in his Volkswagen bus because we were unable to pay the band's transportation costs.

During my tenure (1967–69) as manager of the MC5, I shared with the band my unbridled enthusiasm for Sun Ra's musical message and his cosmic space philosophy. In 1968 the MC5 developed a piece called Starship, a wild space odyssey in the amplified-guitar-and-rock-drums idiom into which the singer Rob Tyner incorporated Sun Ra's poem, "There / is a place / where the sun shines / eternally..."

Starship made it onto the 5's first album for Elektra Records, with Sun Ra sharing composer's credit with the MC5.

In the spring of 1969 I arranged for Sun Ra and the Arkestra to come out to Michigan for a month-long residency. We rented the house next door to our commune at 1510 Hill Street in Ann Arbor for them and presented the Arkestra in concert with the MC5 at several area venues, including Detroit's Grande Ballroom, the Ann Arbor Armory, and at the First Detroit Rock & Roll Revival Festival at the Michigan State fairgrounds, where they headlined with Chuck Berry and the MC5 in a bill designed to showcase the past, present and future of the music.

When I had the opportunity to select the artists for the 1972 Ann Arbor Blues & Jazz Festival, I scheduled Sun Ra & the Arkestra to close the first night's show, following performances by the Seigel-Schwall Blues Band, the Contemporary Jazz Quintet (CJQ), Junior Walker & the All-Stars and Howlin' Wolf.

Sun Ra completely wowed the crowd of 12,000 with the Arkestra's spectacular presentation of space-age improvisational music, brilliant costumery and frenzied choreography. On the Atlantic Records 1972 festival album, the audience can be heard chanting "Sun Ra! Sun Ra! Sun Ra!" for several minutes following the end of the Arkestra's performance.

Sun Ra's 1973 appearance was more highly anticipated than ever before. Now he was incorporating his philosophical disquisitions into the stage show itself, casting his views into verse and presenting them via a three-part vocal chorale to stunning effect.

A new suite based on the previous year's smash success, *Space is the Place*, had been prepared to introduce Ra's concept of an "Outer Space Employment Agency" which would put the idled workers of post-industrial America back into a productive mode outside the tired orbit of Earth.

The Arkestra was again a big hit at the 1973 festival, and they were scheduled to return for the 1974 event when hassles with the Ann Arbor city government impelled us to move the Ann Arbor Blues & Jazz Festival to Windsor, Ontario, just across the river from downtown Detroit.

I was trying to shepherd the Arkestra through Canadian customs when I was singled out and deported back to Detroit on the basis of a marijuana conviction ten years previously.

I went back to my room in the Shelby Hotel and watched myself talking to a television news reporter covering my deportation proceedings.

This experience marked a major turning point in my life when I considered that the farthest-out group of characters I had ever seen in America was allowed entry to Canada, while I was turned back as "too far out".

"You've gone too far," I said to myself. "It's time to turn back now."

That fall I retired from political activism and the rock & roll scene to take up less grueling pursuits, working as an alternative journalist and editor for a couple of years and then opening a small community arts consulting business focused on providing program development and grant-writing services to indigenous jazz artists and organizations.

This led to the establishment of the Detroit Jazz Center in 1979, and by the end of 1980 the Jazz Center was presented with the opportunity to bring in Sun Ra and the Omniverse Jet-Set Arkestra for a week-long residency in downtown Detroit.

Rick Steiger, an aspiring young saxophonist and band leader (Kuumba, the

Sun Messengers, the Sun Sounds Orchestra) from the east side and a regular participant in the Jazz Center's various activities, came to me with an attractive proposal: he had just inherited a couple of thousand dollars from a dearly departed relative, and he wanted to use this windfall to finance a trip to the Motor City by Sun Ra & the Arkestra.

He would engage the band for the week between Christmas and New Year; we would lodge them at the Jazz Center, present the Arkestra in a series of concerts in our after-hours performance space called the Jazz Gallery, and host daily workshops with the band where local musicians could meet, hang out, study and play with the members of the Arkestra.

After a full week of nightly concerts which were carefully taped for posterity, culminating in three shows on New Year's Eve, Sun Ra ended his residency at 6:00am January 1, 1981 by sending band representative Danny "Pekoe" Thompson down to the studio where I was packing up the results of our live recording sessions.

Pekoe asked if we'd like to co-produce an album from the tapes with them, and I was curious as to what that would involve. When he mentioned that they would want us to pay for issuing the record, I explained that there was nothing in the Jazz Center's pitiful budget for such a project.

"Oh, man," he sighed, "Sun Ra says just reach down in that oil money and pull some out—they won't miss it."

And there it was: for something like fifteen years, while I had sacrificed all available funds, energy, and even my reputation at times to present the Arkestra in Michigan as often as possible, Sun Ra had taken me for an heir to the Sinclair Oil Company fortune!

I saw Sun Ra after that many times over the years and never failed to recall that shocking conversation. I would continue to appreciate the music and performances of the Arkestra as long as Ra lived, but the avid idealism which had driven me to pursue these great feats of derring-do would never again return.

INTERVIEW WITH SUN RA

JOHN SINCLAIR: *I guess we can talk about the planet...*

SUN RA: Well, the planet is in such a bad condition that it's inexpressible. It was bad enough but now it's got worse. They're not sure about their religions, they're not sure about their politics, they're not sure about education and philosophy, they're not sure about anything...so you've got complete confusion.

Utter Chaos...

They had utter chaos, then ultra chaos...it's knocking on everybody's door. In the past things came and knocked on a few people's doors, but this is a different age. It's like the atomic bomb, it knocks on everybody's door. That makes a different story. Everybody's involved.

I don't think everybody's caught up in this chaos, I mean I think we both know people who have got something to offer. Instead of that.

Yeah, they got something to offer, but can they do anything about it? That's the problem. Just to have something to offer isn't enough now. So many men and women have come around with something to offer, and some of them became successful, but that doesn't mean anything. Maybe success meaning that they were recognized by the masses or by the rulers, one or the other, but they really don't have any power to retain any success. They're here today and gone tomorrow. If they would come over into another environment or another planet, they wouldn't be successful.

And most of them are caught up in their little bags, in their own little thing, and I call that an eternity—they're over in a cycle, an eternity, a circle...so they stay over in there, because there's comparative safety there—seemingly. And they stay over in there until some unknown force strikes the surface and snatches them out of there and they disappear—they're not on the planet. So they really didn't make it.

Real security means you have protection, I'd say, forever. Even people with guns and all that, like policemen, they don't have any security...something'll snatch them away too. They talk about protecting a state or a government, but they can't even protect themselves. There's something knocking at everybody's door, and it's not to be denied. Governments know it...because people are changing, a lot [of] people are getting so they just don't care, you know, something is happening but they just don't have any go-it-iveness or initiative. So how are you going to rule if you have people like that? If you got people who don't care?

So, actually, the rulers on this planet are in trouble. And I sympathize with them. The people are slowing down more and more, and they're changing every day. So it's gotten to that point now...and this is where a lot of musicians don't really see it. They got their new music, and their new thing, and that's nice, that's a thrill, but what's going to happen after the thrill dies down? What good's music if you don't have people to play it for? When you got people who are hopeless, it's contagious.

So many of the musicians are seeking to escape from all that, I can see that, and for a long time the musicians could escape—but now they're faced with something else. They got to change the way they write, they got to change the way they play, and of course it comes down to strict discipline. The people have had freedom, but they really haven't done anything. I'm not even interested in it, because that doesn't help anybody. The only freedom they'll get is over in the cemetery; then they'll be free. It's a scientific truth: people are only free when they're dead.

So actually, if I was ruling, I wouldn't let the people talk about freedom. I wouldn't let the people talk about freedom, I wouldn't let them fight for it, I wouldn't let them speak of it...I wouldn't let them talk about peace, I wouldn't let them picket for it, I wouldn't let them have anything to do with peace. Because the whole thing is very simple: they're free when they're dead, and they're at rest, and at peace when they're dead. It actually says so: rest in peace.

So when the United States be talking about peace, it's talking about death. They mean that kind of peace. And when the people got a Prince of Peace, the Prince would have to be Death. Of course, this is another kind of mathematics I'm doing...it's something that they can see if they'll just go and look in the cemetery. There's a lot of people out there—it's a city, they got more people out there than they got on the planet walking around. And they are showing you what peace is. Because they at peace—final peace, definite, absolute peace. Now they're free, too—and nothing bothers their freedom. They're free to be dead.

I've had a lot of difficulty trying to tell people that they should investigate that peace and that freedom, because what I'm trying to tell them is too incredible to be true. They say that truth is stranger than fiction, but I know one thing—I balance my equations, and I balance them scientifically, and I know that that's the main thing bothering this planet. It's come out in the open now—not all that power—the power of peace and freedom...and equality.

The only equality they got too, is that all of them die. I notice that all of them don't have the same amount of money, though, or the same amount of opportunity—so it's not really true. I know I never had some opportunities that I should have had—I never had them—probably because I wasn't interested in them. Too limited.

You say you've changed the name of the band from the Myth-Science Arkestra to the Astro-Infinity Arkestra...

Well, actually I didn't change it—that's just one of the dimensions. Because when I play sometimes I use "Myth-Science"—I've got some songs that come under that—and then I had some under the Solar Arkestra...and then I got the

Astro-Infinity—and all of them mean different things to me.

Other Planes of There...

Yes...all of them are based on these other planes, which is actually...I mean I think people need them now. They should be trying them out, see what'll happen. In fact they're gonna have to—because I might be on Jupiter or Mars by then. Because I'm not stopping my program.

Now I got the Solar Arkestra, the Myth-Science, and the Astro-Infinity—and soon I'll have something else. Just like a university—I've got my different courses set up—and they deal with things that are going to be beneficial to people. But it's not religious, like some people are saying—I'm not the least bit religious, I'm not interested in that. Because churches don't do anything but bring people...peace.

What I'm talking about is discipline—striving for things that will never be, they need to discipline themselves so they can do something beneficial for people. But they keep talking about peace. Like I say, the only time they'll be peaceful is when they're dead—they'll look very peaceful then, and they'll BE very peaceful.

Now, my contention is that some people or some intelligence has fixed up words for people, and they got a choice of what they want. There are some words that sound very bad, but they are very good for people. And there are some words that sound very good, but they are very bad. And this is what is really happening on this planet—it's very simple. Some intelligence set up words, and enticed the people to be part of that word. They set up civilizations, churches, educational systems, all based on words. You can see that something is wrong—and if something is wrong, it must be the educational system and what it teaches them to think. It's in the political system, and the religious system, it's even over in the science department so to speak.

What does the music have to do with this, then?

The music...a lot of musicians are ideal, they're in tune with the earth, they're in tune with the people—please the people—they please the people or please the rulers. They're the ones who've got the money. They're playing what the people want, or what they say the people want. But these musicians are really quite afraid—afraid of stepping beyond tradition, into something that would require new ways of thinking and new ways of action.

However, they're not afraid to go out there in space and all, like the astronauts...because it's necessary in these times. And it's necessary for them to keep agitating for peace, and to keep killing each other like they do. That's the main thing about science, that it's set up to find new ways for people to kill each other. And yet I used to think that was so bad…but now, after looking at people, the more I see them I'm not going to condemn them for eliminating each other—not any more I'm not—not when I see what they are. I thought they were very nice and true and spiritual and it hurt me to see them doing what they do.

But now it doesn't bother me, because I'm involved with my other planes of discipline. I'm trying to discipline my self—I mean my other self, because I'm not too worried about my self. Because they teach you not to be selfish anyway, not to think about your self. So I think about my other self—that's the self that's never really had a chance.

The music that I'm playing, that's my other self playing. And that disturbs some people because they never gave that other self a chance. The natural self. So that's my natural self playing. And it's very serious—a lot of people think they can just come on this planet and do what they want to do, be what they want to be, and there's no repercussions whatsoever. But that's not true.

It's not a matter of having no hell—this is hell here—but it's just a matter of, eventually reaping just what you sow. Whether it's good or bad. You set up something, and then it starts to happen. It's like when I started studying, I wanted to find out what was happening on this planet. Then I found out that it's in a worse condition than I ever dreamed of, and I didn't want to have anything to do with it. But since I had set that up as my objective, I can't avoid it.

How did you start studying?

I suppose it started back when I was going to Sunday school…and I just didn't feel like going there. I liked to walk around with my friends in the sun and talk and see each other. That's what we'd do—play hookey from Sunday school and walk around in the sun and talk—three or four of us—I felt happy then, being outside of school, because they taught the same thing every year—it was like a commercial thing—never anything else.

I never learned anything in school—just repeating words. The people in the school were nice—they were nice people—but there was just something wrong. Then I had to really study, read a lot of books. Then I went to college, and that was interesting too, read a lot of books there, but the men who taught me didn't prove anything.

The point about it was, if there wasn't a god, then people wouldn't die. I came to that conclusion, that the only reason people died was because there is a god, and the only reason people are suffering is because there is a god. The way to look at it, the way people die proves that something is killing them—something superior to them always wins. A superior force.

So death is a god, if nothing else, and all people are subject to it, so death's their god. They aren't actually subject to the United States or Russia or anything, they're subject to their god—Death. That's very obvious. The point is, having reached that point, what to do about it? If they ever reach that point, should they be obedient to the god Death or should they be rebels? Because if they're obedient to God and are righteous, then the most appropriate thing to do is to die. Then, when they're dead, they're holy and righteous.

What happens if you rebel?

If you rebel, then you move over into uncharted paths and…and of course they won't like it. What would God look like if his subjects were to rebel? But you don't have nothing to lose—because you don't have anything anyway, really. I don't see anything Death gets people—might send them some flowers, but they can't even smell them. The only thing it offers them is…absolute peace.

It's so ridiculous to say that everybody has to die—it's a waste of time—people with magnificent minds, magnificent talents, why can't they keep on going on? Because it doesn't even make sense that they shouldn't. That's what I'm talking about in my music—all my music really has happiness over in it… and people can listen to it and get that from it.

I know I got something to help people but—I don't know what to do about it. I can put it over in music, the happiness in that or what I call the space feeling—it's in the music and everybody can hear that. I've got some beauty for them too—there's no sadness over in that. Not the way most musicians do…they have very great emotions…I appreciate every musician, I don't care what kind of music they play. I appreciate anything that any musician does on a planet like this one. It's very heartening in a sense to find somebody trying to do something besides killing people.

Like I wrote a number—I think the name of it was If I Had A Hammer—and some gospel group did it. It was a masterpiece the way they did it—they feel it and I appreciate that. But unfortunately some jazz musicians speak against this form of music—the new form of music—and this is very bad because it's very narrow-minded. It's not right.

Because jazz in the earlier days—the musicians were innovators and they were playing something that wasn't according to the status quo and they appreciated one another and anybody who DID something different they appreciated them and supported them—even if they couldn't play it they supported it—they didn't talk about it and all that.

You got a case where a lot of successful musicians and some people who say they are musicians are talking against innovators of music. It's very bad to find that musicians want to restrict another musician. I don't see the artists restricting the artists, I really don't see that. Even in religion I notice the churches—the Catholic Church is getting liberal and changing their rules. Even governments are relaxing their rules and laws.

Now a case like that, where all these diehards and at least the people who just held to the status quo are beginning to see that they're going to have to give in—it's imperative that all musicians stop criticizing their brother musicians because they're innovators and they really should be happening and they really should be taking some of the money they're making and putting up some sums and be right there with them listening or helping because they don't have anything to lose. In fact they could invest in them and make themselves some money.

Now they're trying to be selfish in an art that you're not supposed to be selfish in. Because you can go all the way back and see that the musicians used to be minstrels—troubadors—they weren't selfish—they were out there playing for people. Now a lot of people are getting to say that musicians are trying to be politicians or trying to be religious and all of that, but that's not necessarily true. They're only doing what their brother musicians did, through the ages. They gave what they had to give because they were interested in people and they came out and brought something people needed.

Just like people need music now. Even the Army can't get along without it— they got their band, and the Marines got their band and the Navy and the Air Force got their band and everything has its music. They got to have that. Now why can't people just have bands? They're fighting too, just like any soldier— they're fighting a battle to exist every day and their morale gets low too.

So I would say that if governments are going to have bands to keep up the morale of their soldiers and the ones who pay the soldiers are the people, why can't they have bands to keep the morale of the people up? I think they do deserve something because they're paying so much taxes and they're paying the politician's salary and they're keeping the thing going, so they should not be deprived of music and entertainment…they deserve some entertainment just as much as soldiers do.

I'm not saying that soldiers should not have it. They need it. If they're going to be in the business of murder incorporated. Because that's really all it is and even a simple child knows that…I go by feeling and spirit too. I'm not 'righteous' but I know that spirits can tune in on other spirits, and these people's spirits are plenty low.

So you come down to the point where you've got to have a better world. Now my contribution is in the music. In the first place, I feel that people have got to know—they got to know what happens as is. Now, they've never really been happy on this planet because they didn't ever have anything to be happy about. So then I show them in the music and give a feeling of happiness so they'll know when they're happy and when they're sad.

But I really don't think people know the difference between good and evil and right and wrong on this planet. They simply don't think…Now, to some people it seems like the music doesn't have anything to do with what I'm talking about, but it does. Because music is a language and I'm speaking these things over in it. So in order to understand the music people will have to know some of the thoughts I'm thinking. They'll know what I'm thinking and what I really want, and they will have a better understanding…

Now, my music is about a better place for people to live, not to have a place where they have to die to get there, I'm not talking about that, I'm talking about a place where they can live a method out—my equation is that it's very bad to live and it's very bad to die, because if you live you die and if you die you live… because here's an equation set up that's fooling folks.

Now, the same thing happens in music. There's a certain place a musician reaches where he bases what he's doing on laws. So if you reach a certain point then there's nothing binding or holding you back. If you study long enough, or if you feel in tune with something, you've got a perfect right to express yourself. That's what I've done—I've passed the point of the law, and yet when people really see what I'm doing it does follow the law—it doesn't really break the law, but it's an advanced point of it in a sense…I'm capable of doing it and I do it naturally, and actually I should have had a chance some time ago to write not only for my band, but for other musicians to share what I'm doing as well. So they can learn something too.

Because I know I always learn from other musicians, like when I play in somebody else's band I always learn something, I always appreciated what they were doing. It's wonderful for a musician to write an arrangement, to create something, and you play it and see what his ideas are. It's quite a pleasure. And I certainly played in a lot of bands—they didn't even know that I could arrange, because I never really cared about it. It was just a matter of fate pushing me into other people's eyesight.

Because I do have something to offer them other than music. And they have to face it, because I have to face it you see. They're going to have to really consider it. And that goes for preachers too. I feel sorry for them. I don't know of anybody I feel more sorry for, unless it's the President of the United States or the people who are ruling. Because they got a job on their hands.

Because they're changing ages—one age moves over into another one, and the rulers—they're in trouble. You've got not only a change of age, but a change of laws—the law that has been the law on this planet has moved over to no longer be the law. Now when that happens, and since this planet for thousands of years has been up under that law of death and destruction, it's moving over into something else which I choose to call MYTH, a MYTH-SCIENCE, because it's something that people don't know anything about.

That's why I'm using the name MYTH-SCIENCE ARKESTRA, because I'm interested in happiness for people, which is just a myth, because they're not happy. I would say that the synonym for myth is happiness—because that's why they go to the show, to the movies, they be sitting up there under these myths trying to get themselves some happiness.

And if the actors can indulge in myth, why can't the musicians? They might be actors in sound, they got a right to do that, the only thing about musicians is that I notice they don't do too much sticking together. So with the musicians, I try them out and see just what they can do—because I don't consider myself part of this planet because I don't act like them, and I've noticed that some people treat me very cruel and run over me just like they thought I was a fool. But it wasn't that, I was sympathetic with them and trying to help them because I saw their terrible condition and thought that maybe they could see the point...

I feel that musicians are actually going to have to tell the truth about each other and be honest so they can get some respect from the world—because the world might not know these things like I'm saying, but they can FEEL them. They can feel it when a musician is not sincere, and this is the reason why a lot of people have got disinterested in musicians, because they feel so much phony-ism.

Musicians get it in their mind that they want to be great or they get up there and forget that they're not really great, that there's some musicians who have played things and have done things that had more value possibly than what they're doing, because they were living in a different age and they were much happier. You can get some old records that are beautiful and you'll never forget them. There's a record by Duke Ellington called Jazz Cocktail and I...when I was growing up I always liked to listen to that record, it was really a masterpiece of arranging and had a lot of happiness in it...

It was sincere music, and sincere music is what's happening now. The pretenders and the phonies are all done—they've had their day—and they're producing some nice sounds. It's very strong, but they're not doing anything with it. One thing though, the musicians who are playing the new thing are going to have to learn music thoroughly, that's because I know it thoroughly you see. A lot of people say that I'm just playing around, but it's not like that. I know all the laws of music, I was reared up playing classics and I went to college and studied music for teacher training, so I know music.

But I'm just following my own way, and I know what I'm doing. All the musicians in my band are thoroughly trained, they can read anything, and they have to be able to do that if they're going to work with my band. Every one of them—schooled musicians—in fact, I had to unschool them. And I'm still doing it. That's the way it is.

Do you want to make any last statement?

Yes… You know, I feel that the colleges are looking for something that's different, but I feel that there are some blocks between my music and the people who would understand what I'm talking about and could help me. But some way they have been blocked from it, and know what I know, and they don't know what I know, and they should be trying to find out. I know what they know, too, that's pretty one-sided, I know what they know and they don't know what I know. I took time out to study what they know, and it's nice, and they should take time out to study what I know, and they should compare it to what they know. So they can get someplace. That's what should be happening.

New York City > Detroit
August 1966

#97

"everything happens to me"

for mark ritsema

all my life I've paid
& paid, until my dues card
is punched up
on all 4 sides,

a child
of relative privilege who chose
to 'take the way
of the lowest'—

race traitor & renegade,
beatnik,
dope fiend,
poet provocateur,

living from hand to mouth
& euro to euro,
sleeping on the couches
& extra beds of my friends,

a man without a country
& a post office box in new orleans
for a permanent address,
a pre-pay vodafone

& a laptop computer,
one suitcase stuffed with clothing
& a bag full of manuscripts
& hand-burnt CDs—

to keep my head straight
& my heart right,
to keep up my travels
& carry on the struggle

into another new year,
taking my little verses
& great big world outlook
everywhere people will have me

amsterdam, january 7, 2004 /
rotterdam, january 15, 2004

ART ENSEMBLE OF CHICAGO

Ancient to the Future

A SMALL ARMY of instruments is what you see first—an entire stage full of saxophones, drums, gongs, percussion implements of every description, bicycle horns, hubcaps, xylophones, marimbas, reeds and trumpets almost beyond measure. And you get the picture right away: you're going to hear some people who really came to play!

When the five members of the Art Ensemble of Chicago take the stage to wield this vast musical arsenal, there's no predicting what will come next. They come at you from all over the place, musically, and they open things up so far, in so many different directions, by the time they're done you've been to a lot of places you've never been before—even if you're heard the Art Ensemble many times previously.

It's not that easy to catch them, though, because the Art Ensemble of Chicago doesn't tour so often, and when they do form up and travel, it's a rare year that we get to hear them here in the Motor City. Like so many masters of African American art music, from Benny Carter to Cecil Taylor to the World Saxophone Quartet, the Art Ensemble is far better known in Europe and Japan than in its homeland, and it's still the rarest of things to hear one of their many stupendous recordings on the American radio airwaves.

But they'll be at Music Hall Friday night, October 28, for their first major concert hall appearance in Detroit since their formation some twenty years ago. They'll be here in town in full force, in splendid array, ready as ever to challenge and overcome every conceivable musical cliche and turn the night into pure music. Like Valerie Wilmer says, "They can smoke you away with a breath of air or a wave of the hand"—and what's more, one might add, they most certainly will.

The Art Ensemble's music is a veritable compendium of historical styles, an endless cornucopia of imagination and creativity and artistic intelligence, a vivid panorama of brilliant improvisation, catchy themes, hysterical wit and sardonic humor. They are really playing, in the highest sense of the term, yet they are not playing, which is to say they are as serious as your life about making music that is an accurate and precise registration of the sum of their individual and collective experience as men and musicians here on the planet of Earth.

The Art Ensemble of Chicago has now been a unit for a fifth of a century; its members pursue their own individual paths most of the time, but they come together every so often to take up the music of the Art Ensemble and make it new again, always something greater than the sum of its human and musical parts.

Lester Bowie and Don Moye were just here for the Montreux-Detroit Festival as members of The Leaders, and Roscoe Mitchell is a frequent guest of the Creative Arts Collective, which he helped institute during a stay outside East Lansing in the mid seventies. Joseph Jarman splits his time between Chicago and New York, ever involved in creative projects of many descriptions, and Malachi Favors stays busy working and playing around Chicago.

These are lifetime players, total music makers, masters of modern (or should we call it postmodern) jazz who draw upon the deepest well-springs of ancestral music in order to take their art where it has not yet been. They have opened up the music wider than anyone who came before them, yet they have brought in more historical elements and turned on more people to the glorious past than one would have thought possible.

Roscoe Mitchell (reeds) and Malachi Favors (bass), native Chicagoans, first played together in The Experimental Band formed by pianist/composer Muhal Richard Abrams in the early sixties. Joseph Jarman (reeds), a native of Pine Bluff, Arkansas, and Lester Bowie (brass), a trumpet son of St. Louis, first got together musically with Mitchell and Favors as mid sixties members of The Experimental Band.

By the time these men made their first recordings in 1966, they had become key members of the Association for the Advancement of Creative Musicians (AACM), an African American artists' cooperative founded by Abrams, Phil Cohran, Jodie Christian and Troy Robinson to reawaken and vitalize the Chicago jazz scene.

The AACM and Jarman, Mitchell, Favors and Bowie were soon joined by luminaries-to-be Leo Smith, Leroy Jenkins, Phillip Wilson, Steve McCall, Maurice McIntyre, Lester Lashley, and Anthony Braxton to head up a vast new wave of "free jazz" practitioners who followed in the wake of John Coltrane, Cecil Taylor, Ornette Coleman, Charles Mingus and Eric Dolphy.

These protean Chicagoans who came of artistic age in the late sixties and early seventies brought something to the music that had largely been missing for most of a generation: a reverence for the historical past, and a new understanding of the role of the ancestral forms as a basis for whatever might come out of their postmodern imaginations.

Their music, though more widely various than any previous 'school' associated with a single city, also related strongly to earlier developments of the idiom right there in the Windy City. The AACM musicians took stock of seventy years of jazz accomplishment and integrated the achievements of their predecessors into their own contemporary visions to forge a new approach to composition, improvisation, and performance which put Chicago right back in the middle of the jazz map.

Chicago has always gotten short shrift when people think about African

American classical music—commonly known as jazz—and the ways it has developed. Jazz came to Chicago before the music was even called "jazz" by its originators in New Orleans. Freddie Keppard took the music to Los Angeles early in 1912 with the Original Creole Ragtime Orchestra, dropped the 'Ragtime' in San Francisco, and went to Chicago in 1914. After moving into New York City in 1915 and touring the east coast with the music, Freddie Keppard settled in Chicago in 1918.

New Orleans pianist/composer Jelly Roll Morton was in Chicago in 1912, heading west from New York City. The Roll took the music all over the country between 1905 and 1917, then spent five years in Los Angeles before settling in Chicago in 1922.

Joe 'King' Oliver came to Chicago in 1917, after the US Navy put the clamps on the nightlife scene that fed so many musicians in New Orleans. He brought his band up with him, and soon sent back home for Louis Armstrong to join him there. Johnny Dodds was there, and Sidney Bechet, Jimmy Noone, Paul Barbarin, Wellman Braud, Honore Dutrey, Ed "Montudi" Garland, and a legion of Crescent Citians, playing in gangster joints and plush nightspots and the pit bands of theatres all over the Windy City.

The music was in Chicago early, and the city was on fire with jazz all through the twenties, thirties, forties and fifties. A 'Chicago school' of young white men who literally studied at the feet of the African American masters from New Orleans sprang up quickly and helped propel the music to wide popularity in the years between the two World Wars.

Bebop was big in Chicago after the war, with many visits by Bird and Dizzy and the giants of modern jazz, and a popularized bebop approach by such Chicago-based recording artists as Gene Ammons, James Moody, Ahmad Jamal and Ramsey Lewis met with great approval among black deejays, jukebox operators, and record buyers during the fifties and sixties.

At the same time, a resident musical visionary who called himself Le Sun Ra began to take the music into some entirely new directions. He gathered a nucleus of brilliant young musicians around himself in the early fifties and began putting out records on his own label by a large ensemble he called The Space Arkestra.

Sun Ra's imaginative extensions and permutations of jazz, little known to listeners outside Chicago before he moved to New York City in 1961, had a deep and lasting effect on Windy City musicians as well as on the many musical visitors to that city during the fifties. John Coltrane, for one, spent time with the Arkestra while in Chicago with Miles Davis and learned new approaches to the tenor saxophone from Sun Ra stalwart John Gilmore.

By the time the 'new music' of Ornette Coleman, Cecil Taylor, Charles Mingus, Eric Dolphy, and post-Miles John Coltrane began to twist the public consciousness in 1959–61, Sun Ra's vanguard position in Chicago had been inherited and was being extended by a second generation of musical visionaries led by Muhal Richard Abrams and Philip Cohran.

The Experimental Band, organized by Abrams, and the Artistic Heritage Ensemble, headed by Cohran, picked up on the innovations pioneered by Ra and took them on out, applying his principles of disciplined freedom, orchestrated spontaneity and ceaseless creativity to their own original music. Their young band members were relentlessly schooled in the concept of originality in composition and improvisation, drawing on the vast bank of ancestral music for inspiration in forging their own personal forms in rhythm, melody and performance.

When Roscoe Mitchell, Joseph Jarman, and Lester Bowie began to record under their own names for Delmark and Nessa Records in 1966–68, they demonstrated to an unsuspecting world just how powerful and all-encompassing the music of Chicago had become.

Roscoe Mitchell's *Sound*, Joseph Jarman's *Song For*, and Lester Bowie's *Numbers 1 & 2*—the latter of which brought the four members of the Art Ensemble together on record for the first time—revealed a collective conception as remarkable and stunning in its impact as the Chicago recordings of Louis Armstrong's Hot 5 and Hot 7 in the 1920s.

The Art Ensemble of Chicago itself came together in the fall of 1968, played some historic concerts around the University of Chicago, and left America completely in late May of 1969 to try to find a place to perform consistently in Europe. There they had the opportunity to make several landmark record dates as a drumless quartet, and there they found their missing link—percussionist Don Moye.

Don Moye, a former Detroiter, came from Rochester, NY to study at Wayne State University circa 1965. He learned the rudiments of his instrument and of the jazz idiom at the Detroit Artists' Workshop with Danny Spencer and Ronnie Johnson, left here for Europe in 1969, and finally hooked up with the Art Ensemble in Paris following a chance street corner encounter.

The rest is history, as they say. The Art Ensemble returned to the States in 1971, their reputation made in jazz circles by their series of European recordings. This writer had the pleasure of presenting the AEC in their first major American appearance at the Ann Arbor Blues & Jazz Festival 1972, where they shared a "Music of Chicago" bill with Muddy Waters, Hound Dog Taylor, Mighty Joe Young and Lucille Spann, got over like the Atomic Energy Commission, and were signed by Atlantic Records, which quickly released their festival performance under the title *Bap-Tizum* (Atlantic SD 1639).

Since 1972 the members of the Art Ensemble of Chicago have functioned as worldwide warriors of Great Black Music, embodying their collective concept of

"Ancient To The Future" in performances and recordings as a unit or as leaders of their own 'outside' groups. The Art Ensemble of Chicago has blazed a musical path across the planet that will lead generations of young musicians to explore the past, the present, and their own bright artistic futures with an openness, a dedication to excellence, and a commitment to enlightened self-expression like never before.

DISCOGRAPHY: THE EARLY YEARS
Recorded in Chicago, 1966–1968

Roscoe Mitchell Sextet, *Sound* (Delmark DL-408), 1966
Joseph Jarman, *Song For* (Delmark DL-410), 1966
Roscoe Mitchell, *Old/Quartet* (Nessa N-5), 1967
Lester Bowie, *Numbers 1 & 2* (Nessa N-1), 1967 (with Jarman, Mitchell & Favors: first appearance as a quartet)
Joseph Jarman, *As If It Were the Seasons* (Delmark DL-417), 1967
Roscoe Mitchell Art Ensemble, *Congliptious* (Nessa N-2), l968

ART ENSEMBLE OF CHICAGO
Recorded in Europe, 1969–1970
Roscoe Mitchell, Joseph Jarman, Lester Bowie, Malachi Favors

"Great Black Music": A Jackson in Your House (BYG 529.302), Paris, June 1969
The Spiritual (Freedom FLP 40108), June 1969
The Paris Sessions (Arista-Freedom 1903), Paris, June 1969 (includes The Spiritual)
People In Sorrow (Nessa N-3), Boulogne, July 1969
"Great Black Music": Message To Our Folks (BYG 529.328), Paris, August 1969 82
"Great Black Music": Reese and the Smooth Ones (BYG 529.329), Paris, August 1969
Certain Blacks (Inner City IC 1004), Paris (?), c. winter 1969–70 (add William Howell, drums; Julio Finn, harmonica; Chicago Beau, tenor sax, piano, harmonica)
Phase One (America 30 AM 6116), France, 1970 (add Don Moye, drums)
"Les Stances a Sophie" (Nessa N-4), Boulogne, July 1970 (add Don Moye, drums; Fontella Bass, vocals)

Detroit
October 1988

"in walked bud"

for les reid & john petrie

first there was monk
before the war
& then from further up-
town, in harlem,

from the neighborhood
of coleman hawkins, sonny
rollins, & jackie mclean,
there was bud powell

or earl alfred "bud" powell
on piano, strict interpreter
of dizzy & bird
for the keyboard, fleet

of single line & fast
to abandon
the heaviness in the left hand,
to make room for the bass & drums

& the harmonic
implications
of the melody, the farther
reaches

of the chords, the dizzy
atmosphere
which resulted
from the compression of experience

& the deep urban intelligence
of african-americans
born in manhattan
or brought to harlem as children,

coming up on the streets,
standing outside of bars
& after-hours joints with the whores
& the dope peddlers, straining

to listen
or to hear from the bandstand
or to see the musicians inside
with such aspirations, to get up there

themselves, with they little horns,
behind the drums, or at the piano,
hands on the keyboard
& a room full of people

looking up
from the depths of their lives
to flood the bandstand
with huge waves of love

& warmth, then back out
to the streets, & the ugly
stares, the cold
bitter hatred

of the white people
the nightstick
across the head
in philadelphia, the loss

of consistent memory,
the shock treatments
inside the several nut houses,
a phony dope beef in new york city

& no more cabaret card,
loss of license to work
in the nightclubs of manhattan
or even brooklyn, iced

out
of everything
but the will to make music
out of the guts of a piano,

the amazing bud powell,
the blazing bud powell,
now faltering
& lost, now lucid, now

gone
again, in toronto
with bird & dizzy
& mingus & max roach,

fresh out of creedmore
& more shocks to the head,
may, 1953, on the same night
rocky marciano

knocked out jersey joe wolcott
drunk & crazy bud powell
back in manhattan, a night
at birdland with bird

in the first week of march,
1955, gone all the way out
of his motherfucking mind,
bud powell,

bud powell,
bud powell,
bird's voice ringing in his ears,
mingus pointing his finger

from the bandstand,
"these are sick men,"
he said, "ladies &
gentlemen, please

don't associate me
with this madness," & in
walked monk that night
to catch some music, with his head

set straight on his shoulders
& his feet
firmly on the ground, in control
of his faculties

IT'S ALL GOOD

like few men of any time,
1955, just a week before bird
would leave us here
& bud would stagger on,

the scene changes,
time waits,
exile in paris
from 1959 to the end

of his life, but on this night
at birdland there they are,
bird at the microphone
intoning his name & bud

staring off into space, & monk
taking it all in,
crazy
too, like a fox

to say to bird & bud, "i
told you guys
to act crazy, but i
didn't

tell you
to fall in love
with the act. you're *really*
crazy now..."

louisville, ky
october 12 , 1985 /
detroit
december 7–14 , 1985

THE PROPHECY OF JACK KEROUAC

"Kerouac sees himself as the Prophet
and Charlie Parker as God."
—*Herb Gold (c. 1958)*

AMERICA AFTER WORLD WAR II was well on its way to becoming the kind of ugly, spiritually desolate world it is today.

The mental and moral landscape of America had been flattened and irradiated like Hiroshima and Nagasaki when the warplane Enola Gay dropped the atomic bomb on human beings in Japan, and the fabric of American life would remain terminally warped forever after—or at least until that day when the Americans finally face up to their terrible history and offer their most humble and sincere regrets in abject apology to the peoples of Earth.

The dehumanization of American civilization began in earnest when they dropped Fat Man and Little Boy on the people of Japan and flew smugly away, back to the Land of the Free and the Home of the Brave.

And after the bomb began the homogenization and commodification of our culture, spearheaded by a legion of real estate developers desperate to reshape America in their own image and driven by an insatiable greed to begin the process of draining and abandoning our nation's beautiful teeming urban communities to establish their endless networks of suburban modules designed to house the white people in an ever expanding ring of once open land outside the limits of our nation's cities.

Here too began the rigid economic stratification of our society which has created a tripartite modern reality in America—the rich get richer, the people who are allowed to work for them prosper in suburban bliss, and the uneducated, racially segregated underclass is left to wage a bitter struggle for simple survival in the vast urban ghettos which remain as the ruins of our great industrial centers.

Small pockets of resistance gathered and stood bravely against the raging tide of conformism and conspicuous consumption which swept over post-war America—tiny clumps of intellectuals both street-level and academic, left wing agitators and apathetic drop-outs, jazz musicians, poets, honkers and shouters, bluesmen, painters, mad bebop dancers, the operators of tiny independent record companies that specialized in documenting and disseminating the popular music of African America, and a handful of inspired writers determined to chronicle the joys of modern life as well as measure the relentless disintegration of the nation's human and emotional resources during this ghastly period of decline.

The greatest of all these writers was Jack Kerouac, a literary prophet who illuminated post-war America with his epic tales of ecstatic and complicated life outside the narrowing cultural mainstream. Jack Kerouac left our humble planet for places unknown on October 21, 1969 at the age of forty seven.

That day also marked the fifty second birthday of the [then] very much alive John Birks "Dizzy" Gillespie, genius of modern jazz, born in 1917. Kerouac's birthdate, March 12 (1922), coincides with the death of the great Charlie Parker, one of Jack's idols and prime artistic influences, on March 12, 1955 at the age of thirty four.

It is not at all strange that these three contemporaries, born within a five-year period, should be linked by their vital dates on the great wheel of karma. Together they forged a complete revolution in the sound of modern music and prosody.

The shift in verse and prose forms pioneered by Kerouac and his literary comrades moved American writing after World War II to follow the rhythmic and harmonic revolution in jazz waged during the years of war by Charlie Parker, Dizzy Gillespie, Thelonious Monk, Kenny Clarke and their contemporaries.

Kerouac, first attracted as a football scholarship student at Columbia University to the sound, intelligence and drive of tenor saxophonist Lester Young, was an habitue of the after-hours sessions at Minton's Playhouse and Clark Monroe's Uptown House in Harlem, where he heard Monk, Bird, Dizzy, Max Roach and other young jazzmen wrestle nightly with the problems involved in moving the music to a higher level of complexity, intellection and rhythmic thrust.

Kerouac spent the rest of the forties trying to infuse his own writing with the wild methodology of bebop, finally succeeding in 1951–52 with *Visions of Cody*, *On The Road* and *Dr Sax*.

Kerouac, the Great Rememberer, "Memory Babe" as his boyhood friends called him, allowed the size, weight and relentless rhythmic thrust of Bird's brilliant improvisatory music to shape the flow of his incredibly detailed recollections and propel him through great flights of imaginative fancy.

He attacked narrative writing as an exercise in epic poetic composition driven by the imperatives of an inspired bebop saxophonist—to make it happen, *say something* and make it *swing*.

Bird and Dizzy and Monk are playing inside Kerouac's ears as he writes: sometimes he's a tenor saxophone, other times he's the singer, then again he might be the drummer whacking and boomping away beneath the horns.

But the music is always there, in the writing, and all around it, defining it, all ways, always there.

"You guys call yourselves poets, write little short lines, I'm a poet but I write lines paragraphs and pages and many pages long," the bard insisted in a letter to Allen Ginsberg, Gary Snyder and Philip Whalen in the mid fifties.

Or, to Donald Allen in 1959: "The rhythm of how you decide to 'rush' your statement determines the rhythm of the poem, whether it is a poem in verse-separated lines, or an endless one-line poem called prose...(with its paragraphs).

"So let there be no equivocation about statement, and if you think this is not hard to do, try it."

Let there be no equivocation about statement. *Say something*, brother man, and make it *swing*. If you think this is not hard to do, *try it*. Bird made it sound so easy, but you can hear hundreds of players every night, sixty years later, all over the world, still trying to get inside Bird's sound.

Kerouac's brilliant series of novels—*On The Road, Dharma Bums, The Subterraneans, Visions of Cody*—detailed the exploits of "the mad ones, the ones who are mad to live, mad to talk, mad to be saved, desirous of everything at the same time, the ones who never yawn or say a commonplace thing, but burn, burn, burn like fabulous yellow roman candles exploding like spiders across the stars..."

Blasted on marijuana, benzedrine or cheap wine, Kerouac sat at his typewriter and captured the spirit and frenzy of the 'mad ones' he encountered between the early years of the war and the end of the 1950s, the mad ones and the improbable lives they devised for themselves in a sort of jazz and dope and poetry underworld of their own fabrication—an underworld which maintained a precarious existence on the cutting edge of urban civilization, living outside the law in the rotted underbelly of the beast, feeding on the excess produce of the hostile world of commerce around them and transforming this purloined energy into magnificent works of personal expression in music, dance, painting, poetry and prose.

On The Road, Kerouac's best known work, written in one continuous burst of creative energy in 1952, chronicled the beginnings of what has come to be known as the beat generation during its formative years just after the war, tracing the physical and spiritual journeys of a small group of manic friends in New York City who fanned out all over America—and later the world—to seek out kindred spirits and enjoy new and different experiences with them despite the tightening noose of middle-class life and the suburban wastelands springing up all around them.

This group—Jack Kerouac, Allen Ginsberg, William Burroughs, Herbert Huncke, Neal Cassady and others of their acquaintance—also formed a dynamic literary collective that produced groundbreaking works in prose and poetry which had an impact on American life well beyond the frontiers of the world of literarature.

When *On The Road* finally found publication in 1957 it exploded onto the scene as a sensational bestseller and Kerouac was hailed—or, more often, sneered at—as the spokesman for a new generation.

Beat: tempo, pace
    strike, hit repeatedly
    take advantage of, steal from, burn
    beatific
    tired, worn out, burnt, cheated

"Once started," William Burroughs pointed out, "the Beat movement had a momentum of its own and a worldwide impact. In fact, the intelligent conservatives in America saw this as a serious threat to their position long before the Beat writers saw it themselves. A much more serious threat, say, than the Communist Party.

"The Beat literary movement came at exactly the right time and said something that millions of people of all nationalities all over the world were waiting to hear...

"There's no doubt that we're living in a freer America as a result of the Beat literary movement, which is an important part of the larger picture of cultural and political change in this country during the last 40 years."

The great Kerouac persona has relentlessly been reduced over the years to the well known caricature of the graceless drunken beatnik lout. Bullshit! Kerouac, my friends, was full of grace, and a "great creator of forms that ultimately find expression in mores and what have you".

> *This was what Charlie Parker said when he played:*
> *'All Is Well.' You had the feeling*
> *of early in the morning,*
> *like a hermit's joy, or like the perfect cry*
> *of some wild gang*
> *at a jam session*
>   *Wail! Wop!*

Yes, All Is Well. Or like the end of the *Blues and Haikus* session, when producer Bob Thiele asks Kerouac if he can get home okay.

"Yeah," Jack says. "We got a car."

"Oh, good."

New Orleans
October 21–24, 1992 /
January 20–22, 2000

#75

"brilliant corners" [16]

for steve hager & paul krassner

out of the darkness
of the second world war
before the soldiers came back
to turn america

into a vast suburban wasteland
dreamed up by real estate developers
with huge dollar signs in their eyes
& nothing at all in their hearts—

out of the darkness
of american life
in the first half of the '40s
when the only rays of light

were cast in nightclubs
& after-hours joints
illuminated by the music
of the most adventurous of americans—

thelonious monk at the piano,
charlie parker on saxophones,
dizzy gillespie on trumpet,
kenny clarke at the drums,

brilliant corners
of modern civilization
flooded with light
& intelligence,

IT'S ALL GOOD

a bright beacon
ahead
through the desolate landscape
of post-war america

& sitting in the corner
at minton's playhouse
in the middle of the night
digging the band like crazy,

a hip football player
& would-be sportswriter
from lowell, massachusetts
who also wrote stories

for the school paper, like
"lester young
is 10 years
ahead of his time,"

so well known at minton's
in harlem
that the musicians on the set
named a song after him,

"kerouac,"
jean-louis known as ti-jean
or jack, the great bard
of modern america

who would turn
the genius rhythms of bebop
into dynamite literature—
"on the road,"

"doctor sax,"
"dharma bums," "the subterraneans,"
"mexico city blues," "the scripture
of the golden eternity"—

a vast trembling body
of visionary writings
that re-shaped american life
in every possible way,

& allen ginsberg,
fellow student at columbia,
son of a poet schoolteacher
& a mad red housewife,

incipient bard of the future
from paterson, new jersey,
who would see the specter of blake
in his dormitory room

& hallucinate a solitary rose
on the clothes hanger in his closet
& inscribe great visionary odes
on the windows of our skulls—

"howl,"
"america,"
"sunflower sutra,"
"kaddish" & hundreds more—

kerouac & ginsberg
looking for their kicks
among the petty criminals
& dope fiends of times square

    (kerouac was arrested
    as an accessory to murder,
    ginsberg went to the nuthouse
    to beat a stolen property beef)

& they met up with their mentor
in this seedy milieu,
a street-level philosopher
& junkie & queer, a renegade

IT'S ALL GOOD

from the genteel environs
of upper middle class life
in the city of st. louis,
a member of the family

that invented the adding machine
& on his mother's side,
the man who founded
the public-relations industry,

william seward burroughs
turned the language
around
& pointed it back

at the squares
who had stripped it
of its meaning, & blew up the sky
with his revolutionary writings—

"naked lunch,"
"nova express,"
"the soft machine,"
"the ticket that exploded"—

 kerouac & ginsberg
& burroughs
in new york city
in the years after the war

when bird ruled the music
with his magnificent recordings for dial
& savoy, & dizzy's big band
was playing "things to come"

& "cubana bop," & thelonious monk
would make the first recordings
of his incredible compositions
in the fall of 1947

& a young man from denver
blew onto the scene
straight off the front range
of the rocky mountains

with enormous western energy
& fast-talking wit, & the ability
to park a car
anywhere he wanted—

neal cassady
drove across the landscape
like a metaphor
for change, turning literature

inside out, & making life itself
a complex work of art,
immortalized by kerouac
in "on the road"

& "visions of cody," & by ginsberg
in "howl" as 'cocksman
& adonis of denver, secret hero
of these poems,'

author of "the first third"
& a human bridge
who connected the '50s
with the '60s

from behind the wheel
of a bus named "furthur,"
pushing america farther
than it had ever gone

before, with a new vision
of a new world
given life
by the practice of its dreamers,

propelled by allen ginsberg,
tireless proselytizer
for the creations of his friends,
who schlepped their manuscripts

from publisher to publisher
for 10 years, until "on the road"
& "naked lunch"
were finally brought to press

& "howl" was arrested
& tried for obscenity
& the beat generation
was in "time" magazine

& young people in america
suddenly wanted to know
where
they could get some marijuana—

& a road out of the stasis
began to open up
& out
in front of us—

   & we followed it

*   & we followed it*

new orleans
november 15-19, 1999 /
amsterdam
november 20–22, 1999 /

new orleans
december 11, 1999 >
january 31 > february 8, 2000 >
january 11 & 14, 2003

rotterdam
january 8, 2004

ROBERT LOCKWOOD JR.

Blues from the Delta

THE MISSISSIPPI DELTA, that fertile strip of silt-rich land stretching south from Memphis to Jackson on the east and Vicksburg on the river, has for a hundred years produced a swift-flowing stream of deep, emotionally-charged music which gradually came to flood the entire world with the sound and feeling of the blues.

Created and developed by self-taught African American guitarists and singers out of the materials and conditions of slavery, share-cropping and the Jim Crow South, this rude indigenous musical form struck a universal chord in the human heart everywhere it could be heard.

The blues breathed life into ragtime and made it come out jazz. It crept into the pale corpus of American popular music and added muscle, rhythmic thrust, depth of feeling.

The blues gave birth to rock & roll and went on to sire an even larger second generation of rock musicians all the way across the Atlantic Ocean whose blues-based offerings have transformed popular culture for an entire quarter-century.

The inventive giants of the Delta blues have long passed into legend: Charley Patton, Robert Johnson, Skip James, Son House, Rice Miller (Sonny Boy Williamson), Howlin' Wolf, Muddy Waters, Willie Dixon, Little Walter, Jimmy Reed, Guitar Slim, Elmore James, Magic Sam and a legion of fellow creators who are no longer among us.

Living masters like B.B. King, John Lee Hooker, Albert King and Little Milton Campbell are known now far beyond the strict precincts of the blues ghettos, while lesser-known titans like Sunnyland Slim, Jimmy Rogers, Johnny Shines and David "Honeyboy" Edwards elicit awe and admiration from music lovers of all ages and stations.

One of the greatest surviving Delta blues originators, Robert Lockwood Jr, has never received the acclaim accorded to his peers, although his contribution to the development of the modern blues idiom is immense.

As Robert Palmer insists in his epochal work of scholarship, *Deep Blues*, Lockwood "was the first Delta guitarist to popularize a jazz-influenced, single-string lead guitar style". His influence has been felt in the work of the great guitar heroes of the second half of the twentieth century, including Muddy Waters and Riley "B.B." King, as well as among their legions of followers in America and England.

125

Robert Lockwood Jr was born on a family-owned, 160 acre farm between Aubrey and Marvell, Arkansas (around twenty five miles north and west of Helena) on March 27, 1915. His mother and father split up while he was very young, and when Robert reached school age his mother brought him into Helena to live with her and attend the local schools.

He started entertaining as a kid dancer on the streets of Helena and learned to play the family's organ at home "before I got on that guitar".

His guitar studies were inspired by the legendary Robert Johnson, the Delta blues virtuoso who had taken up with Lockwood's mother and spent his time in the Helena area largely as a guest in the Lockwood home.

Robert Jr would pester his mentor for instruction and quickly developed his guitar skills under the supervision of the master, who soon began to allow Robert Jr to accompany him as second guitarist in his travels around the area.

Lockwood's development as a guitarist suffered when Robert Johnson abruptly lost his life in the summer of 1938, the victim of poisoning by a juke-joint operator near Three Forks, Mississippi, whose wife had made a play for the popular, good looking musician.

Robert Jr was devastated; as he told Palmer, "It took me a year and a half before I could play in public. Everything I played would remind me of Robert, and whenever I tried to play, I would just come down in tears. That's what really inspired me to start writing my own material."

Lockwood left the Delta briefly in 1940 for Chicago, where he recorded several of his new compositions for 78 rpm single releases on Bluebird Records: Take A Little Walk With Me, Black Spider Blues, Little Boy Blue and That's All Right, all now regarded as classics of modern blues.

But his first stay in the Windy City was a short one; soon he was back home in the Delta, where he hooked up with harmonica great Rice Miller, soon to become known as Sonny Boy Williamson, whom Lockwood had often accompanied as a teenager.

"I left Chicago in 1941," Robert Jr recalled for Robert Palmer, "after I made those records. When I got back to Helena, I remember I was walkin' on Elm Street when Sonny Boy spotted me. He grabbed me, had me up off the ground, and said, 'You ain't gonna leave here.' And I was stuck with him for about two years."

By this time Lockwood had begun experimenting with the still-new electric guitar, just beginning to be popularized by pioneers like Eddie Durham, Charlie Christian and Aaron "T-Bone" Walker. He was also leaning away from the crude harmonies and straightforward melodies of the traditional Delta blues, opening his ears to the sounds of jazz and searching for ways to bring them into the blues idiom.

"I never really listened to guitar players after Robert Johnson," Robert told Bob Palmer. "I listened to horns. I'd tune in Count Basie or somebody like that and sit and try to copy the licks the horns were playing... That's where all the good electric guitar players get their ideas, from other types of instruments."

In November of 1941 Sonny Boy, always a canny self-promoter, made a deal with radio station KFFA in Helena, Arkansas that put Williamson and Lockwood on the Delta's musical map in a big way. Starting in December the two bluesmen would appear on KFFA every weekday at noon to play fifteen minutes of their own material and announce the times and locations of their local engagements.

The Interstate Grocery Company, manufacturers of King Biscuit Flour, signed on as sponsors of the show, and Robert Lockwood became "the first electric guitarist heard over the radio in the Delta, and the first many younger guitarists in the area heard anywhere".

King Biscuit Time opened the radio airwaves to the sound of the blues, and the program quickly became immensely popular throughout the upper Delta. When the King Biscuit Entertainers added James "Peck" Curtis on drums in 1942 and Robert "Dudlow" Taylor on piano soon after, Sonny Boy and Robert Jr helped create the prototype for the modern blues band that would dominate the scene throughout the 1950s and sixties.

Robert Jr finally tired of Sonny Boy's erratic and cantankerous ways and left the King Biscuit show in 1945 to begin his own KFFA program under the sponsorship of Mother's Best Flour. He formed a band utilizing piano, bass, drums, trumpet and trombone, mixing in jazz with the blues and novelty numbers featured on the show and reflecting the new trends in rhythm & blues then evolving on the east and west coasts.

Lockwood left Helena again later that year to take a railroad job that would lead him to Wyoming and Nevada, where he ended up playing with an assortment of groups before returning to the Memphis/West Memphis area around 1947 and signing up with pianist Bill "Destruction" Johnson's jump blues band, which featured two saxophones, piano, bass, drums, and Robert Jr on guitar and vocals.

Johnson got steady work for the group in North Little Rock, Arkansas, where the band also broadcast over KXLR. It was here that Bill Johnson turned Robert on to using the guitar pick instead of his favored finger-style approach, saying, "Goddamnit, you gonna use it".

With this move, as Palmer puts it, "Lockwood's transformation into the Delta's first modern lead guitarist was now complete", and before long he would move to Chicago to take his place in the center of the burgeoning urban blues scene for the next ten years.

Although Robert Jr never enjoyed the popularity of fellow Delta refugees like Muddy Waters, Howlin' Wolf, Little Walter, Sonny Boy Williamson, B.B. King, John Lee Hooker, Jimmy Reed and Elmore James, all of whom developed substantial followings as a result of their recordings for Chess, VeeJay and Modern Records during the fifties, he played a big part behind the scenes as a top studio guitarist and artistic role model.

His tasteful, intelligent, jazz-influenced guitar can be heard on many of the best blues recordings of the period, including the bulk of the masterworks cut by Sonny Boy and Little Walter for the Chess brothers' Checker Records imprint.

Lockwood left Chicago at the end of 1960, moving with Sonny Boy to Cleveland, Ohio and blues obscurity. When Sonny Boy returned to Chicago a year later, Robert Jr remained behind and brought his family to join him in Cleveland, where he has resided for the past thirty years almost completely outside the national limelight.

From time to time Lockwood can be moved to accept an invitation to perform for modern day audiences at blues festivals and special events, where his magisterial presence, authoritative manner and timeless, emotionally rich blues playing and singing never fail to delight listeners of every persuasion.

"Ain't too many left," Muddy Waters said to Robert Palmer, "who plays the real deep blues." Robert Lockwood, dear friends, is one of the few surviving innovators of the deep-down Delta blues, one of the men who started it all with the sound of his single-string electric guitar lines played over the driving pulse of a pounding rhythm section, bringing the blues into the modern era and propelling its sound around the entire world.

Don't miss this rare chance to observe and enjoy one of America's greatest living musical treasures while we're still blessed with his presence here on the planet.

Detroit
Summer 1990

"21 Days in Jail"

for Bob Howe & John "Chinner" Mitchell

Robert Lockwood Junior
was born on a farm
between Aubrey & Marvell,
Arkansas, around 25 miles west
& north of Helena,
on March 27, 1915.

As a young man
living in Helena with his mother
around 1928 or '29,
Robert Lockwood
had the good fortune
to meet his mentor,

Robert Johnson,
who had big eyes
for young Robert's mama
& hung around the house there
long enough for Robert Junior
to pick up on his music. Robert says:

"At the time, my ambition
was to play a piano
or an organ. I had heard
a lot of guitar players,
but I wasn't interested in 'em.
But then Robert came along,

& he was backin' himself up
without anybody helping him
& sounding good. He would go somewhere
to play for people
& tear up the house. So I got
right on top of that. By him

having a crush
on my mother
I got a chance to be around him
a little bit. I think I'm about
the only one
he ever taught."

    2

Around 1934 or '35
Rice Miller began to appear
at Robert Lockwood's door
seeking his mother's permission
could Robert Junior ac-
company him

           (Rice Miller,
later known as
Sonny Boy Williamson,
"secret hero of these poems,"
the greatest harmonica player
of all time). So Robert says:

"I started going to places in
Arkansas with him, but he
worried my mother
for about two years, before she
let me go to
Mississippi with him. And sure enough,

we had some pretty strange experiences there. One time
we left the Delta
& went up into the hill country,
& in Sardis
they put us in jail

for vagrancy
for 21 days. That was
on a Friday. On Saturday
we went up to the second floor
& raised the jailhouse windows
& started playing. In a matter of minutes

the jailhouse was surrounded
with people. There was a little
fence down there, about as big
as the one
by the side of my yard,
& the people started throwing nickels

& dimes
& quarters & dollars
over that fence. The trusty went out there
& picked the money up
& we knew he didn't bring it all to us.
We knew he got fat,

but when he turned it in to us,
we had made four hundred dollars.
That day.
         The next night
the high sheriff
& the deputy sheriff

came & asked us
did we want to go out
& make some money. Sid & Ed
was their names. And
for the next
21 days, they took us out

to serenade for the whites,
every night but Sunday. They'd take up
the money for us
pass the hat, make the people not put
nothin' less than a dollar in it.
And then they'd take us back

& put us in jail. Now,
mind you,
they was bustin' places
for corn whiskey
left & right, & they gave us
a whole gallon of that. We had girls

comin' to the jailhouse
& spendin' the night. We was eatin'
from a hotel down the street.
So it really wasn't
like bein' in no jailhouse.
But it was terrible

because it was against our will.
See, this particular
part of Mississippi
was really starved for music.
And the police officers,
they liked the way we sounded

& just took advantage
of bein' police officers. They knew
the only way
they was going to be able
to enjoy us
was to lock us up.

Sonny Boy
was doing quite a few country &
western things—
'You Are My Sunshine'
& stuff like that— but we would
do the blues

for them, too.
Them white people down there
always did like the blues.
They just didn't like
the people
who created the blues.

3

   "Well,
by the time
our 21 days was up,
we had close to a thousand dollars
apiece. So old man Ed
asked me & Sonny Boy

at the same time,
'Look,
if I turn y'all loose,
what y'all gonna do?' And I mean
I'll tell you the truth,
even if it hurt me. I grew

up like that. I said,
'Mr. Ed,
I'm getting' the hell outta here.'
Sonny Boy said,
   'Whoahhh,
I'm gonna st-st-

st-stay around awhile.'
They laughed &
let us out. Knew damn well
he was lying. And as soon
as we got out,
we hit the highway."

Detroit
March 22, 1982

WILLIE KING

The Secret History of the Blues

" You talk about terror—
I been terrorized all my days"
—Willie King, Terrorized

THE BLUES has never been about what's on the surface. It cuts deep below the crust of everyday life and reaches straight into the heart of things, from where all feeling lives and never lies.

It speaks of bad luck and trouble, desperate love and abandonment, good times and bad times and every emotional shade in between.

But at the very bottom of the blues is the terrible sadness people feel when they are unjustly and mercilessly beaten down every day of all the years of their lives by the people over them.

The brutal harshness of life as a landless, cruelly exploited or jobless and discarded American of African descent is what the blues is all about, and the things people do to make a life for themselves within this crushing social framework so that they may enjoy some small measure of happiness as relief from the constant battering.

But, in the long American experience of the blues people, there is and always has been great danger in speaking forthrightly where the white people might hear you and take offense, because their response to what they do not want to hear has never been nothing nice.

So the blues has always talked about everything but the oppressor in the second person—it's addressed to the mean woman, or to the neighbor who's taken your mate, or to the gods of chance and fate. Rarely, rarely has the blues been about the wicked master who steals your labor, takes your woman or wants to end your life—the upstanding citizens upon whom the fates have smiled by making them your social superiors in every goddamned way.

This point is drawn very finely in a remarkable conversation between folklorist Alan Lomax and three Mississippi bluesmen who came up in the 1920s and thirties, Big Bill Broonzy, Memphis Slim and John Lee "Sonny Boy" Williamson, recorded in the mid 1940s but never released under their own names until a dozen years ago or so, when all three men had passed on to their greater reward.

After the bluesmen describe the hopelessly severe social conditions under which they were raised in the Deep South, they are taken aback when Lomax suggests releasing the recording: "Oh, no," they gasp, "we still got people down there."

In the modern world, where life in America's vast urban ghettos is even more brutally oppressive than the years of slavery and then of sharecropping in the South, where even children may be heavily armed and human life is at no premium whatsoever, it is commonplace to hear the rap artists talk about anything they want to, including their intentions toward the people who keep them down.

But in the blues, which continue to be sung and played by people who cling for their lives to an earlier aesthetic, the subject of the blues remains masked under the rubric of interpersonal relationships or the vagaries of fate.

It is simple to conclude that this misdirection is what lends the blues its poetic force, and this writer would be the last to argue that point. The blues is powerful in its rootedness in the circumstances of daily life in America, and the general absence in its lyrics of the oppressor who is always present in real life adds another layer of poetic depth to the idiom.

That's as true for the great bluesmen and women of today as it was for Bessie Smith, Charley Patton, Memphis Minnie, Son House, Robert Johnson and Muddy Waters.

But when you hear a blues singer say it right out, like Willie King does on this album of northwestern Alabama blues direct from the twenty first century, it raises the power of the blues to an even higher level, and you might even say to yourself, "Oh, yeah, so that's what they were talking about."

It sounds so natural, to hear Willie King talk about all the places he's worked and how little he has to show for it, or how working in the rural environment seems not really to have changed since the days of slavery, even though it's almost a century and a half later now.

It sounds so natural, because that's what you were hearing all along, as a subtext to the lyrics of the blues. Willie King brings it all down front, as they say, and in his songs reveals the secret history of the blues.

Born in Prairie Point, Mississippi, in 1943, Willie was raised by his grandparents and has lived and struggled in the Deep South for most of his life. He's worked in the fields plowing mules, in the sawmills, as a traveling salesman of shoes, cologne and notions, but he's never been resigned to accepting his mandated lot in life.

Thus he's been a civil rights activist for more than thirty years now and a student of the techniques of community organizing in the rural setting as taught by the professional agitators at the Highlander Folk Center in Tennessee where Pete Seeger, Guy Carawan and other important folk artists have been active for well over half a century.

A musician since he was a youth—he was playing a one-string guitar at the age of nine—by the late 1970s Willie had started playing the blues in rustic local nightclubs and juke joints as a way to bring the "struggling songs" he was writing to the people of his community, hoping to inspire them to join the movement to gain more control over the terms of their lives.

He made music at night, and by day he organized the Rural Members Association, sponsoring classes in music, woodworking, food preservation and African American cultural traditions and providing transportation, legal assistance and other much needed services to the RMA's constituency.

Described as "a field hand turned Field Marshal", King has combined his musical mission with his community organizing activities to give voice to the deepest feelings of his listeners and make a significant impact on their lives.

Willie's songs are remarkable: never harsh nor doctrinaire, they state the realities of real life in the ordinary language of the blues, matter of factly telling the truth about the way things really are and tempering the songs of social criticism that call for serious change with tender pleas for love and compassion—remembering, in the phrase of Che Guevara, that a true revolutionary is guided by great feelings of love.

Willie's music is wholly rooted in the blues tradition, and he utilizes the forms, rhythms and grooves endemic to northern Mississippi and Alabama which are familiar to his listeners through the works of Booker White, Howlin' Wolf, John Lee Hooker, Junior Kimbrough, R.L. Burnside and other bluesmen native to the area.

The band of musicians he has recruited to play his music are beautifully united around the vision of its leader and support King's voice, songs and guitar with a warmth and empathy that is almost palpable. Willie's long-time partner and closest comrade is second vocalist Willie Lee Halbert, who echoes and underlines King's phrases in a manner which seems to be unique in the blues idiom to this particular ensemble.

Guitarist Aaron "Hardhead" Hodge and drummer Willie James Williams are fellow veterans of countless Sunday night stomp-downs at Betty Jean's jukehouse and other favorite local venues, sticking with King and Halbert through every sort of thick and thin.

Keyboard man Henry Smith and bassist Robert Corbett—at nineteen he is twenty years younger than anyone else in the band—are fairly recent additions, and alto saxophonist Kevin Hayes, a truck driver from Louisville, Mississippi, joins them when he can.

Willie calls them The Liberators, and watching the ensemble begin to assemble in the funky little Memphis recording studio where they've driven from northwestern Alabama to make their new album, it's easy to see that this is not your standard-issue blues band.

The core members have been together a long time and their easy camaraderie is readily apparent, while the newer guys are made to feel equally welcome. They set up around their leader and get right to work, their familiarity with the material through regular performance giving them the kind of confidence needed to make things move along without a hitch, and by the end of their third day at Easley McCain Recording they're ready to pack up and head back home with the whole album safely in the can.

One of the reasons everything is able to proceed so smoothly is the production team, headed by Willie and Rooster Blues founder Jim O'Neal and aided and abetted by Rooster staffers Jeff Loh and Brian Factor. Willie met O'Neal at a blues festival in Eutaw, Alabama, in 1987 and kept in touch with Jim over the years.

Willie signed with the label at the turn of the century and cut his first Rooster Blues album, *Freedom Creek*, which garnered almost unanimous critical acclaim and was named Album of the Year by *Living Blues* in 2001. Willie was also named Blues Artist of the Year in the same poll, and the new album is eagerly awaited by everyone who had the good fortune to hear *Freedom Creek*.

Well, no one will be disappointed here, because *Living in a New World* builds on the considerable strengths of the live album—including great songs with a unique focus, soulful playing by a well-seasoned ensemble, and an overwhelming feeling of oneness with the audience—to deliver an impressive program of music that's deeply steeped in the blues tradition yet as fresh as today and tomorrow.

All the songs here are Willie King compositions (his friend Peter O'Hare contributed the lyrics to Ain't Gonna Work), and the lyrics are full of King's trademark topics: the rigors of life as a working man with nothing to call one's own, the stultifying lack of progress toward social and economic justice, the need for oppressed people to unite under the banner of compassion and common purpose. And the band sounds even better in the studio than live on stage, which is not always so easy to achieve.

Willie King knows the secret history of the blues all too well, and he reveals it here so plainly and so naturally that there's no possible room for doubt.

"The blues have always been part of me," he sums up in the monologue that ends the album. "I live it every day. And it's about love—sharing, helping each other, caring for one another, that's what the blues life is all about.

"I'm holding on to the blues life, because I found out that it's a good life to live. I just want to keep passing it down."

New Orleans
March 31, 2002

"Fattening Frogs For Snakes"

for Dennis Formento & Arthur Pfister

Coming out of Mississippi,
out of the mouths
of the children
& grandchildren of slavery
right around the turn
of the 20th century,

calloused fingertips
pressed down on the strings
of beat-up guitars
on small town street corners
or broken down back woods joints
in the darkness of Saturday night,

or on a bright Sunday morning
in a ramshackle clapboard church,
making music
to praise the Lord, & give thanks
for another back breaking week
in the cotton fields of the Delta

      (for this was music created
      as much to escape
      the rigors of share cropping
      & brutal manual labor
      as to shape a new form
      of expression through song)

& the Delta blues sounded forth
out of Mississippi
on crude recordings
cut in make shift studios
by enterprising white men
from the North, & sent out

on 78 rpm singles
from Paramount & OKeh & Columbia
to enter & reshape the lives
of people of every description
all over the world—the Delta sound
ringing all up & down the line

like a National steel guitar
frammed in some little jukehouse
in the middle of the woods,
or the amplified blast
of an electric guitar
plugged into the wall

in a nasty street corner bar
on the South Side of Chicago,
the sound of Mississippi
carried up from the Delta
into the factories & tenements
of the cities of the North

where peoples could make a living
outside the cotton fields
& be paid in cash dollars
at the end of every week or two
& conduct their lives
in the ways that they saw fit

& the music sustained them
as it had in the South, transforming the industrial noise
of the urban landscape
through amplified harmonicas
& pounding pianos

& the crashing of drums
& the Fender bass—a music
of such great power
& incredible beauty
& depth of emotion, so deeply rooted
in the lives of the people

that their bitter experience
could be shaped into art
of the highest possible order
that would inform all of popular music
for the rest of the century—

but their rewards
would never come, & the white man
would reap the fruits
of their artistic labors
as if they were bolls of cotton
in a 9-foot croaker sack

& the music of the Delta
would be appropriated
& exploited beyond measure
by the descendents
of the slave holders, & their bank rollers
to swell their bulging coffers

IT'S ALL GOOD

& nothing would be returned
to the people of the Delta
& their music
would be taken away
& they would be left
to face the terrible future

of life in the ghetto
with nothing to sustain them,
nothing to carry them
through the horrors of modern life,
nothing but the watered down sound
of what was once their music

played back at them by white people
on every television set in America,
nothing from the billions of dollars of profits
to be realized from their creations,
nothing to the creators,
nothing to the people who created them,

not even the dignity
of being recognized
for the enormity of their contribution
to the cultural life of our nation,
nothing to the blues men,
nothing to the blues people,

this is what they mean
when they talk about the blues,
this is what the blues is all about—
"fattening frogs for snakes"
& watching the mother fucking snakes
slither off with the very thing you have made

New Orleans
March 7, 1998 > August 31 > September 12–14, 1999 /
Ferndale, MI
October 22–24, 1999 /
New Orleans
November 13–16 > December 18, 1999

NORTH MISSISSIPPI
HILL COUNTRY BLUES

WHEN YOU HEAR the word "blues" you're bound to think of Mississippi. The phrase "Mississippi blues" leads at once to thoughts of Clarksdale and Greenwood and the music of the Delta. But when you hear them say "North Mississippi blues", you know they're talking about the hill country to the northeast of the Delta and the distinctive African American music that's developed there over the past two centuries.

The music of the North Mississippi hill country is thriving today like never before, and the whole world is being exposed to the sounds of R.L. Burnside, Kenny Brown, the Rising Star Fife & Drum Band and the North Mississippi All Stars. Even more important is the evidence that the music continues to exist and develop and grow in its natural habitat—in Marshall, Tate, Panola and Lafayette counties, where it came from.

Perhaps it would be best, before we go any further, for you to unsheathe your copy of *Hill Country Revue*, the new album by the North Mississippi All Stars recorded live at the Bonnaroo Festival last June, and pop it in your CD player. Here Luther and Cody Dickenson and Chris Chew present the entire spectrum of hill country blues, from the raw West African rhythm sound of the Rising Star Fife & Drum Band to the funky blues & hip hop fusion of Cody Burnside.

R.L. Burnside, the patriarch himself is there, ensconced in a throne of a chair, singing his classic Jumper On The Line and shouting encouragement and blessings throughout. Burnside progeny Duwayne, Gary and Cody Burnside add their contemporary takes on R.L.'s nasty trance blues to the mix, effortlessly exhibiting the family's magical ability to preserve the highest tenets of the tradition while extending the eternal verities of the hill country blues into the present future.

The Rising Star band has survived the death of its own patriarch, Othar Turner, and kicks ass way into the twenty first century with its wild ancestral drumming and infectious exuberance on the fife and drum standards Shimmy She Wobble and Station Blues. And Luther and Cody proudly introduce their own father, legendary Memphis pianist/producer Jim Dickenson, who's featured on the J.B. Lenoir song popularized in North Mississippi by Oxford's Kudzu Kings, Down In Mississippi, and introduced by Jim as "a little song about where me and the boys come from".

"We came up from a community of musicians and different types of roots music from Mississippi and Memphis," Luther Dickinson told John Metzger in 2002.

"Musically, as kids, every once in awhile our father would have [us] to back him up on a show. So we would have to learn all different types of roots music—early rock & roll, soul, rockabilly, country—all types of different roots music, because that's his bag.

"It took a long time, but eventually I came around and became fascinated with the hill country blues. I'd been playing slide, finger-pickin', and open-tuned guitar all my life, but when I finally came to it from my own angle, it was very natural because I grew up with it. I don't play blues—I'm a rock & roller—but we just can't help it. We've been musicians all our lives, and we just keep growing."

"We got to try to keep it going," R.L. Burnside emphasized in a 1999 conversation with Ed Mabe. "Don't want it to end right now. There's a lot of young people going back to the blues once they found out that the blues is the roots of all the music. They going back to the blues.

"It took 'em a long time to find out where the music started from. But once these kids found that out, it's good now."

THE NORTH MISSISSIPPI hill country blues has a sound all its own. It carries all the emotive force that powers the more familiar Delta blues, but its roots extend directly back to the ancestral music of the West African slaves who were brought to the area between 1840–60 to work the extensive farms and plantations operated by the local cotton barons.

Here as in New Orleans and nowhere else in the South, the African roots of the blues have been faithfully preserved at the core of the music evolved by the American slaves and their descendants.

You can hear the entire spectrum of the North Mississippi sound on *Hill Country Revue*: the fife and drum marching band music that's reputed to be at the very core of things; the elemental, hypnotic, trance-inducing slide-guitar-and-drums blues of the North Mississippi countryside; the relentless back-woods boogie workouts that drive people to the dance floor—all the rhythmic concepts and formal constructs first developed in West Africa that have survived intact in this obscure little corner of the American South.

These roots have grown a common repertoire that's been passed on from generation to generation, often within the same family, from slavery times and the years immediately following Emancipation through the entire twentieth century and now into the twenty first: fife and drum songs like Shimmy She Wobble and Jim And Jean; Booker White's Shake 'Em On Down and Po' Boy A

Long Way From Home; Mississippi Fred Mcdowell's Write Me A Few Of Your Lines and You Gotta Move; Junior Kimbrough's All Night Long and Keep Your Hands Off Her; R.L. Burnside's Jumper On The Line, Old Black Mattie and Going Down South.

These songs are renewed, extended and reconstructed as they are passed along from father to son to daughter to grandson and great-granddaughter, each generation adding something and taking something away but never straying far from the deep root structure that goes all the way back to West Africa.

This music is played and heard and danced to in the context of family and community life, at picnics and family gatherings and church services, in crude juke joints like Junior Kimbrough's old place near Chulahoma or the present Burnside Blues Café off Highway 7—always present and alive, always throbbing and pulsing with the life of the people who created them and speaking directly to the cares and concerns of the people who receive them into their own hard-scrabble lives in the hill country of North Mississippi.

Otha Turner's spirit persisted on Earth for ninety four years and lives on in the drumming and fifing of his sons and daughters and their own children, like the teenage fifist Sharde and drummers Rodney, Andre and Aubrey. Booker White's musical creations were amplified and passed on by Fred McDowell to his neighbor R.L. Burnside and thence to R.L.'s children and grandchildren and to his "adopted son", guitarist Kenny Brown, who performs around Oxford and the area with R.L.'s grandson Cedric Burnside on drums. Junior Kimbrough is gone now, but his music is carried on by sons David and Kinney and their siblings, and by his students, like guitarists Eric Deaton and Luther Dickenson.

The renowned Hemphill family of Choctaw County and around the Tate and Panola county line perhaps best illustrates the family tradition in the music of North Mississippi. Singer, guitarist and drummer Jessie Mae Hemphill, born in 1934 (or either 1937) in Senatobia (or either Como), Mississippi, spent her first six decades making a name for herself in the local community and later throughout the blues world before a stroke in 1993 left her paralyzed on her left side and unable to play guitar.

Jessie Mae came up under the tutelage of her grandfather, Sid Hemphill, a popular fiddler in hill country string bands, fifist and quill player in the area's fife and drum bands, and reputed master of nine instruments—panpipes, drums, guitar, piano, banjo and fife among others—whose music was documented by the Library of Congress in 1942 and again in 1959.

Sid, born in 1878, was indoctrinated by his own father, almost certainly a member of the first generation of post-Emancipation African American musicians and a renowned North Mississippi fiddle player and multi-instrumentalist himself.

The generation in between Sid and Jessie Mae Hemphill saw the emergence of Sid's daughter Virgie Lee Hemphill (Jessie Mae's mother) and her sisters Sidney Lee and Rosa Lee, another versatile musician who played drums and guitars and made several well received recordings.

Her mother and aunties started Jessie Mae on guitar at age seven or eight and soon inducted her into the snare and bass drum choir in Sid Hemphill's popular fife and drum band.

Blues scholar Barbara Flaska, writing of Jessie Mae in an article titled 'The High Water Mark Keeps Rising,' called her music "idiosyncratic. Her playing ignores the standard 12-bar blues progressions and relies instead on the open-chord tunings and repeated riffs typical of the folk blues of her native Mississippi.

"Her open tunings are rhythm-powered and enhanced by an occasionally hypnotic drone. Her guitar style is over-driven, a little roughed-up and coarsely textured, but very natural sounding. There's not too much in the way of turnarounds or doubling back.

"Her songs are driven by a relentless rhythm [and] powered by a fierce strum, with a slide up one string and down the next for accent. Hemphill plays way up the neck, with both barred and fingered chords, and bends a string when the mood strikes her. The stomping guitar parts act as a rhythmic echo to the words and percussion.

"Her songwriting often wedded the stomp and march rhythms of the fife and drum bands to her amplified guitar work. When she played outdoors, people are reported to have climbed dancing into trees while others still on the ground turned handstands and danced on their hands." This pithy description might well characterize the music of the hill country in general.

THE NORTH MISSISSIPPI hill country has always been a special place. It remained under the fierce control of the Chickasaw Nation, whose tribal headquarters were in the Old Fields near Tupelo, until 1832 when the Chickasaws were tricked out of their land by the federal government and evicted from Mississippi to make room for white planters and their African slaves.

The Chickasaws had successfully resisted the Spanish invaders, ousting DeSoto and his troops from the Pontotoc area in 1540, and 200 years later they vanquished the French forces led by Bienville and D'Artguette when the Chickasaws refused to surrender the warriors of the Natchez Nation who had fled to them for sanctuary following the Natchez victory over the French settlers at Ft. Rosalie.

But after another century the Chickasaws' long reign finally came to an end at the hands of the Americans, and the first white settlers marched into the area over the Pidgeon Roost Road built by the United States for removing the Indians to lands west of the Mississippi River.

More settlers came down from Memphis on the Chulahoma Road and on the Memphis and Tuscumbia Road, a course between the Mississippi and Tennessee Rivers that had been beaten out by buffalo herds and used by the Chickasaws for centuries.

By 1850 this migration had brought 29,000 residents—more than half of whom were slave laborers of African origin or descent—to the area around Holly Springs, which had been established half a century earlier as a storage depot for voluminous shipments of corn whiskey that came on flatboats down the Mississippi River from the territories to the north. After the Chickasaws were ousted, Holly Springs was named seat of Marshall County, which soon became known as the "empire county" of Mississippi due to its fertile soil and high yield of cotton that in turn made quite a few local planters fabulously wealthy.

Following Emancipation the population remained stable, but in the rural areas the black percentage grew considerably higher. Astute planters had in many cases selected captive crop-growers and herdspeople from West African tribes like the Arada, Dahomey and Fulani for their indentured workforce, and these slaves and their descendants continued to farm the hill country land after the vicious share-cropping system replaced the feudalistic form of slavery which had prevailed prior to the Civil War.

Living in relative isolation, farming their little plots of land and struggling for barebones survival in the hill country, the ex-slaves and their families continued to draw spiritual sustenance from the ancestral forms of music and worship that had been brought to America from their native lands and nurtured in relative secrecy during the long cruel years of slavery.

The planters had proscribed the use of communicating instruments such as drums and horns as well as every other manifestation of African culture in their relentless attempt to achieve the dehumanization and utter isolation of their human chattel for purposes of total control.

But the African Americans of the hill country managed to preserve crucial aspects of their culture by masking them with New World forms of music and worship.

The African love of hypnotic musical repetition as a means of confronting and transcending the exigencies of earthly existence lived on in the devotional forms that were allowed to develop under the aegis of the Christian church services organized by the plantation owners as a putative force for 'civilizing' their captive 'savages'.

It also found expression in the unlikely form of military marching music that served to lead virtually all militia units into battle from the Revolutionary War through to the time of the Civil War.

In a 1972 essay titled 'Fife and Drum Music in Mississippi', blues scholar Dr David Evans reports that "a large number of black fifers and drummers served in the Union army during the Civil War, and there is even one recorded case of such a group in the Confederate army...

"After the Civil War," Evans explains, "fife and drum bands declined in importance in the military and were largely superseded by marching brass bands. In the South, the fife and drum bands since the Civil War have been black.

"African tradition was in great part responsible for the popularity of the fife and drum band among blacks, and it would seem to have introduced considerable syncopation and polyrhythm into the drumming... The African concept of 'talking drums' has also had some effect on Afro-American fife and drum bands.

"In general, the drums are primary in the ensemble and do not simply play a rhythmic accompaniment but actually beat out complex patterns of polyrhythms with considerable variation and improvisation on set themes, strongly emphasizing the idea of making the drum beats correspond with the syllables of the words and thus representing another close link with the African tradition.

"These musical ties are reinforced by the dancers," Evans concludes, "who 'salute' the drums with pelvic movements not unlike traditional dances still seen in Africa, Haiti and the West Indies."

"In a time when drumming by slaves was strictly forbidden for fear of illicit communication," Bill Steber adds, in 'African-American Music from the Mississippi Hill Country', "the fife and drum was an acceptable outlet...

"But in the hands of slaves and their progeny, the stiff, formalized music used to direct military movements was transformed by the same African syncopations and polyrhythms that eventually gave birth to jazz and blues."

> *"How old it is? I don't know. They said it's African,*
> *back in African times, that's what they say."*
> —*Othar Turner*

ALL POPULAR MUSIC TODAY is informed by the rhythms and forms developed by the African American slaves and their descendants. Blues and spirituals are thought of as the root forms of this music, but a lotta people don't know about the formative role played by the fife and drum bands of the agrarian South in shaping the music that was to follow.

"The music of the North Mississippi Hill Country predates the Delta blues," Dr Evans points out. "The rhythms and percussive drive of fife and drum music had a 'strong influence' on the development of Hill Country blues guitar, since most early bands performed fife and drum, string band music and/or blues— depending on the occasion and desire of the audience."

The black string bands performed ballads, reels and old-time music on fiddles, mandolins, banjos, string bass and guitar, playing in a style that many now think of as exclusively Caucasian in origin. But, as Jessie Mae Hemphill told Evans, "That white guy what play that fiddle about 'Turkey in the Straw,' all of that come from my granddaddy [Sid Hemphill]. Wasn't no white band playing nothing like that. What they playing now, all that come from my granddaddy."

The music crossed over both ways, as the post-bellum fife and drum bands of the South interpreted both military music and the popular songs of the day within an African rhythmic framework. "Jazzing up" marching music would soon pass into the province of the black brass bands of New Orleans, but the pop tunes would persist as part of the repertoire of the fife and drum ensembles, like the four fife and drum pieces by Sid Hemphill's band cited by Dr Evans that were recorded by Alan Lomax in 1942: Jesse James, After The Ball Is Over (in waltz time), The Sidewalks Of New York, and a piece called The Death March.

"The latter title," Evans says, "suggests that Hemphill's band may have marched at funerals, though Lucius Smith, its surviving member [in 1972], does not recall doing so nor do any other fife and drum players among my informants. Some even seemed shocked at the suggestion."

But to the contrary, Otha Turner testified to Bill Steber: "They say drums was a-calling. If a person ceased, and you carry them to the cemetery, loaded in the wagon, all them drums get behind them and marched, just like it was a hearse, and they brought them to the cemetery, playing the drums."

Annie Faulkner of Abbeville, Mississippi, remembers when her father Lonnie Young played, "They would not start their picnic unless the drums came and kind of sanctified the area," she told Steber. "They always wanted the drums to come and bless the area."

As for the secular side of things, Dr Evans draws a vivid picture of the role of the fife and drum bands at public occasions. "The musicians really dance and sway while they play," he writes. "The 'march' is usually led by a dancer who emerges rear-end-first so that he is facing the musicians. He is followed by the fife blower and the snare drummer or drummers. The bass drummer brings up the rear.

"Sometimes the musicians break their single file and bunch up. The fife player rocks and sways and sometimes sings a line or two. He may be joined by the moaning or whooping of one of the drummers. The main requirement of any vocal effort in such a situation is volume, since the drums can be heard six miles away on a calm night.

"Spirituals constitute only one part of the repertoire of the fife and drum bands. Some commercial blues hits of the last few decades are now played, like 'Sitting on Top of the World' and 'My Babe.' Another group of songs consists of old minstrel pieces such as 'Granny, Will Your Dog Bite? No, Child, No,' and 'Mama's Gonna Cook a Little Shortenin' Bread.' A final group of songs is known by the generic name of 'Shimmie She Wobble,' which was a popular dance of the 1920s."

"A lot of people say that the blues sounds like fife and drum music. All the blues, they say, started from fife and drum bands."
—*R.L. Burnside*

BY THE turn of the twentieth century, the 'Jim Crow' segregation laws introduced in the 1890s to ensure poor housing, substandard education and extremely limited job opportunities for the South's black citizens resulted in their near-total disenfranchisement, and the sharecropping system efficiently kept blacks in virtual economic slavery.

"The way people was treating us back in those olden days, that's what the blues is all about," R.L. Burnside explained to Ed Mabe. "Working for the man, you couldn't say nothing, ya know. Couldn't tell him what he done wrong, but you could sing about it."

The blues passed back and forth in the hill country from the fife and drum outfits to the string bands, which were often comprised of the same musicians playing a whole different set of instruments. The music was anchored in the hard life and ancestral folkways of isolated African American sharecropping communities, gave expression to their thoughts and feelings, and provided a jubilant means of escape from the omnipresent oppression of everyday life in their shared circumstances.

The blues of the Delta region was exhaustively documented and widely distributed from the early days of blues recording in the 1920s onward. But, with few exceptions, the music of the hill country remained largely unnoticed and undeservedly obscure for the next seventy years, finally emerging on record in the 1990s by virtue of well-promoted CDs by R.L. Burnside, Junior Kimbrough, Jessie Mae Hemphill, Othar Turner and the Rising Star Fife and Drum Band.

Yet the music of the hill country retained every bit of its vitality and effectiveness throughout this entire period of outside inattention, constantly renewing itself by means of total immersion in the cultural life of the region and enjoying continuous artistic growth as it was passed on from generation to generation.

The first of these hill country generations to grow up with the blues as its principal means of expression sprang up between 1900 and 1910 and included as its key figures the fife master Othar Turner, the hard-hitting guitarist and singer Booker White, and the late-blooming exponent of the electric slide guitar, the man known as "Mississippi" Fred McDowell.

Othar Turner was born in 1907 in Jackson County, Mississippi. His parents were sharecroppers, and he grew up plowing the fields and chopping cotton. He took up the drums at seventeen and taught himself how to make and play a fife, closely observing local players like John Bowden.

"He'd get on that fife, man—it'd get late over in the evening, folks was running, hollering, 'Blow it, John,'" Turner told Bill Steber. "That son of a gun would get to blowing, kept his cap sideways, and I'd be walking along behind him. That son of a bitch would blow it for them."

Before long Othar was playing the fife and drums at rustic picnics and local celebrations and performing with Sid Hemphill and Napolian Strickland, two of the greatest North Mississippi reedmen, before forming the Rising Star Fife and Drum Band. The Rising Star became a permanent fixture in the hill country and continues to perform the traditional fife and drum band repertoire despite Othar's passing in 2002 at the age of ninety four.

Othar made his first album, *Everybody Hollerin' Goat*, for the Birdman label in 1998, and followed up the next year with an incredible recording called *From Senegal to Senatobia* which teamed up the Rising Star Band with Jim, Luther and Cody Dickenson and a group of musicians brought over from West Africa to create an amazing new African American musical fusion.

THE DISTINCTIVE SOUND of the hill country blues was first introduced to the outside world by a powerful singer and guitarist named Booker T. Washington White.

Booker White was born sometime between 1902 and 1909 in Houston or Aberdeen, Mississippi, His father worked on the railroad and played the mandolin, piano, drums and saxophone, and his mother was a preacher's daughter who exposed her children to the music of the black church.

Booker's father gave him his first guitar at the age of nine and taught him how to play. He started listening to blues artists George "Bullet" Williams and Charley Patton and began playing local parties and juke joints while still working as a field hand.

He left the hill country in 1920 and moved to St. Louis to play the streets and blues clubs, returned to Houston but left frequently to hobo through Cincinnati, Cleveland, Baltimore, New York and other cities.

White augmented his musical activity by playing semi-pro baseball with the Birmingham Black Cats and fighting boxing matches for money.

He made his first recordings (as Washington White) for Victor Records in Memphis in 1930, although only two of the fourteen sides saw release.

He finally hit with Shake 'Em On Down on Vocalion, recorded in Chicago in 1937 shortly before he was removed to the Mississippi penitentiary at Parchman Farm to begin serving a sentence for assault.

While White was incarcerated at Parchman, folklorist Alan Lomax recorded a pair of his songs—Sic 'Em Dogs On and Po' Boy [Long Way From Home]—for the Library of Congress Archive of Folk Songs.

Booker was released from prison in 1940, did some more recording for Vocalion in Chicago and then settled in Memphis in 1942, where he worked as a laborer into the early 1960s.

Booker White was rediscovered during the folk-blues revival of the sixties and made a series of well-received new recordings and concert and festival appearances, touring Europe with the American Folk Blues Festival in 1967, playing at the Olympic Games in Mexico City in 1968, and appearing with his first cousin, B.B. King, at the New Orleans Jazz & Heritage Festival in 1973.

White suffered a series of strokes in 1976 and passed away the next year. His classic recordings include Shake 'Em On Down, Parchman Farm Blues, Stranger Woman Blues, Dirty Mistreatin' Blues and The Doctor Blues, and his concept of "World Boogie" was adopted years later by the North Mississippi All Stars as their slogan for global conquest.

BOOKER WHITE'S exact contemporary, the great hill country bluesman "Mississippi" Fred McDowell, was born on January 12, 1904 in Rossville, Tennessee, a small farming community just east of Memphis and just north of the Mississippi border. He began to hobo around in the 1920s, hitchhiking from town to town and playing for spare change on street corners.

"I was about twenty one when I left Rossville," Fred told an interviewer. "There I was plowing with a mule. My father was a farmer and I worked with him. We were working twelve acres, growing cotton, peas and corn. I went to Memphis from there. I just got tired of plowing.

"After I got there I started working the Buckeye Oil Mill, sacking corn. I worked for the Dixon brothers hooking logs on the track. Worked in Chickasaw stacking logs for barrels. Worked at the Illinois Central shop in Memphis building freight cars.

"All this time I was picking up guitar. I was just a young man when I started playing guitar, but I didn't get a guitar of mine until 1941."

In his late thirties Fred finally settled down on the 51 Highway near Como, where he farmed during the week and played local fish fries, juke joints, parties, picnics and dances on the weekends. He developed a highly personal approach to the music, mastering the bottleneck style and composing tunes to showcase his unique style.

"I made up a lot of the songs I sing. It's just like if you're going to pray, and mean it, things will be in your mind. As fast as you get one word out, something else will come in there. When I play—if you pay attention, what I sing the guitar sings, too. And what the guitar say, I say."

Although he spent nearly half a century perfecting his musical approach while playing for friends and neighbors in the hill country, McDowell wasn't discovered until the late 1950s when Alan Lomax and Shirley Collins spent several evenings at his home near Como recording his entire repertoire.

A series of albums made with Chris Strachwitz for Arhoolie Records in the mid sixties followed to great acclaim, giving Fred the opportunity to compose new songs and perform at clubs, universities, the Newport Folk Festival and on European concert tours.

Fred McDowell was diagnosed with cancer in 1971, retired from playing and passed away in July 1972 at the age of sixty eight. His recorded legacy includes modern blues classics like Write Me A Few Lines, 61 Highway, You Gotta Move and spiritual numbers like When I Lay My Burden Down and "Ain't Gonna Be Bad No Mo'.

Two other first generation blues contemporaries usually identified with the Delta have roots in the music of the hill country that are rarely examined but clearly apparent in their playing and compositions.

Howlin' Wolf, born Chester Arthur Burnett on June 10, 1910 in the area around Aberdeen and West Point, left the hill country at the age of thirteen for the Delta, where he learned to play guitar under the tutelage of Charley Patton and studied harmonica with Rice Miller.

Wolf's music is a completely idiosyncratic blend of deep Delta blues and the hypnotic African drone characteristic of the hill country blues, reflecting the influence of Booker White and the fife and drum bands as well as the imprint of his mentor Charley Patton.

John Lee Hooker, born in 1917, is a Clarksdale native, but his mother remarried to a man from the hill country who played the guitar and instructed his stepson in the rudiments of blues performance. Like Wolf, the creator of a unique amalgam of Delta blues and hill country trance music, Hooker would introduce the world to the throbbing sound of the North Mississippi boogie with his string of hit recordings that stretched from The House Rent Boogie"of the early 1950s to his Endless Boogie collaboration with the Canned Heat Blues Band twenty years later.

THE SECOND GENERATION of hill country blues players was spawned between 1926 and 1937 but had to wait until the 1990s for its music to be widely heard outside of North Mississippi.

The eldest and the patriarch of this second generation was guitarist R.L. Burnside, born in Oxford to a family of sharecroppers on November 23, 1926.

"I grew up in the rough times, ya know," he told Ed Mabe. "I started trying to play when I was sixteen, but I was twenty one before I started getting out in the public playing. I grew up around Fred McDowell and Rainie Burnette, and I just always have wanted to play. Didn't nobody never teach me nothing, I just kept trying it and watching people till I learned.

"Fred McDowell was the first guy I saw play the blues. We didn't live over half a mile from him at one time. We'd be going to gin some cotton with my grandaddy and we'd be coming back in the middle of the night or in the evening and we'd stop by there and listen to Fred.

"When I got up to where I could play, about eighteen or nineteen, I'd go out with him on Saturday nights at them house parties, ya know."

Burnside also frequented the hill country picnics where fife and drum music was performed and found a way to get the African drone and drive of the drummers into his sound.

After half a century of regional musical activity he was finally recorded with his family band by David Evans' High Water label in 1979 for an album titled *Sound Machine Groove*.

But his music didn't meet the international blues public until 1994, when Fat Possum Records released the magnificent *Too Bad Jim* album produced by reedman and blues scholar Robert Palmer.

Burnside reached out beyond the traditional blues audience with *A Ass Pocket O' Whiskey*, his 1996 collaboration with the Jon Spencer Blues Explosion, and solidified his new base in the alternative rock movement with *Mr Wizard* (1997) and *Come On In* (1998), both featuring R.L. in reconstructed electronic settings devised by punk rock remix experts provided by the Oxford-based Fat Possum label.

Burnside's close friend and neighbor, David "Junior" Kimbrough, was born on July 28, 1930 in Hudsonville, MS, and learned to play guitar by listening to records by Delta bluesmen. Kimbrough combined the droning, emphatic rhythms and powerful beats pioneered by Booker White and Fred McDowell with his own eclectic musical sensibilities to create a music that forged a new identity for the hill country guitar style.

And, like Burnside, Junior Kimbrough drew upon his extensive family—he claimed to have fathered thirty six children—to bring his music to life. He is considered to have personally trained, or at least influenced, most blues musicians in the Marshall County area during his long career as a local legend.

"People just loved the rhythm of his music," says Junior's son and drummer Kinney Kimbrough. "It make them move. You know, it's like a hill country funk blues or something."

Junior Kimbrough was introduced to contemporary audiences by Robert Palmer's 1991 documentary film, *Deep Blues*, which also featured fellow hill country favorites R.L. Burnside and Jessie Mae Hemphill, and by Palmer's Fat Possum CD productions *All Night Long* (1992) and *Sad Days, Lonely Nights* (1993).

Kimbrough also maintained a popular juke joint at his ramshackle home near Chulahoma, where he and Burnside and their offspring held forth every weekend for years. Junior suffered a fatal heart attack in January 1998 shortly after the release of his third Fat Possum collection, *Most Things Haven't Worked Out*.

The tremendous personal impact of Kimbrough and Burnside can be felt and heard in the music of a third generation of hill country bluesmen, this one made up of young men of the Caucasian persuasion who have taken the North Mississippi sound as their own—guitarists Kenny Brown, Eric Deaton, Lightnin' Malcolm, Richard Johnston and Luther Dickenson—as well as the sons and grandchildren of Othar Turner, Junior and R.L. who keep their ancestral music alive and well.

In their hands the blues and fife and drum music of the North Mississippi hill country continues to flourish into a new century, steadfastly renewing its base in the traditional African American culture of years past and taking the original World Boogie to new audiences all over the planet.

Amsterdam
January 4, 2005

IT'S ALL GOOD

Sources

R. B. Henderson, 'Marshall County secured from Chickasaws,' in *The South Reporter*, Nov. 25, 1965).

Martha Fant, in *Biographical and Historical Memoirs of Mississippi* (Goodspeed Publishing Company, 1890), pp. 256–58.

Dunbar Rowland, L.L.D., 'Marshall County,' in *Mississippi, The Heart of the South, Volume II* (Chicago-Jackson, S.J. Clarke Publishing Company, 1925), pp. 787–91.

Greg Johnson, 'Othar Turner' in *BluesNotes* (May 2003).

Bill Steber, *"They Say Drums was a-Calling": African-American Music from the Mississippi Hill Country* ©1999 Bill Steber.

David Evans, 'Black Fife and Drum Music in Mississippi,' in *Mississippi Folklore Register*, vol. 6, no. 3 (Fall 1972), pp. 94–107.

John Metzger, 'Straight from the Mississippi Mud,' in *The Music Box*, vol. 9, no. 6 (Jun. 2002).

Greg Johnson, 'Napolian Strickland 1924—2001,' in *BluesNotes* (September 2001).

Max Haymes, 'Background to the Blues,' 2000.

Peter L. Patrick, 'Mississippi' Fred McDowell: Biographical Information, AAVE website.

Barbara Flaska, 'The High Water Mark Keeps Rising' at popmatters.com.

Talisha R. Davis, 'Biography of Jessie Mae Hemphill'.

Chris Nelson, 'Junior Kimbrough Obituary,' *Addicted To Noise* (Jan. 20, 1997).

Ed Mabe, 'R.L. Burnside: One Bad-Ass Bluesman,' Nov. 1999. (Interview with R.L. Burnside at Nick's Upstairs, Philadelphia, May 11, 1999)

Scott Barretta, "Hill Country' a Family Affair,' *Jackson Clarion-Ledger* (Oct. 28, 2004).

"Scuze Me While I Kiss the Sky"

for Jimi Hendrix

Up from the skies
over Seattle
like a Boeing jet
out of Mississippi,

guitar blazing fire
out of Elmore James
& Muddy Waters, Chuck Berry
& Little Richard,

taking stage after stage
back & forth across the country,
laying it down for the Queen
of Rock & Roll,

then it's Jimmy James & his Jammers
at the Cafe Wha
in New York City,
Greenwich Village stylee,

guitar paratrooper
dropping from the skies over America
with the bomb
in his front pocket

& Miles Davis
on the phone, Gil Evans
listening
& taking notes,

Every guitar player
in England & America
tuned in to his frequencies
for everything they're worth—

IT'S ALL GOOD

Jimi Hendrix, baby,
blowing up the music
into something as vast
as the inside of his head,

fitting the music
around his pounding heart
& the explosions going off
inside his nerve endings,

the colors on the wall,
on his back & in-
side his cranium, the colors
of all colors,

colors of rhythm,
colors of blues,
colors of guitar string
& Marshall amplifiers

stacked up high
over his head,
colors of explosions
& bombs bursting in air—

Jimi changed the music
forever, in so
many different ways,
he changed the music

like it's never been changed
in all the years since, he took the colors
of everything in life
& put them right in the music

where they belong
& made it sing colors
without end, kissing the sky
again & again & again

Ursulines Street
New Orleans
February 17, 1994

156

THE SOUNDS OF NEW ORLEANS

WWOZ on CD

WELCOME TO the wonderful musical world of WWOZ Radio New Orleans, a wildly improbable twenty four hours a day media outlet for the sounds of the Crescent City and the music and culture of the surrounding region.

Established in 1980 by a pair of brothers from Texas, Walter and Jerry Brock, WWOZ has grown from its most humble origins to serve a steadily increasing listenership with the full spectrum of jazz and heritage music: blues, gospel, New Orleans R&B, cajun music and zydeco, reggae, world music, traditional and modern jazz.

Now licensed to the New Orleans Jazz & Heritage Foundation, WWOZ Radio beams out at 90.7 FM from Louis Armstrong Park in the Treme Musical District and boasts a special commitment to the music, both historic and contemporary, of the surrounding community.

WWOZ is where our recording and performing artists invariably bring their new CDs and tapes to be played or come on the air themselves to talk about their life's work or their upcoming engagements.

But why am I telling you? If you've got this CD in your hands, you're already bound to be a listener to WWOZ, since this record is a limited edition pressing made especially for Friends of WWOZ who have committed their pledges of support to our Spring 1994 fund drive.

There is no commercial edition of this set in sight, so the holder is in possession of one of only 500 copies of this special collection of live music from the 1993 New Orleans Jazz & Heritage Festival.

JazzFest '93 was a very special occasion for WWOZ: for the first time the station was able to broadcast the festival live from the fairgrounds from start to finish.

Our live broadcast mixed music from several stages with ringside coverage of the passing spectacle, including artist interviews, impromptu on-mike performances by visiting musicians and singers, conversations with passersby, appearances by many of the station's seventy five volunteer program producers, and the unmistakable sounds of the Social Aid & Pleasure Clubs and their brass bands second-lining by the WWOZ broadcast table.

The JazzFest broadcast pushed the station's handful of full-time staff members to every possible limit, but our krewe of volunteers of every description came through in every important respect and the show went on with great aplomb, sending out the sounds of JazzFest to anyone in the Greater New Orleans Area in the proximity of an FM receiver.

What's even better, WWOZ's undauntable team of engineers and sound technicians managed to get large segments of this music down on tape—some thirty six hours of music in performance all told, recorded direct to Digital Audio Tape under the direction of Mark Bingham and preserved for our edification and delight.

The music presented on this disc was first selected to be used in a special two-hour radio program, the *WWOZ Mardi Gras Special*, produced by Tim Green and this writer to be distributed nationally during the summer of 1994.

Then our general manager and Big Chief, David Freedman, came up with the brilliant idea of making a limited edition CD to be given away as a premium in the station's spring fund drive.

Now it stands by itself as a representative sample of WWOZ's regular broadcast programming—what we call "The Sounds of New Orleans".

Modern brass band funk on a Jelly Roll Morton theme by the Dirty Dozen Brass Band, swinging contemporary vocal jazz by Ms. Germaine Bazzle with the Alvin 'Red' Tyler Quartet, *a capella* gospel by First Revolution (featuring WWOZ Gospel Train host Bro. Larry Bell), second-line bebop by Charles Neville & Diversity, down-in-the-alley zydeco by new star Beau Jocque & the Zydeco Hi-Rollers, deep Mississippi blues by Robert Lowery & Virgil Thrasher, the Professor-Longhair-plays-Hank-Williams sound of John Mooney & Bluesiana, jazz improvisation on a popular R&B theme by the Fred Kemp Quintet featuring the great Smokey Johnson, and a Mardi Gras Indian chant by Big Chief Donald Harrison Sr. and the Guardians of the Flame combine here to draw a brilliant audio portrait of our fiercely idiosyncratic radio programming.

I think I can speak for the entire WWOZ family when I say: thanks for your support, welcome to our ever-growing membership, and we hope you enjoy listening to this music as much as we enjoy playing it for you over the airwaves.

And, as always, our special thanks to the musicians of the Crescent City and environs for making it all possible.

Let this be the first of many such special products as we all continue to grow together in the music.

VOLUME TWO

JAZZFEST 1994 marked another high point for WWOZ. Thanks to some last minute special funding by the Jazz and Heritage Foundation, BET-On-

Jazz Television, and the city of New Orleans though its City Council, WWOZ was able to broadcast live from the fairgrounds all seven days of the festivities there, bringing the sounds of music in performance, artist interviews, festival actualities and impromptu performances to listeners throughout the New Orleans area from 11:00am to 7:00pm daily.

Initially faced with an utter lack of funds with which to underwrite the costs of the festival broadcast, general manager David Freedman had virtually written off the project until a last minute infusion of cash was suddenly made available.

We had exactly one week to design and plan this relatively mammoth undertaking, yet we were on the air the first Friday morning of the Fest with full-scale coverage from our broadcast trailer.

But this wasn't quite enough. Once the JazzFest broadcast was set, the fertile minds of WWOZ's staff and volunteer programmers went into overdrive, and a series of remote broadcasts from community venues was hastily scheduled for nights after the fairgrounds shut down and days between and after the fairground performances. All the performances were intended for live broadcast, although several never made it onto the air for one reason or another.

Several of the recordings in Volume Two resulted from this series of guerrilla sessions conducted by WWOZ's Michael Kline and this writer at diverse Crescent City venues during JazzFest 1994. Most of these cuts were recorded by Tony Brooke and Cory Smith—two young men who came in from California on a wing and a prayer, crashed on Dave Freedman's floor for ten days, and volunteered their services to engineer and record the string of live broadcasts from which these selections were drawn.

The series started with Earl Turbinton & Friends from the By-Water Barbeque on Friday, April 22, and continued through Monday, May 2 with a live program from Tower Records on Decatur Street featuring Kermit Ruffins & The Barbeque Swingers, the Zion Harmonizers, the Tony Dagradi Trio, the Hackberry Ramblers and the Bluerunners.

On Saturday night, April 23, we were at the House of Blues at 225 Decatur Street for the annual BlackTop Blues-A-Rama show, starring Earl King, Guitar Shorty, Robert Ward, Grady Gaines, Carol Fran & Clarence Hollimon, W.C. Clark, and Big Dave & The Dynaflows.

On Sunday we broadcast the Creole Blues Revue with Deacon John, Chuck Carbo, J.D. Hill and Danon from the Cafe Istanbul on Frenchmen Street.

On Monday it was Doctor John plus the Heavy Metal Horns from Tipitina's, at Napoleon and Tchoupitoulas uptown.

On Tuesday there was another in-store presentation at Tower Records starring the great Charles Brown.

Wednesday brought a live doubleheader, both ends of which were tragically blocked from the airwaves by a previously-scheduled WTUL broadcast from the Howlin' Wolf club which utilized the same portable transmitter frequency we had planned to use for our own signal.

The first concert, Trombone Shorty's Second Annual Treme Brass Band Blowout at the Louisiana Music Factory on N. Peters, struggled from noon to 3:00pm to get on the air before we threw in the towel.

The mounting confusion resulting from the jammed broadcast precluded the achievement of a proper mix inside the record store, and our single selection from this presentation, the Chosen Few Jazz Band's Salty Papa Blues with Lady Linda Young on vocal, made it onto tape only when a visiting radio producer, Steve Rowland, witnessing our many difficulties on-site, whipped out his portable DAT machine and a stereo microphone and planted himself in front of the stage with his mike stuck out at the music.

That night we moved uptown to Tipitina's for the Professor Longhair Foundation's *6th Annual Piano Night*, a gala invitational concert that had long been promised to our listeners.

But the WTUL broadcast kept our transmission from Tipitina's off the air all night, and we had to be content with the recording of the evening's proceedings captured by Tony Brooke and Cory Smith and eventually produced for actual broadcast in June.

Piano Night yielded three selections for this CD: the opening rendition of his 1955 hit, I'm Wise, by the great Eddie Bo (then recorded as Slippin' And Slidin' by Little Richard); the premiere solo piano performance by David Torkanowsky, who improvised this emotional tribute to the late Danny Barker as the opening salvo in an extremely powerful performance; and the soulful Jon Cleary reading of his composition Been And Gone, initially featured by Marva Wright on her CD *Born with the Blues* and positioned here to close out the program.

Door Poppin', the spritely offering by former Dew Drop Inn regular Carol Fran and her husband, Clarence Holliman—legendary guitar star of Bobby 'Blue' Bland's thrilling Duke Records singles of the 1950s—was recorded at the *BlackTop Blues-A-Rama* at the House of Blues. The original studio recording of this hip little song can be heard on Carol and Clarence's current BlackTop CD, *See There!*

Bruce "Sunpie" Barnes & his Louisiana Sunspots were the hit of the Jubilee CityFest in Montgomery, Alabama, this past May, when a production team from WWOZ was engaged by Alabama State University station WVAS-FM to direct their live broadcast from the Montgomery riverfront. Engineer Keith

Top Magdalene Arndt & John Sinclair, Detroit 1964.

Bottom John Sinclair in Leni's apartment, Detroit 1964 or 1965.

Top Allen Ginsberg
preparing to introduce
john Sinclair as "the
Angel of Detroit" at
the Berkeley Poetry
Conference, July 1965.

Left Partners in Crime:
John Sinclair & Charles
Moore, Detroit 1965.

Top Thelonious Monk at Cobo Hall, Detroit, January 1967.

Bottom John Coltrane & John Sinclair backstage at Cobo Hall, January 1967.

Top Sun Ra.
Bottom MC5, "Black To Comm," Community Arts Auditorium, Detroit 1967.

Previous page, top John Coltrane.
Previous page, bottom MC5, Ann Arbor 1968.

Photos © Leni Sinclair

Top Trans-Love Energies gathered on the roof of the Detroit Artists Workshop, 1967.
Bottom Trans-Love Energies picking up Tim Leary from the airport, Detroit, 1967.

Next page, top Wayne Kramer Salutes the Flag, Ann Arbor 1969.
Next page, bottom John Sinclair fixing a cocktail in front
of the Guerrilla poster, Ann Arbor 1968.

Top John Sinclair captured by the Oakland County Police, 1968.

Bottom John Sinclair beaten & under arrest in the Oakland County Jail, 1968.

Top Ann Arbor cop, Lt. Eugene Staudemire & John Sinclair backstage
at MC-5 free concert, West Park, Ann Arbor 1968.

Bottom Members of the Detroit Chapter of the Black
Panther Party at a "Free Huey" rally, Detroit 1968.

Top Pun Plamondon, John Sinclair & Wayne Kramer in the
basement at Trans-Love Energies, Ann Arbor 1969.

Bottom Leni Sinclair and Genie Plamondon, Trans-Love Store, Detroit 1968.

Top Bob "Righteous" Rudnick, Minister of Propaganda, & Ken Kelley, Minister of Information, White Panther Party, Ann Arbor 1970.

Bottom Red Star Sisters at White Panther Party Headquarters, Ann Arbor 1970.

Photos © Leni Sinclair

Top Abbie Hoffman
& Bob "Righteous"
Rudnick, Chicago 1971.

Left Member of the
John Sinclair Defense
Committee, the
great Mitch Ryder,
Ann Arbor 1971.

Top CIA Conspiracy Trial Defense Team with William Kunstler, Genie Plamondon, Terry Taube, Pat Richards, Lynn Gaines, Neal Bush, David Sinclair, Leonard Weinglass, Ken Kelley, Buck Davis, and Ken Mogill, Detroit 1971.

Right Yoko Ono and John Lennon Press Conference, New York City 1972.

Photos © Leni Sinclair

Top John Lennon at the John Sinclair Freedom Rally,
Crisler Arena, Ann Arbor, December 10, 1971.
Bottom Bob Seger at the John Sinclair Freedom Rally,
Crisler Arena, Ann Arbor, December 10, 1971.

Next page, top John Sinclair,
Ann Arbor 1969.
Next page, bottom Sunny, Celia &
Leni Sinclair, Ann Arbor 1970.

Left Muddy Waters onstage at Otis Spann Memorial Field at the 1972 Ann Arbor Blues & Jazz Festival.

Bottom Leni Sinclair in front of the camera for a change, Ann Arbor 1971.

Keller captured this fresh breath of Louisiana Saturday Night during Sunpie's triumphant appearance on the opening night of the festival there.

The Earl King recording of his timeless Ace Records classic from 1955, Those Lonely, Lonely Nights, comes from another guerrilla recording of a concert that never made it onto the air, the WWOZ Mardi Gras Party in Congo Square on February 20, 1993. The Marcia Ball Band opened the show, which featured Tommy Ridgley & The Untouchables with special guests Ernie K-Doe, Al "Carnival Time" Johnson, and the one and only Earl King, and engineer Mike Pelopolous managed to get the proceedings down on tape.

The rare recording of pianist/vocalist Sammie "Ironing Board Sam" Moore was a welcome last minute addition to the CD and resulted from an impromptu appearance by the pianist on this writer's New Orleans Music Show during the week when the music for this disc was being selected for mastering.

Ironing Board showed up at the station on a rainy Wednesday morning in late July and quickly laid down a series of musical treats, including his poignant tale of marital woe and resultant 'Non-Support' proceedings in front of the judge.

Tony Dagradi and his mighty trio with Jim Singleton and Johnny Vidacovich performed their sinewy version of the Thelonious Monk composition Nutty during an in-store concert at Tower Records the day after JazzFest '94. An entire program of the trio's magical ensemble improvisations can be heard on Live at The Columns, the recent release from Turnipseed Records.

The Zion Harmonizers' selection, Brother Moses Smote The Water, was recorded at the same Tower Records engagement and was also broadcast live on WWOZ. A great set of this historic group's current repertoire, along with the studio version of this cut, can be heard on Best of New Orleans Gospel, Volume Two, on Mardi Gras Records.

For the next selection, the producer has exercised his prerogative to include a verse-and-alto-saxophone performance of his poem Spiritual, accompanied by the legendary Marion Brown during his brief residency in the Crescent City between early January and late April, 1993. This piece was recorded by Mark Bingham and an early edition of the WWOZ DAT Patrol at the Louisiana Music Factory as part of the record shop's vigorous Mardi Gras Week festivities.

A stellar edition of Michael Ray's Cosmic Krewe is featured here with the entirely improvised performance which closed out their three-and-a-half hour presentation at the Voo Doo Boo at the late, lamented Charlie B's nightclub on October 30, 1992, just after the conclusion of WWOZ's live broadcast. Tony Dagradi delivered the muscular tenor solo heard here while dressed in a Batman costume, his saxophone poking out in front of a standard-issue bat mask.

This new CD is the product of the work of many, many people and most of all of the New Orleans-based musicians who have donated their performances to this effort.

These are some of *The Sounds of New Orleans*—just a sampling of the infinite musical resources that abound in the Cradle of Jazz and the Home of the Blues.

VOLUME THREE

THE SOUNDS of New Orleans is a continuing project of WWOZ Radio. Its several facets include recording and broadcasting live music from several stages at the New Orleans Jazz & Heritage Festival; making live recordings and broadcasts of New Orleans musicians performing at other community venues; producing radio programs from these tapes for national distribution; and making this music available to WWOZ listeners through special broadcast programs and our semi-annual Fund Drive premium CDs, of which this is our third offering.

The music on *Volume Three* was recorded at JazzFest '94 and was first broadcast from the fairgrounds as part of WWOZ's seven day, eight hours a day live coverage of the New Orleans Jazz & Heritage Festival each spring.

Several of these selections were also featured in the *WWOZ JazzFest Special*, a two-hour radio program hosted by Wanda Rouzan which is currently being aired by stations all across the country as part of our first major attempt to export the *Sounds of New Orleans* via radio syndication.

A second, one-hour program, the *WWOZ Mardi Gras Special with Dr John*, was released at the same time. Both were produced for broadcast by the producers of this compact disc from live recordings made for WWOZ Radio.

Our first three CDs in *The Sounds of New Orleans* series spotlight New Orleans-based artists in performance whose current work in many cases is not readily available on record.

The artists featured on *Volume Three* join the impressive roster of Crescent City musicians established with *Volumes One and Two*. Our program opens with the traditional Wild Indian prayer, Indian Red, offered by Big Chief Monk Boudreaux and the Golden Eagles as part of their JazzFest performance on the Congo Square Stage. In real life Indian Red can be heard at the opening and/or closing of virtually every Indian practice and public ritual. The Golden Eagles' original recording of Indian Red can be heard on their Rounder Records album *Lightning and Thunder*, recorded by Mark Bingham 'in context' at the H&R Bar at Second & Dryades in 1988.

Alvin Batiste & The Jazzstronauts follow with Music Came, a stirring Batiste

A John Sinclair Reader

composition given a powerful reading by vocalist Muriel Jennings. The all-star Jazzstronauts line-up includes Keith Loftus on tenor saxophone, George Fontenette on trumpet, trombonist Danny Heath, pianist LaShaun Garry, Roland Garon on bass, the mighty Sir Herman Jackson on drums, and special guest Mark Whitfield on guitar.

The ReBirth Brass Band is featured in a hard-charging performance of tenor saxophonist Roderick Paulin's composition You Move Ya Lose, recorded in the driving rain at JazzFest '93. The studio version of this popular new tune can be heard leading off Re-Birth's latest release, *Rollin'*, on Rounder Records.

Bassist Walter Payton's Snap Bean Revue is one of the city's best-kept musical secrets, but the cat gets let out of the bag every year at JazzFest when Mr Payton brings out his special ensemble to put on a show. Diminutive vocalist Sharon Martin gets the feature spot on our 1994 selection with the Sugar Pie DeSanto classic, Use What You Got, featuring solo turns by alto saxophonist Jules Handy and guitarist Louisiana Bill.

Guitarist Steve Masakowski & Friends dedicated their opening day set to a program of music from Steve's Blue Note CD, *What It Was*, and the lovely song Southern Blue to Steve's friend Mr Danny Barker, who had just recently passed away. Bassist Bill Huntington is especially soulful here, and Masakowski's tender guitar is beautifully abetted by the sensitive touch of drummer Johnny Vidacovich.

The timeless Mr Eddie Bo and his band are next with a 1994 update of his 1961 classic, Check Mr Popeye, spotlighting Eddie's rollicking piano, lusty vocal, and hilarious lyrics. Saxophonist Red Morgan and guitarist Leo Williams sparkle in support. You can hear the original recording of Check Mr Popeye (Parts One and Two) on the Rounder CD of the same name which collects Eddie Bo's wonderful 1959–62 singles for Ric Records.

The one and only Snooks Eaglin and his power trio with bassist George Porter Jr and drummer Terrence Higgins blast out Larry Williams' Dizzy Miss Lizzy with a crispness and authority the Beatles could only hope to approximate in their well known version of thirty years ago. Snooks prefaces his performance with a call out from the stage to this writer, who was indeed sitting on his butt in the WWOZ broadcast van, beaming Snooks' set out over the airways from the House of Blues Stage at the fairgrounds. Snooks' studio recording of this song can be found on his great BlackTop CD from 1991, *Teasin' You*.

One of the real high points of our 1994 live broadcast was Deacon John's magnificent set of Elmore James, B.B. King and J.B. Lenoir compositions with his All-Star Blues Band featuring tenor saxophonist Fred Kemp, pianist Robert Dabon, bassist Charles Moore and drummer Oliver Alcorn. Deac's virtuoso reading of Elmore's rarely heard Happy Home from the early 1950s is more a re-creation of the classic Broomdusters sound than simply a cover version of a blues masterwork.

Bourbon Street stalwarts Willie Lockett & The Blues Krewe sign in with a definitive performance of the Jesse James favorite I Can Do Bad By Myself, with their horn section much in evidence and a tasty guitar outing by Michael Sklar. Look for the Blues Krewe's first CD to be issued in 1995.

WWOZ's Brother Larry Bell, host of the Gospel Train programs heard every Sunday morning (8:30–10:00am) and evening (8:00–10:00pm), helps close out the program with his gospel ensemble, the First Revolution Singers, and bass singer Jerome Alexander's fresh *a capella* arrangement of Leave That Liar Alone. This performance was recorded April 28 in the WWOZ broadcast van as the five members of the group crowded around the microphone to send a song out live to the people listening to the station's JazzFest coverage.

Once again we'd like to thank all the musicians whose participation has made this project possible, especially the players who have donated their performances to be shared with our members on this compact disc.

Special thanks go to Keith Keller of Chez Flames Recording, who organized the taping of the JazzFest 1994 performances on a few days' notice, secured excellent recordings, and edited and mastered these selections from the DAT master tapes for this album.

We'd also like to thank the underwriters who provided funds for WWOZ's JazzFest 1994 recordings: the New Orleans Jazz & Heritage Foundation, BET-On-Jazz Television, and the City of New Orleans through a grant from the New Orleans City Council.

And finally, thank you for pledging your support to WWOZ. Your contributions and donations, along with the completely voluntary services of some seventy five on-air programmers, make the continued pursuit of this noble experiment in community radio increasingly possible. This record is just another example of the wonders we can work together.

New Orleans
March 28 > August 30 > December 26, 1994

"We Just Change the Beat"

for Johnny Evans & Martin Gross

"You know,"
Willie Dixon says,
"when you go to changin' beats
in music,
you change the whole style.

The difference in blues
or rock & roll
or jazz
is the beat. The beat
actually changes the whole

entire
style." The beat actually
changes
the whole en-
tire style. Where you

put that beat, be
careful
or you'll change the whole
change the whole
change the whole entire

when you go
to changing' beats you know
you can
change
you can go to changin'

you can change the whole style

2

Now Frank Frost
of Lula, Mississippi
puts it like this. He says:
"In other words,

we taking the down blues
& bring it up tempo.
I don't know what
you would call it.

Just take the cotton-picking blues,
I would say,
& bring it up to modern music
today. I guess that still be blues.

The onliest difference
between the cotton-picking blues
& what we doing today
is the tempo. . . . Let me see

if I can give you something
to remind you
of back in those days"—
[& he plays a few notes]

"Now that's just the old,
ordinary
original way, you know.
That's just the cotton-picking blues

that way. Then we change up
just the tempo
& the beat. That's the dance tempo
you hear now. Just something

they can dance to
these days. That's the same blues.
We just change the beat.
It's no different!

Detroit
March 21, 1982 /
New Orleans
December 7, 1995 / March 5, 1998

WALTER "WOLFMAN" WASHINGTON

The Wolfman is at Your Door

WALTER "WOLFMAN" Washington has followed a rough and rocky road through the vicissitudes of the music business since his induction as a teenage guitar player into the house band at the legendary Dew Drop Inn nearly forty years ago.

Wolfman emerged as a band leader himself in the early 1980s and delivered a series of critically acclaimed albums for Rounder Records: *Wolf Tracks*, *Out of the Night* and *The Wolf is at Your Door*—and one for Pointblank, *Sada*, each featuring his passionate soul-funk- blues singing and playing backed by his crack horn band, The Roadmasters.

Washington's trials and tribulations as a band leader carrying his own horn section have often seemed endless, including a seven year period without a US recording contract and the release of only a single European album, *Blue Moon Rising*, featuring the Roadmasters augmented by the J.B. Horns.

But Wolfman's persistence with the band has paid off big time, and their new release, *Funk is in the House,* boasts a fiery, skintight ensemble sound, a repertoire of tastefully selected soul classics and intense, highly personalized original compositions, and an overall level of performance which places Wolfman unequivocally at the top of the class as a contemporary urban blues vocalist and guitarist.

Born in New Orleans in December 1943, Washington first sang at Sunday gatherings at home and in church with the Friendly Five Gospel Singers. He started playing guitar as a member of the True Loving Four Gospel Singers and soon entered the rhythm & blues ranks backing up his cousin, Ernie K-Doe, who had just scored a Number One hit with Mother-In-Law.

The young Wolfman was mentored at the Dew Drop by singer Johnny Adams and got his first taste of road life during two and a half years with Lee Dorsey.

He returned to New Orleans and worked for two years with Irma Thomas, then spent several years as guitarist for the Tick Tocks, a singing group made up of former members of Huey "Piano" Smith's indomitable Clowns.

Washington pursued his further musical studies as guitarist and lead singer for six years with David Lastie & A Taste of New Orleans, a group of Ninth Ward all-stars which included guitarist Alvin "Shine" Robinson, trumpeter John Brunious, and drummer Walter "Poppee" Lastie.

Emboldened by his years of apprenticeship, Wolfman then formed a series of bands with drummer Wilbert "Junk Yard Dog" Arnold and a succession of bassists, backing up Johnny Adams and performing on their own as the Force, the Mighty Men, the First Amendment, and eventually the Solar System.

Discouraged with the band's lack of progress after the release of its album on Senator Jones' Hep'Me label (now available on CD from Mardi Gras Records as *The Best of New Orleans R&B, Volume Two*), Wolfman signed on as a sideman with his song-writing partner, vocalist Timothea Beckerman, and began to meet the men who—with Washington and Arnold—would form the basis of the Roadmasters: bassist Jack Cruz and saxophonist Tom Fitzpatrick.

Nearly fifteen years of constant playing and touring through all kinds of thick and thin have shaped the Roadmasters into a gleaming, well-oiled blues machine that combines and recombines the soul, gospel and urban blues roots of its music into a smooth, soulful synthesis of everything that's good about all three.

Wolfman sings like a man truly possessed, reaching new heights of expressiveness and power over the band's churning rhythms and form-fitted horn commentaries. His jazzy, urban guitar lines and relentless rhythm parts shine continually in solo and in section, and the entire ensemble performs with bristling intensity and absolute assurance throughout.

After chasing Wolfman for this interview for about six months, we finally sat down at his uptown home just days before each of us would leave New Orleans for a European tour—my first, Wolfman's too many to be counted. I had heard the band at its CD release party at the House of Blues only a few days before and was fairly gushing with praise.

Our conversation turned at once to the new Roadmasters album, the first release under Washington's new long-term contract with Bullseye Blues & Jazz Records.

WOLFMAN SPEAKS:

THAT NEW ALBUM—man, that is something else. Believe it or not, we spent, like, six months back and forth just working on the rhythm tracks. And sometime the horns would come in, after we'd done laid the rhythm tracks down for them, they'd come in and get together and study their little parts.

So it was easy for us to go in the studio and do this album. Like, in two days we had put the whole rhythm track down—in two days. And we let [producer] Scott [Billington] do all of the mixing and the stuff what he had to do. So that Friday—we went in there that Monday and Tuesday, and it was Friday, I musta went in about 12:00 that day, and by 8:30 that night I was through with all the tracks.

What I did was—I just sung. I just sung all the way through. I sung with the album, but I did the final thing that Friday, because I needed time to study everything, and make sure it was, you know—complete.

So it was kind of easy for me to deal with that. What I did was, I just went on in there about 12:00 and added my couple of little things, my drinks and stuff, you know, and I just went in there and to my surprise—I didn't realize how open my voice was that day. Because me and my lady had went out, you know, just to celebrate for a couple of days, and when I got up that Friday morning, I felt kinda good, you know, but I didn't realize that I felt that good.

But everybody really contributed to this album. That was what made me [feel] more comfortable about it, because it was like—they normally would do it where the rhythm section would go in, boom, we'd cut our little thing and go. And then the horns would come in and do their little thing. And then I would come in.

These eleven years that the boys been together, you know, it done paid off. It's payin' off pretty, you know, because I feel comfortable. It comes from everybody talking. You see, you've got bands that don't wanna talk. We have— all these years we've cried on each other's shoulders, we done talked about each other's problems, and so forth. No matter what it was, it was easy for us to communicate.

Now I feel like King Arthur and his court—I got my Round Tables, you know? [Laughs] I got the boys. Now I just want to talk the Roadmaster people into giving us all a Roadmaster. [Laughs]

Another thing is, I wanna write more serious stuff. You know, more reality— real stuff. Instead of writing what's in the fantasy of my mind, write what's really happening That's where I'm comin' from, you know, the whole point of where I'm coming from, because I listen to this album now, and all of this stuff is reality stuff. That's all I want to write now. I don't wanna go off into another thing. I've been able to start back to preachin' again, you know, it's like the mind is being able to be active within the spiritual sense of my life. It's been a big difference, really.

This group has opened a lot of doors for me—especially for myself, because I really didn't think I'd have the band that wanted to stick with me that much. You see, the roots that I've been trying to create with this band have been roots that's been way back in the day. You don't find bands that's playing the kind of music I'm playing. You find them playing this other thing—all mechanical stuff going on, you know—and cats is not really communicatin' the way they supposed to—used to do at one time, you know.

You got a song, you don't discuss that song now, because somebody gonna talk about one song, and somebody else gonna talk about another song, but we playin' somebody else's song, but then everybody's talkin' about somebody different, you know. Everybody's gotta be discussin' that one song and learning about discipline of bein' able to communicate.

It's just like havin' a concert, or a conversation, you know—when you're amongst a bunch of people that everybody talkin' about one subject, everybody can't talk about that one subject at one time. Okay, you got one person that takes the floor, and you talk. Then, next somebody else after that, you know? That's the discipline that cats nowadays—in my band, I can see it in my band, because those cats are givin' it to me.

I look at James Brown's horn section—you know, Maceo and them—man, look, them cats, that's when I really knew I was on the right thing, when them cats said, "Hey, wait a minute, man, we doin' the same thing. I wanna play with you too. Let me be on this album [*Blue Moon Rising*]." And that opened that—I said, "Hey, yeah, okay, I can do this. I know I'm in the right vein," you know?

But there are very few of us. Very few of us. And I realized it takes a lot of patience, it takes a lot of understanding, and when cats understand one another and respect one another in that sense of direction, quite naturally you're gonna have a good organization. And I think that I could have an organization just like that, you know? It just makes me feel good to see this.

At one time, when I was singing spirituals—I was with the Friendly Five Gospel Singers—and those cats, man, they had Walker (he's deceased now, God rest his soul), and Big Bill (he's dead now, God rest his soul). These cats, man—Walker was the youngest one, and Bill was the oldest, you dig, but Walker had more soul than Bill. But, do you think Walker would make Bill feel that he wasn't in front, that he wasn't the first...?

That respect was there, man. The rest of them cats, they gave each other that respect, you see? When Bill decided, 'Man, I just can't handle it, I just can't be in front,' Walker didn't say, 'Well, hey, man, I'm glad you're gone,' you know? No. No, man. 'Thank you for the position.' Okay. But before he could say thank you, everybody else say, 'Yeah, Walker, you in that position.' To see that kind of communication goin' on, man—and wasn't nothin' down on paper, you know. This was word of mouth—gentleman's agreement, we called it. That code thing, you know what I'm saying?

So I grew up with that kind of discipline, you know, and I went through about six or seven bands before I got this band, you know. This is the longest I've ever had my own band—the longest I've ever had a band [before] was five years. That's the longest I ever kept a band.

The first band I had was called Force. It wasn't but me, a drummer, and a bass player. The drummer was Wilbert [Arnold], the Junk Yard Dog. That's my sidekick—that's like Cisco and Pancho, you know? [*Laughs*] But the bass player just couldn't hang, because the kind of music that I wanted to play, he could see it, but he couldn't play it, because he wanted to play too much of this other thing. He wanted to play Jimi [Hendrix] stuff, you know?

You see, I have developed myself to a point now where I want to project what I've learned from Lee [Dorsey], from Fats [Domino], from all of these cats, you know—Bobby, B.B.—I wants to express that now. Because I got a band that wants to play the hell out of music. I mean, you got cats that don't wanna play that kinda foundation music. They wanna play the house—they don't wanna play that foundation.

So, it grew up in me that way. I've always felt—because, see, when I came in, and cats that was older than me that was into this music, especially New Orleans cats, like David Lastie, all these cats, you know, and Snooks [Eaglin] and all these cats, you know, man, I was the youngest motherfucker in that shit, you know. I'm talking about when I got into my real age, about twenty five, twenty six, something like that.

I had been on the road with Lee [Dorsey], I had spent two years with him and something, and then I came to be with Irma [Thomas], and hung out with her. But then, when I got back, I started gettin' recognized by these elders—cats that was here, that was makin' big money, not leanin' on nobody but themselves, and I pulled in.

Like the Off Limits, when the Off Limits was really poppin' then, and they had that place down there on Tupelo and Galvez, down in the Ninth Ward, they had that place open where all these cats would hang out at, these musicians—I mean heavy musicians. George Herron, [Eddie] Bo and all of 'em.

That's when I started into gettin' introduced to Bo and all these cats, that was playing the foundation. The Founders, in fact. I was the youngest that was hangin' around with them cats, you know what I'm sayin'? You know, like Chuck Badie and all these cats, Half-A-Head and all these cats. I had met so many when I was out there with Lee and them—meetin' Billy Butler, and Jerry Butler and all these cats, you know, and I thought I was meetin' somebody. But see, when I come home, and I seen that all these cats was big cats, they was the founders of New Orleans music, and these cats is gonna accept me?

And my first gig that was gave to me that made me feel that important, was Shine—Al Robinson—he gave me my first gig, with the Settlers. They were like older cats that were playin' shit, and I'm just tryin' to get into this shit, you know. David Lastie and them, and the Taste of New Orleans, them cats—now, them cats was playin' some music, man.

And all I knew was just the regular chords, you know, like the majors, and a couple of the minors, and just so many of the diminished, you know, and to get a chance like that to play with cats like that—and then these cats started recognizin' me, like Piansky (Emile Vinnette], you know, and John Brunious and all these cats, man. All these cats was recognizin' me, like, "Yeah, man, Walter, you can play, man."

But then I started thinking—wait a minute, I wasn't tryin' to get out there and try to play like these bad cats, you know, this weird music. I wanted to play that down-to-earth blues and funk. So these cats, that's what they were playin', you know. A lot of cats said, "Man, they playin' heavy, heavy jazz." Yeah, it's jazz, but it's some groovy jazz! I liked that shit, and I just wanted to stay right there in that thing. I didn't wanna move.

And, as I got bands after that, you know, they just didn't want to play that shit. They wanted to be in their age bracket thing, you know what I mean? And I wanted to play the old kind—Misty, and Jumpin' The Blues, and stuff like that. Couldn't find cats to play like that.

And then finally I found [bassist] Jack [Cruz], and then Wilbert came back. Jack said, "Man, I like that kind of music. I wanna play that." I said, "Oh, you do?" I brought him though all kinds of changes—all kinds of changes—and he said, "I'm gonna stay right here. I ain't goin' nowhere." Wilbert, he came back, "Yeah, I'll play this."

I likes to venture too, but I needs a band to help me to venture. You can't venture by yourself. So we just had Jack. Then Tom [Fitzgerald] came: "Yeah, man, I like to play that shit too, bruh." Then Larry [Carter]. But I just couldn't keep a keyboard player. Man, every keyboard player wanted to change the rules. You know, they wanna go this way, they wanna go that way.

So I said, "Naw, I'd rather play guitar by myself. I don't need no keyboard player." So, Luka [Frederickson] came, and he had been studying all our albums, and he came and sat in one night while we were playing at the Dream Palace. And I just called something out at random, and you know that cat knew it? Everything I called, he knew it. I said, "Okay, you're hired," right there.

You know, one time I was playin' at the Apollo with Lee—that was our first gig with Lee Dorsey, at the Apollo Theatre—and, man, they had King Curtis, he was the band leader at that time, and his trumpet player—the trumpet player came to the gig, boy, and he was fucked up. He was fucked up, man. We were playin', and the cat looked at him and said, "You're fired. Pack your shit up."

Right then and there. He looked in the audience and—I'll never forget this— he looked in the audience and said, "Anybody can play trumpet can come up here and play the part." Do you know they had a cat jumped up and said, "I got my horn ready. It's already tuned." And he jumped up right then and there. Now I said, "That is what you call some heavy stuff."

They used to talk about New York, but look, New York has some heavy musicians, and when them cats be doin' that, they be doin' that for real. And when I saw Luka, that made me thought about that. You know, he was right there, and I needed a keyboard player at that time anyway, to start—you know, another level. All the cats were all for it, too—there wasn't nary a squawk about hiring him. He's been with us for about a year now.

But it's been my dream to have my own band. I've always wanted a show band, you know. Like most bands, you know—like Bobby "Blue" Bland's band, B.B. King's band. When I saw big bands—the real first big band that gave me the idea of really havin' a big band, was Betty Wright. I saw her in Rock Hill, South Carolina, on this festival, and I was right close to her at the bandstand, and I had never seen a band like this before. She had about twelve, maybe twelve or thirteen pieces, and believe it or not, it sounded just like you were sittin' in your living room listening to the stereo—that's just how they was playing, with control.

I said, "Lord, if I could only get a band like that." That's when I saw Bobby "Blue" Bland and them—that was the next big band I saw, Bobby "Blue" Bland, B.B. King and them on the showboat. They had a concert, and I looked up there and said, "Lord have mercy, yes, that's what I want." Ever since then, I've been workin' toward havin' a big band.

And now I got a band now that is really comin' to that point where they can really be like that. I don't want 'em to be jumpin' out there and just dancin' and all that stuff. That's not necessary. Play that music! And play it with soul. And have fun with it—yeah, have fun with it. That's the way I like it. But you know what I love now? What I love now is, the way they are presenting the mind, the thoughts, of what I want. They got the understanding of the understanding.

They tailormade these horns. I mean, if you listen to the horns on these tracks, they tailormade it. It's like, they just created that blanket. And it just made me [feel] good, just knowing they wanted to do these things.

It really makes me feel good when I think back to when I was comin' up, and my mama and them used to bring us to church—me and K-Doe. Nobody know his name is Cholly Jr, that's his nickname. They used to bring me and him to church, at that New Home Missionary Baptist Church at Jackson and Prieur, and my mama and them was in the choir—all my aunties and all them used to sing in the choir—and every now and then they let Cholly Jr sing. I used to be sittin' on the benches there, just watchin', thinkin', 'Lord, I wish I could do that'.

So one Sunday evening—all the groups used to come over, all those groups that used to be on WBOK, on Sunday mornings they'd have their thing on WBOK, and then they'd come over to my mama and them's house, all the groups—my uncle would invite 'em. See, the Friendly Five, most of 'em was my cousins and uncles. The Rocks of Harmony, all them was my cousins, you know, and stuff. So they used to come over to the house and eat breakfast, you know, after they'd leave from the studio.

So this particular Sunday, they was singin' the Our Father prayer, you know, and I told 'em I felt the spirit. I just felt it. I told 'em, I said, "Let me sing it. Please let me sing it. I wanna sing it." Because I was raised up on the Our Father prayer, and I used to love to hear Archie [Brownlee] sing it, and I sung that song that day.

From that day forward, I knew I could sing. Because, man, I had tears comin' out my eyes—everybody in the room had tears in their eyes. "Junior, we didn't know you could sing." And every time they go to church from then on, mama and them would let me come up in the choir too. I musta been about eight, nine years old. They let me come up there and sing, and stuff. That was kicks.

That's when I formed—we had a group called the True Loving Four Gospel Singers. And we would sing in the back yard and stuff. Yeah, we would get together—there wasn't but four of us: me, Robert Lee, Richard, and Mitchell Ross—his daddy used to sing with the Chosen Four or the Chosen Five Gospel Singers. He would come and coach us. Robert Lee was the lead singer. He was a little short dude, and he'd put his little head back, and he'd be gone. There wasn't but the four of us in the room, and he'd be goin' on.

Mr Ross used to come over and guide us and coach us and stuff, and we'd have some good harmony too. And then one Sunday morning, my uncle told me, he said, "Junior, y'all wanna come"—'cause they heard us in the back yard over a couple [to] three weeks, you know—he said, "Y'all wanna come over to the radio station and sing a song?" We said, "Yeah, we sure would!" Man, that was the thrill of life, man.

So they brought us to the radio station, and we sung our song. We sung the song, Jesus Is A Rock In The Weary Land. [*Sings*] Man, look, everybody was comin' in to see what we looked like. And what tripped me out, mama and them heard us, you know, because they was at home listenin' to the radio, because they knew we was gonna come on. So when we got home, mama told me, "Now Junior, you wanna sing spirituals, do ya?" I said, "Yeah, mama." "But you're not baptised." I said, "Huh?" "You got to be baptised if you wanna sing gospel. I don't think you're ready yet."

I didn't think so either, but man, I started singin' and singin' and singin' and prayin' and askin' God, "What do I feel? How do I feel this?" I knew what mama and them was talkin' about, but—I was kinda scared of that water. They'd dip you down in the water and raise you up. So I finally asked God, "Show me do I have that—that religion?" And it come to me in the strangest way.

I was sittin' in the church, and it looked like I just couldn't keep still. Reverend Dunn was talkin' about all the different books in the Bible, and how they represent so much of the disciples and the teachers that was going on in this world before us. And all of a sudden, man, something just hit me—I just couldn't sit there.

The next thing, I was in front of the church: "I want to be baptized." And mama say, "Uh huh! He ready now!" And man, look, I got baptized, and it looked like—it was like a dark cloud, a dark cloud had been lifted. When I come out that water like that, the dark cloud that I had over me was gone! It was gone, man. And, I mean, all good things just started happenin' to me.

We started gettin' a lotta programs, you know, my uncle and them used to bring us places where they was, and that's when I learned how to play guitar. See, all the groups that was doin' it, we was only singin' *a capella*. We didn't have no music instruments. And nobody in the group wanted to learn no instrument or nothin'—they just wanted to keep their hands free so they could move 'em.

So I volunteered, you know. I knew how it would sound, so what I did was, I tuned all my strings up to a chord, you know. It wasn't [A-]440, but it was a chord, you know—[*sings*]. And, man, I was playin' that one finger. I played with that one finger almost a year—that one finger, bruh. It got sore, man! I only could make one chord, you know, that was that major, I mean the seventh chord—I love sevenths, you know—that's the only chord I could make with that one finger.

So, man, one Sunday mornin', the Zion Harmonizers, they asked my group to come in on their program, and they had a guitar player there, !bruh, this cat—this cat was playin' with all his fingers. He was playin'—hittin' that treble, and walkin' that fretboard—[*sings*]. Why, I sit there and watched that cat for an hour—for a whole solid hour I watched that cat, bruh.

And, man, when I went home, I tried to play the same thing—it wouldn't sound like that, though. Because, see, I had my guitar tuned up different from what he had his guitar tuned up. Man, I was cryin' and tryin' to play them chords, and cryin' and tryin' to play them chords, and I said, "Mama! I can't get these things. I can't get 'em. I just can't get 'em."

So there was this old man called Uncle D, used to stay down the street from us—that son of a bitch could play some guitar. I was stayin' on Derbigny Street between First and Second, 2419 S. Derbigny, that's where I was at. And this cat, he was stayin' in the next block, and this cat could play like all of them—he was playin' Lightnin' Slim stuff, and all that stuff. He could play with that music. And man, I was sittin' on the porch, and this cat came by, and he said, "Junior! What is that you playin'?"

I didn't have nothin' but a little cigar box, you understand. I had made it. My mama couldn't buy me none. See, they didn't think I could play, because I only played with that one finger. I took my cigar box, bruh, and put me a clothes hanger in there about that long, and had that right there, and twisted me about two or three rows of rubber bands on there.

So he said, "Man, what you tryin' to do?" I said, "I'm tryin' to make me a guitar." And he said, "Look, man, look—that's not a guitar. That's not a guitar."

So he went to his house and got me a guitar. He had two—one old, old hollow body—and he brought it to me and he said, "Junior, I'm gonna sit you down and show you how to tune it. Take the one string, tune that one to that one, and then take the next one, and so forth. Now that's how you tune it."

And I started playin' with it—I tried them chords, and there they are! You know? I started lookin' at my fingers and I said, "Man! Look at me!" I knew three chords—three chords: that was the minor chord, and the major chord, major seventh, and the four and the five. You know? And I knew how to make that minor, that minor on the four. Man, look—from then on, I was hell. I just couldn't pick, but I could play me some chords. I'd scare you half to death with them chords, man. I was playin' some chords.

We stayed together all through high school—all through junior high, all through senior high, with the group. Finally this cat came to school when I was in high school, in the eleventh grade—Erving Charles, he was in my class, and Ervin Williams, they call him Punchy. Both of 'em play bass. Erving plays with Fats [Domino] now. Man, them cats used to come to school, bruh, with rolls of money, like this [gestures]. We all was goin' to Booker T. [Washington].

And I said, "Hey, bruh, where y'all get that money from?" "Hey, man, we play music." "Yeah? Where y'all play music at?" "Aw, we play in night clubs and stuff." "No shit, bruh? I didn't know that!." I say, "Can I come by y'all sometime and listen at y'all practice?" They said, "Yeah, man, sure."

So, man, I started going by their house, because they was stayin'—Erving Charles was stayin' in the projects back there on Calliope, and Ervin Williams was stayin' right there on Washington between Galvez and Johnson—right there. So, they all would go by Ervin's house after school, and they'd get the guitars, and they'd be jammin'.

So they invited me by there one evening after school, and I didn't stay that far—I could walk from there to home. Man, them cats got in there and started slappin' that shit, man. I said, "Wow, y'all sound good. Show me that shit," you know? They would never say, "Well, look, man, you put your chords here, and you play this here." They just said, "Here, watch it, man. You just watch it—see what we're doin', brother."

They'd be playin', and I watched it. Man, I got to listenin' at that shit, and start playin' that shit just like that, and I'd go home and practice on my little guitar. I didn't have no electric guitar, you know, I just had that one that Uncle D gave me.

So Cholly Jr, he was—that's when Mother-In-Law was out then. Yeah, Mother-In-Law was out, hittin', you know—so he said, "Junior, you wanna play a guitar?" I said "Yeah." That cat went and bought one of these Rickenbacker amps, about this big, you know, and a Gibson one-pick up guitar, with the solid body? Man, I couldn't wait to get around by Erving and them.

Hey, man, look, I rolled that son of a bitch for miles to his house, just to show 'em that I had a guitar and amp, you know. I rolled that thing to their house, and Erving was sittin' on the porch—it musta been about 6:00 that evening—and Erving was sittin' on the porch, him and Punchy, you know, they were out on the porch, playin' that shit.

I come down the street rollin' my shit, you know, and "Hey, man, he comin', man, he comin'!" "I got it, man, bruh." And they helped me hook it up, and I started showin' them what I knew. And do you know, from that day forward, they started playin' bass! They stopped playin' guitar. Ask Erving Charles. "Man, I'm not playin' no guitar no more."

I wasn't even soloing—I was just chording, you know, I was just chording. But I knew what chords I was playing now. I was just usin' those fingers, you know. "Man, we're not playin' no guitar no more, uh uh, we playin' bass." And from that day forward they started playin' bass. You know?

But look, John, from there—that's when I started playin' with Cholly Jr and them. He had [Ernie] K-Doe and the Matadors. They called him Cholly Jr because my uncle was named Charlie [Joseph]—he married one of my aunties—and he loved that Uncle Charlie. Everywhere Uncle Charlie went, he would follow him around, everywhere.

K-Doe is my first cousin—his mama and my mama was sisters. We came up in the same house, man. His mama stayed down on Third Street, but Cholly Jr stayed with us because we had more room in our house. See, his real daddy was named Ernie, Ernie Kador, you see, but Cholly Jr didn't like to be around his daddy a lot.

It was nice of him to do this for me, but after I learnt—he got this group called the Matadors, K-Doe and the Matadors. It was like me, Peter Rooster—we used to call him Peter Rooster—played drums, and Beaver played bass. Man, I didn't have to solo too much, but I played them chords, you know. Man! I didn't play on the records, but on the gig, I played just what was on the record. Whatever they had on the record, I would play it. All of K-Doe's stuff—everything, from Mother-In-Law on down.

After I spent that year with Cholly Jr, when I quit from them, by then I had learned some nice stuff, you know—learned a little more chords and things, and we had been workin' around in the area, like Baton Rouge, Port Allen, like that. But after I left him, Johnny [Adams] wanted me to play at the Dew Drop [Inn, at LaSalle and Washington]. So I joined the band, the house band at the Dew Drop, and I wanted to play me some music, you know.

I knew a little bit, and I didn't have to worry too much about soloing—Sammy Berfect was playin' organ, and he was doin' most of the soloing, and they had Hawk on trumpet, and they had Mel on tenor, and Sugar Daddy was the drummer. Sammy was playin' bass on the foot pedals and the keyboards at the same time. We were the house band—we did all the shows, behind any group that come in there, or any artist that come in there.

Like at that time they had Big Joe Turner, he was comin' through, and Charles Brown, he was comin', and Esquerita and the Esquerettes, they were comin' through, and the Inkspots—they used to stay at the Dew Drop. Earl [King] used to hang out there all the time. Bobby "Blue" Bland used to come through there, Little Johnny Taylor—we'd play behind all these guys that didn't have their own band. All they'd do—they'd say, okay, at least play the chords, see. And what I didn't know, I just made out, see, because Sammy knew all that shit. He took care of all of that. So I just played with him, you know, for a while. He was doin' that church thing by day and playin' at night. And it was nice, man, real nice.

The Dew Drop was poppin' then, bruh—whew, was the Dew Drop poppin'! That was the only black club in Uptown that you'd find any musician that was a musician would come through—any musician. I'm serious. Any musician. They had the Tiajuana, but that wasn't hittin' on nothin'. They had the Rocket, that wasn't hittin' on too much. The Shadowland, they wasn't doin' nothin'. But the Dew Drop had everything sewed.

You know, in them days, Frank Painea—when Frank said you come in there, you come in there. That's when I met Little Milton—he had just started in there. Tyrone Davis, all them bad motherfuckers used to come through there. And I played with 'em. If they had their own band, we'd play the first set. Oh, man, them was the days, though. But it still was on the tail end of learnin' these cats, and learnin' the foundation of where I wanted to be at.

And when I really started tryin' to perform, the only thing I could solo was somethin' like what Jimi Hendrix would do, you know, all that wild shit, stuff like that. And they didn't wanna hear that shit. All they wanted to hear was chords. "Yeah, give us some nice chords," you know.

Johnny [Adams] is the one that gave me that start at the Dew Drop. He gave me that position. Oh yeah, he gave me that position. You know, 'cause Johnny was the singer, and he was stayin' at the Dew Drop hisself, that's when he first got married, and when I told him—I said, "Well, look, man, I just can't hang out. Mama want me to go back to school," and I didn't wanna go back to school, you know. I didn't wanna go back, I just decided I wanted to play music, you know. And Johnny said, "Come on."

At that time, I was playin' with all them cats and I was makin' nice money, man—eatin' pretty, you know. Yeah. I didn't have to worry about payin' for no food, because all of the musicians that stayed at the Dew Drop, that worked at the Dew Drop, you ate free. You drank free. You know what I'm sayin'? So it was no problem eatin', you see. And you didn't have to pay but $7.00 a week for a room, and the room didn't have nothin' but a bed, a radio, a table, and a place to hang your clothes, and you had to use one bathroom for the whole place.

They had about thirty rooms there, and the majority of the rooms were owned by musicians. Earl [King]—Oh, Lord, I hate to say this, but—Earl got a book of everything that happened there. Earl had bored holes in each one of those rooms so he could spy on them people! That's right! Oh, man, everybody got that paper. Earl had somethin' on everybody around there—everybody around there. That was somethin'. And they'd sit down there in the restaurant and wait until he come down, and he'd say, "Uh huh. I know about that. Yup. Uh huh. And I know about you too." He would do that. He was like that.

But then Lee [Dorsey] came through there, and Lee liked the way I played. And Lee said, "Hey, man, do you wanna go on the road?" And I'd never been on the road like that, you know, outta the New Orleans area. And I said, "Uh, yeah." And Lee's tours was going all over the United States. He had Ride Your Pony out then. Ride Your Pony was hot. I mean, it was hot!

So he says "Well, look, man, I can pay $700 a week, plus board—all you wanna eat, and anywhere you wanna sleep. You ain't gotta worry about nothin'." "Yeah!" And all I could play was [sings guitar part to Ride Your Pony]. That's all I had to play. That's all. And plus, just play the chords, you know what I'm sayin'? He didn't want no solos—just chords. So, "Okay, I'll go for that."

Man, I went out there on that tour and, boy, the first place we went was the Apollo Theatre. The Apollo Theatre. Nothin' for me to do but meet up with some cats that had came to New Orleans, that I had played with at the Dew Drop, because they didn't have no guitar player, and every time they'd come to the Dew Drop they wouldn't have no guitar player, so I had a chance to play with these cats. That was Joe Tex's band. He had his band. They went with Joe Tex when Lee came and got me. So, man, I cried and they cried—"We don't know when we're gonna see each other again," and all that.

Come to find out—we're sittin' there and Lee says, "Man, we playin' the Apollo Theatre in New York." We was in a red convertible Cadillac—me, Richard Dixon, a cat named Peanut, and Lee's girlfriend. Man, we drove from here all the way to New York City, nonstop except for gas.

So we got to New York, and the thing that tripped me out, bruh—guess who was at the hotel? Joe Tex and his band. And, man, look—for two weeks we had some fun. Because, see, Joe Tex was the star, and Lee Dorsey was the co-star. It was kicks, bruh—for two weeks that was the best fun I had in a long time. We had our own valet, bruh—the cat would come through and fix our hair and everything, you know. I had hair—Lee wanted all of us to have, you know, hair like his, but it was straight, you know.

So mine—in them times, I had me a big old bush, you know, big bush. So the idea was, when I had it fixed, from here I could take the back of my hair and put it all the way to here [*covers his face*]. That's just how long it was. And it was curly—curly, curly, curly. So, see, we'd be on stage and I'd just flip it over while I was playin', see, and throw it back, and it'd all fall right back in place. Man, you talk about some fun.

Shit, for two years and six months I was like a king. We didn't play, like, no joints or nothin'—it was all theatres, and these parks, and all these big places like that. Nothin' but big shows. Thing that got him over: that trick shot. See, when it come time for him to sing that Ride Your Pony, he'd take these two pistols out and "Pow! Pow! Pow!" That'd wrap the show up. He'd take it all then. That's all. That cat was dangerous. He was dangerous. Oh, he was dangerous.

Lee was the nicest dude you'd ever wanna meet. We never had to worry about nothin'. I mean, any of the time. So, after a year or so, the band started gettin' bigger. We wound up with about four horns. It was me, Richard and Peanut, and then we added the horns—we had Leroy Derbigny, he played trumpet; we had Shep [Fred Sheppard] in the band, and Joe Gardner was in the band at that time. We didn't have no keyboard player, just bass and drums, and guitar.

At that time the band started gettin' bigger, and we finally hooked up a job in Chicago. The last six months of the tour—see, I was out with him for like two years and six months, but after a year we started gettin' the big band, and then we got this big, big show while we were stationed in Chicago for like six months.

Man, look, it was in the winter, see, and it was snowin'. It was snowin', bruh. It wasn't nothin' nice. Not that. So I decided I can't take this. After that I decided, "Hey, man, I'm goin' home now." Everybody started gettin' in trouble and shit, you know, and me and Dixon was the only ones who—we had our own loan-out thing, you know, like when we get paid, we were loanin' a dollar on a dollar to the cats, you know. The cats would fuck around and spend up all their money, you know, and then they could borrow it from us.

We were sendin' our money home. We would take like $100, maybe, and we would live off of that $100 for a whole week. See, because Lee was payin' for the hotel, and all the food, all we was buyin' was our wine—we didn't have to worry about no weed, because Lee kept a whole big grocery bag full of that. But these cats was just buyin' shit all the time, and they never had any money.

I got tired of that, so I said, "Look, I'm goin' home." I came home—I caught the next train out of there—I came home and I asked my mama, I said, "Mama, how much money I got?" 'Cause I always sent my money home. Mama said, "You got $43,000." Out of two years and six months, that's what I came home to. She kept it all—didn't spend nary a damn penny. I was sendin' home $600 a week all that time. And do you know I had to beg that woman to let me have any of that money!

So that's when Irma [Thomas] asked me to start workin' with her. So I started workin' with Irma. I went out with Irma for two years, mostly around the city, and sometimes we would travel a little. We had our own van she bought us. She had this cat named Victor was her manager at that time, and he bought everything—bought us a van, bought us a trailer, bought our instruments. We had to rehearse all the time. She was doin' real good, but she just didn't wanna do too much traveling with us. She wanted to do something totally different. But she didn't wanna really do anything right, in that sense, and even today she's not recognized.

When I got with Irma, Irma didn't have a band. Irma was trying to make a band. That's when the Shadowland was really, you know, into bloom, and they wanted to have bands there. But she didn't wanna really do anything else with that band—she wanted to do a different thing. Joe Dunn was on drums, because Peanut had cracked up, and he went to Mandeville.

Me and Joe Dunn was in that band, Roger Lewis on baritone, a cat named George Poche played tenor, Dave Barnes, he played bass, and we had a cat named Lionel Richardson on trumpet. And no keyboards—just us. We worked with that for a long time, and then after that—the last gig I worked with Irma, we played Tampa Florida, and Wilson Pickett was on the show at that time.

She was nice about lettin' me and Dave sing—you know, we would always sing before she come up. I'd sing like mostly Bobby "Blue" Bland stuff, or Tyrone Davis stuff, or either Dave would sing mostly Otis Redding, and we would both get together and—remember Sam & Dave? We would wind up singin' that before she would come on. We'd end up with that—Soul Man, that one and When Something Is Wrong With My Baby, them was the two we would sing. We'd do them two.

Look, the Toronados was nothin' nice, now. The Toronados was nothing nice, you hear me? And, see, when Irma come out, all Irma would have to do was walk across the stage—she done tore the house down right then and there. It's Raining, she was out there with that, and she had about three or four of 'em that she was really doin' at that time. Ruler Of My Heart, all her big hits was out then. But she didn't have no band, and we was really a hittin' band.

And this Tampa gig was with Wilson Pickett—we had to play behind Wilson Pickett, because Wilson Pickett was starrin' that night. In Tampa Florida. We had to play in front of him, and they put us in some kind of Army barracks. They didn't have no hotels for us. But we fixed 'em. We fixed 'em. See, what we did was, when we got off that stage, boy, look, in the dressing room, I mean they had boo-koo women. They were all outside the door and everything.

So when we left that stage, we took all the women out of his dressing room, that was supposed to be with him, we had 'em piled all on the back gate of the station wagon. We had 'em all on that, all on top of the hood, and we went back to the Army barracks and we had our own party. When Wilson and them got off that stage, they didn't have no women in their dressing room—we had all the women. Irma came back to the barracks: "What's all this in here?" She had her flashlight. "All y'all got two womens apiece!"

That was the last gig I played with Irma. I came back home, and my days was just settlin' down. I had wanted to just jump out there, but now I wanted to be back home and try somethin' else. I went with the Tick Tocks at that time—they had just left Huey Smith. It was Huey Smith and the Clowns, and then they changed. They left Huey Smith—John, Allen, and Eugene, they all left him. Bobby Marchan, he was with them. So I went with them for a while—oh, about three or four years. That's when I really started gettin' out there.

But the Tick Tocks, they wasn't really doin' nothin'. They didn't have no hit record out. They was workin' mostly around town. They had this club called the Dooley-Bop Club, and we rented the club for oh, for about six months, and put on our own shows. We stayed in the club and everything—played the show at night, and jammed in the daytime.

I played with them a while, and then I said, "I got to quit this", and I left that. There wasn't nobody in the band—it was just me playin' guitar, and sometimes Buddy Williams would come in and play drums sometimes. Erving, he played bass for us for a little while, but we mostly traveled to different clubs and played with the house band. I was only just the guitar player with the singers.

Them cats was dangerous, man. Them cats would do flips and shit, man, oh lord. Gerri Hall would come and sit in with 'em—she hung out with Scarface John for a while, they was tight. Me and Allen hung out a lot. Eugene, he was always gettin' in trouble somehow—he stayed in trouble. He stayed in trouble.

I mean, look, man, the cats that I hung with at that time, they was cats that was down to earth, man. Regular cats. There wasn't no weird, out stuff. But I had to leave 'em because they were always gettin' into too much trouble. I left 'em then, and that's when I got with David Lastie and A Taste of New Orleans. I got with them—Shine [Alvin Robinson], and Wallace on bass, David [Lastie] on tenor, John Brunious on trumpet, Walter Lastie on drums. Oh yeah. And Piansky [Emile Vinette] on keyboards.

They were playin' at this club called the Clio Tavern, back there on the other side of Melpomene, by the project over on Clio Street. I went over there, and he said, "Man, I heard you're a bad guitar player." I said, "Well, yeah, I try to play good, you know." He said, "Well, look, man, I'm fixin' to go to California, bruh, you want a job?" I said, "What? Playin' with who—these cats?"

These cats was heavy, man. These cats was heavy. "Oh, man, you can play it. You play Ray Charles stuff, don't you? You know a little Bobby 'Blue' Bland stuff, don't you? Yeah, you'll play it." He said, "We're playin' at the Off Limits on

Saturday and Sunday mornings, startin' at 2:00 in the morning." I said, "What? Oh no, I don't play at no 2:00 in the morning." I just be tryin' to get me some sleep at that time. But he said, "Man, look, come on down, audition."

So he brought me down there, and man, them cats was jammin'. Boy, they had their pistols on the fuckin' table—this was the Off Limits, at Dumaine and Claiborne—man, these cats had their pistols on the table, bruh, knives all over the place, half pints on the table. These cats was bad, man. These cats was playin' some music. Man, I got there and I start auditionin', bruh, they said, "Yeah, man, you all right, boy." And I was with them cats for about, almost six years. A Taste of New Orleans.

That was my first group that I went to Europe with. We played the North Sea Jazz Festival. I was doin' the singin'—that's when I started singin' on my own, there. Man, I never will forget that. We had five days, you dig? We only had to work one day, dig? We started off in Amsterdam and, man, look, that was some kicks. We found a place that was a coffeeshop—that was the first time I heard about the coffeeshops. You look on the wall there and they got all kinds of weed. I looked at that and said, "Man!" They said, "You can walk around with twenty five grams, or somethin' like that, on you—like in a bag." It was like twenty five guilders for one of them.

So I said "Okay", and I got me some of this African gunji—check this out, bruh—and I smoked me some of that shit, and some time later Poppee [drummer Walter Lastie] said, "Why don't you try some of this skunk?" "Okay." Man, that shit was more powerful than that African. So what I did was, I bought me a little bag of that stuff, and for two whole days I was walkin' around and my feet could hardly touch the ground, bruh, I felt just that good.

So the night of the gig—the night of the gig, Poppee said, "You all right, bruh? Don't get too high, you dig? Don't get too high." So I fooled around there and smoked about two of them bags and, bruh, look, I got on the gig and the fellas was jammin'. And all of a sudden I got sick. I said, "Oh, man." I was just that fuckin' high, bruh. And I knew if I just threw it up, I'd feel a whole lot better. I'd be all right.

So I eased over to David, and I said, "David"—we was playin' I Got A Woman, you know what I'm sayin'?—and I said, "David"—when David got ready to take a solo—I said, "David, look, man, I got to throw up, man." David say, "Man, what's the matter with you?" I said, "I'm sick, man, sick." So David said, "Okay, I'm gonna hold my solo as long as I can."

I went to throw up, and I come back, and I say, "Man, how am I gonna get back up on that stage? How I'm gonna get back?" And something said to me, "Crawl on that motherfucker." Well, I got down—I got down, you hear me, and I crawled. And, man, look, it tore the house down. It tore the house down!

Man, look, I got up there, I got up there, and I crawled to that guitar, and as David was comin' out of his solo, I started into a solo. Man, I tore that shit down, and when we come off that fuckin' stage, bruh, we got a standing ovation. David said, "Man, have you ever did some shit like that before?" And I said, "No." He said, "Well, you sure did a good job on this one."

The last gig I played with them, we played this bowling alley in Mobile [Alabama]. We played the bowling alley there—three nights we had to play there. And Buddy Williams had brought some of this golden leaf weed—man, that was some good weed. Ooooh, shit! Man, look—we had a whole cereal box full. On the way out of town I started smokin' one, and when we got to the gig—I was smokin' all the way until we got to Mobile. I played the gig. All I drunk was Cokes—a few Cokes, and smoked weed.

I sit up all night Friday night, playin' my guitar and smokin' weed. All day Saturday, I was sittin' there smokin' weed, playin' my guitar. All night Saturday night, playin' guitar and smokin' weed. For three nights and three days, I just sit up and smoked weed and played guitar. And drank Cokes. And that was the last time I played with them. The last night I really just decided that it was all over, and that I had to leave.

One night we had played across the river, and Poppee died that night. We was playin' When The Saints Go Marching In, and when it came to his solo, he just went like that [*slumps down in his seat*]. This was in the early eighties. And it just took me out. I spent some very wonderful times with them cats, man.

Those cats used to come and pick me up in the morning, show me how to— Piansky would show me how to solo. He would just take me off, and he would show me how to hear how the drum was supposed to be playin' with different instruments, and David would let me know exactly what's really happening with hearin' the voicings and stuff, and plus the spiritual intake, you know. It was so much fun tryin' to get involved with these cats.

They used to come and pick me up in the morning, about 9:00, get home about 7:00, 8:00 at night. We'd be jammin' at different people's houses. Cats would keep their instruments in the car, you know, and we'd travel. I couldn't leave my house without my guitar. Everywhere I went, they had an amp there for me.

Them cats taught me to understand what it means to know the feets and meats of this world. You know? The feets and meats of the world. You got your feets that—they the leaders, they in front, they direct 'em. And you got your meats— they're the followers. You know? They told me, "Man, if you don't understand what it means to be a follower, how could you understand what it means to be a leader?" You know? Once you learn how to be a follower, and understand all the little things a leader have to go through, if you really want to be a leader, you have to learn all of those things.

You know, you gonna ask questions, often enough until somebody even wants to say, "Well, yeah, man, this is what this is for, and this is what that's for." And it took the longest to understand all that—the feets and meats of the world. You know, it sounds kinda weird, but it's the truth. Life is a motherfucker. You got to pay attention to what's really out there with the people that's goin' on, and the people that you be workin' with. And it took me a while to understand what it means to have something, and to understand what I had.

When I got with the group Force, it just opened up a lot of doors for me, you know—for myself. And it gave me a lot of confidence in myself. I tried to record with cats, but the only group that really had that potential to make me want to do it was Solar System.

I made those records for Senator Jones with Solar System—that was me and Dog [drummer Wilbert Arnold, the Junk Yard Dog], and a cat played second guitar—I can't think of his name right now, but he could play—we called him Half Pint, he was a little short dude—and then Darryl Francis on bass, and I'm playin' guitar. We had a little cat—I can't think of his name—playin' keyboards, but he got bored.

After we did that album [for Senator Jones], they asked us to play on the JazzFest, and we had the horns—they was called the Little Big Horn Section. There was a cat named—they called him Sweetwater—on tenor, and I forget who it was on trumpet, but anyway they called 'em the Little Big Horns. They was bad cats. We went on right before Allen Toussaint.

Then after that it was the Mighty Mens, and it was the same cats, same rhythm section, but with different horn cats. I had a cat named Frank, Little Frank, playin' trumpet, and I forget his name playin' tenor, and that was a nice group. The Mighty Mens was somethin' else. But then after that I just said, "Nuh-uh." And then they started breakin' off, okay, just started goin' through different changes and stuff, so I said, "Well, I'm gonna give it up."

That's when we were playin' in the [French] Quarters, and I started playin' with Timothea, during that time. And that's when we got Jack [Cruz], and we started workin' this trip together. I was her guitar player, you know, and we'd hire different cats to play, and stuff like that. That's when I got the Roadmasters.

Before that, I had worked with Johnny [Adams] on and off with all three bands—the Force, Mighty Men, and the First Amendment—I'd say within, like, sixteen years. The last group I worked with Johnny was the AFBs. That was right before I got Force. And then Johnny started comin' with us then—altogether like sixteen years. Every time he had a gig, he'd call on me—every time.

Johnny was like my mentor—he actually taught me. All the things I had learned from these cats, Johnny taught me how to deal with these cats—all these different cats. That was how I came to be accepted by the elders, because of the discipline Johnny had taught me. You used to couldn't tell me shit, because I knew it all. But I learned that in order to get somewhere you have to be able to work with intelligence.

And Johnny would say, like, "Hey, man, you don't know it all. You don't know what it means to get to where you are yet, and all it means to get there. And if you don't, you gonna stay right there where you at." And I saw a lot of cats that didn't listen to Johnny, and they'd fall by the wayside. Johnny'll tell you that I'm the only cat, out of all the cats that he had taught, that he would admire and respect. I'm the only one.

Man, Johnny has a way, man—this cat, man, he might appear to you like the most difficultest person to get along with, but Johnny will give you heart, soul, and mind. He's a beautiful cat. Johnny bought my first outfit—my first uniform. I mean, I got a black guitar that I bought myself—my first guitar that I ever bought of my own—it cost me $800, and he helped me get it. That was my very first guitar of my own, and I been playin' that guitar almost twenty seven years.

The Roadmasters—that was a group that I had tried to form, and then I met Jack [Cruz]. I found out how close Jack could understand what I'd been sayin' about the mental state of musicians, and how that discipline will carry you a long ways if you know self of understanding discipline.

You know, people can reach out to you if you have a way of reaching out to them. If you feel that you're gonna hold back, they'll hold back too, no matter what. But they'll reach out to you till they find out that you're gonna hold back. Jack had showed me that he was like a brother, in a sense. When me and Jack first got together, me and Jack created a language between each other, and we didn't have to say a word—just start playin'. We played for about three hours, just playin'—everything that come out of my heart, we just played.

He told me, he said, "Now, give me one year—just one year—and I'll be with you for the rest of my life." And from that day to the first day of that next year, he knocked on my door. He didn't let nary a day pass from that year—because he was there every day. And when he came, he said, "I'm ready now." And he's been with me ever since.

Then Timothea went and got Wilbert [Arnold], because I had got tired of tellin' him, "Hey, man, I got a band that's gonna stick together, and you can relax now", and all that stuff. I just got tired of it, because it just didn't happen. So Timothea got him. And I said, to me—I didn't realize until after the Solar System that I really wanted to have a band. But at that time I couldn't find the right cats that wanted to deal with that—cats that was compatible to each other. Because I always believed in my signs, I believe in the compatibleness of people—and everybody's not compatible with each other. But when you get the right signs that understand that philosophy, it just makes things gel right, you know?

And when that happened, then Tommy [Fitzpatrick], he came in and he said, "Well, man, I wanna play." You know, he came and sat in, and he sounded so good that I could see the potential. He couldn't play half as good as he does now. He was playin', but he wasn't phrasing—he was just playing. There were no periods, no quesion marks, no exclamation points, no nothin'—none of that. You know what I'm sayin'?

So he got in, and everything started workin' the same, and I said "Okay", and that's when Jon Cleary came in. But I could tell Jon wanted to be, you know, as I am—a leader. And he stuck with it, and he changed his ideas and everything. We went through some heavy mind trips. And we talked about that, and when he decided he wanted to go out on his own, there was no bad feelings or anything, it was just, "Hey, man, just go for it."

And then Craig [Wroten] was with me for a while, but Craig had that same idea of bein' out there. Craig got us started with some nice stuff, but Craig wanted to be the boss and I couldn't go for that. Craig and his wife, they wrote the music for the *Sada* album, but he wanted to do his own thing, you know, and I wasn't gonna let nobody take over what I had started.

No matter how strong they was, you can believe one thing: this is mine. You wanna take it, you better get your own. So that's when I decided I wasn't gonna have no more keyboard players—I was just gonna deal with it myself. I said, "Well, I'm not gonna deal with nobody but horns."

So I started adding horns. That's when Larry [Carter] came in, and Larry wanted to do the same thing—he wanted to do some arranging and stuff. That's when David [Ellington] came in, and David, he just showed me right off that he wanted to play, you know. So then I had what I wanted—them three horns. I had that three right horn players. And then everybody started gellin'. And then [keyboardist] Luka [Frederickson]—I said, "Here comes the right one." Now I had all the right cats—I had the right blanket.

I know I got a few more colors that I'm gonna add on, but that's gonna be next year. I wanna add on a rhythm guitar, I wanna add on the percussion, and I wanna add on some vocal singers, and some back-ups for the band. But that's gonna be for the big shows. So when the time comes for me to have that show there, I'll have it! I'll have it. And I intend on havin' that. Yeah, man, I intend on havin' that.

You know, I've always paid attention—always paid attention. I always wanted to learn more, wanted to feel more, in my music. Keep an open mind—that's the only way it'll happen. If you don't keep an open mind, ain't nothing gonna really come to you like it's supposed to. You'll always feel that you're in the dark. I'm glad I came up in the era that I came up in. It really taught me the right things, you know.

New Orleans, May 27, 1998 /
Eugene, OR, July 18, 1998

"Thank You, Pretty Baby"

for Allison Miner

As the last days of 1995
gather & scatter, never
to be seen
again,

our hearts reach out
to the spirits of our friends
who have passed
in the last year, with grateful thanks

for everything they meant to us
& the contributions they made to our lives
as they passed their years
in our midst—

with special thoughts
of my beloved rabbi,
The Righteous One,
Stanley Bob Rudnick,

& just now gone from us,
the one & only Ms. Allison Miner,
master presenter
of modern & ancestral music

in all its splendid guises,
champion of Professor Longhair,
co-creator of the New Orleans Jazz &
Heritage Festival,

archivist, documentarian,
fund-raiser, development specialist,
pioneer of WWOZ Radio,
manager of the ReBirth Brass Band

& Big Chief Bo Dollis
& the Wild Magnolias
of the Mardi Gras Indian Nation,
indefatigable second-liner,

singer of songs, triangle player
& mother of sons,
benefactor to thousands,
friend & inspiration to so many—

Thank you, pretty baby,
as Professor Longhair would trill
"for Allison & her party" at Tipitina's—
Thank you, pretty baby

    until we meet again

French Quarter
New Orleans
December 30, 1995
for Jonathan & Rashi Kaslow

Music by Professor Longhair,
House Party New Orleans Style
(The Lost Sessions 1971–1972)
on Rounder Records

IRMA THOMAS

An Audience with the Soul Queen of New Orleans

AS HER LENGTHY REIGN as the Soul Queen of New Orleans extends into the twenty first century, the great Irma Thomas continues to grow as an artist, band leader, record producer and human being, ever gaining in accomplishment, grace, regal bearing and artistic stature.

During the first year of the new millennium, Ms Thomas is celebrating her forty second year in showbusiness with the release of her new Rounder CD, *My Heart's in Memphis*, a program of tailormade Dan Penn compositions produced by Penn and Scott Billington.

The stark outline of Irma's complicated biography is well known to modern-day music lovers: the New Orleans native was a mother at fourteen (and four times a mother at nineteen), a cocktail waitress at sixteen who began her musical career sitting in with Tommy Ridgley & the Untouchables at the Pimlico Club in Central City New Orleans. Tommy took her to Ron Records to cut her first single, the classic You Can Have My Husband (But Don't Mess With My Man) (Ron 328, 1959).

The dynamic young singer was soon snatched up by Minit Records, where she starred in a series of stellar Allen Toussaint productions including Cry On (Minit 625), I Done Got Over It (Minit 642), It's Raining (Minit 653), and Ruler Of My Heart (Minit 666).

After the New Orleans label was acquired by Imperial Records, Irma had some success with Wish Someone Would Care (Imperial 66013) and Time Is On My Side (Imperial 66041), but she never managed to cross over into the mainstream of popular music like her contemporaries Aretha Franklin, Gladys Knight and Dionne Warwick.

Irma recorded an album's worth of material in Muscle Shoals for Chess Records in the mid sixties, but only a couple of singles were unenthusiastically released by the Chicago firm at the time (now on CD as *Something Good*, MCA/Chess, 1990).

She recorded briefly for Atlantic but was told she "didn't have it any more". She made an album with Jerry Williams (aka Swamp Dogg) in the early seventies that wasn't finished or released until twenty years later (*Turn My World Around*, Shanachie, 1993).

Soon Irma abandoned her pursuit of a career in the performing arts and took a day job at a Montgomery Ward store in California while she raised her four children as a single mother.

Summoned back to New Orleans in the late seventies to appear at the New Orleans Jazz & Heritage Festival, she generated considerable interest in reviving her career and, under the direction of her new husband and manager, Emile Jackson, began the torturous process of re-establishing her hegemony as one of the true Soul Queens of the twentieth century.

Producer Scott Billington brought Irma to Rounder Records in the mid eighties to begin a long and fruitful association that's produced a string of outstanding albums: *The New Rules* (1986), *The Way I Feel* (1988), *Simply The Best: Live* (1990), *True Believer* (1992), the gospel album *Walk Around Heaven* (1993), *The Story of My Life* (1997), and a special project called *Sing It!* (1998) which featured Irma with fellow singers (and Rounder artists) Marcia Ball and Tracy Nelson.

The live album, recorded at Slim's 333 Club in San Francisco in 1990, was nominated for a Grammy as Best Contemporary Blues Recording, and *Sing It!* got its own Grammy nomination in 1999.

Born Irma Lee in Ponchatoula, Louisiana, February 18, 1941, Irma Thomas hasn't slowed a step but instead continues to increase her remarkable powers as a singer and performer. She shares production credit with Scott Billington on most of her albums and remains in vibrant form at the head of her responsive, well-polished ensemble, the Professionals.

She and Emile own a cozy nightspot, the Lion's Den, on Gravier Street near Broad, where she entertains—and cooks for—friends and visitors on special occasions. What's even more remarkable is her imminent graduation from college—at age fifty nine!—with a degree in business.

Early in the new century, ace photographer Barry Kaiser and I were summoned to Irma's New Orleans East bungalow to talk and take some pictures with the Soul Queen of New Orleans.

Just back from entertaining the New Year's Eve crowd in San Francisco, Irma wanted to stay close to home to attend her ailing husband, and she soon made us comfortable in her sunny front room while Barry snapped his photos and I asked her about her earliest influences.

IRMA THOMAS: I came up in a good time, I think, for music. It was a growing time. I didn't have a lot of female vocalists to style myself after, but I took from those I did learn from, which was Mahalia [Jackson], she was the gospel side of me, and Pearl Bailey was my showmanship side.

I didn't know the Bessie Griffins and the Bessie Smiths, because they were way ahead of my time. I knew of them, but there wasn't a lot of their music being played when I was growing up, in the areas where I lived, but I became aware of them as I got into the business. And they were great artists in their own right.

You know, it was very raw—their material was very raw. If someone would have told me when I was six years old, in the middle of the strawberry patch, dancing and singing Boogie Chillen, that I'd ever be on the same stage with John Lee Hooker! I mean, it was, like, "God, I'm in awe of this guy"—and I'm not in awe of very many people, but I was in awe of him.

And to actually be doing a show with Lowell Fulson—my dad had most of his records, even when they were on 78s, okay, so to grow up and be a part of the same venue with these people is, like, mind-boggling, you know. And I really consider myself blessed, really truly blessed, because I never thought I would be sharing a stage with these people.

JOHN SINCLAIR: *What about the R&B area? Were you listening to Annie Laurie and people like that? Faye Adams?*

Annie Laurie, she was okay. I liked some of her stuff. I didn't listen to her a lot. Believe it or not, when I came up—oh, I listened to Faye Adams, Ruth Brown had some stuff going back when I was coming up, getting into the business, LaVerne Baker, there were so many—but, basically, I cut my eye teeth on male vocalists. [*Laughs*]

There were a lot of groups going, like the Ink Spots was one of my favorites, and don't ask me why, I have no idea, but I think because I went to a movie one time and they had these little short subject movies, and the Ink Spots was one of the shorts that they used to show all the time.

And then I had an opportunity to go to the movie theatre and see the Coasters. I saw them for fifty cents on a Sunday afternoon matinee—it was a combination movie and show, and the way they used to do shows then, where you had a featured act, a shake dancer—yeah, at the Ritz Theatre, which is now a church—you had a shake dancer, you had a comedian, and you had a featured act, and of course the MC, and then the movie. And they would alternate. It was fun. And then, when I became part of that alternating series, I played the Apollo Theatre, and then I says, "God, I remember going to the movies and doing this". [*Laughs*]

Who were the male vocalists you listened to?

Brook Benton, he was around, of course; John Lee Hooker; and I did Percy Mayfield—my dad used to play a lot of their stuff. My dad had a lot of their records, and so he played, on Saturdays when he'd be around the house, at home, that's what you'd hear, on what they called the record player back then, 78s, and

45s was just coming into the scene in the late forties and the fifties, so that's what I grew up on.

Then when I lived in the country, I had that country music side. I lived in Greensburg, Louisiana, and also in Hammond for a while, because my father's people were from that area. I didn't live with my mother's people that much, because my mother was born in Anacoco, Louisiana, which is west of here, west of Alexandria, around Fort Polk, and I didn't spend a lot of time with my grandparents on my mother's side, but I spent a lot of time with my father's people, because, being an only child at that time, they both worked, so they sent me to the country, and that's where I heard a lot of—on Sunday you heard gospel, and you heard the country music.

And, as a child, I can remember listening to the early years of John R[ichbourg, the great R&B deejay on 50,000-watt WLAC out of Nashville, Tennessee], late night, and I never thought I'd be having my records played on John R.

Course I never thought I'd be in the business—to be honest with you, it was not something that I aspired to. I liked it, I knew I enjoyed singing, and I knew I wanted to be on stage and that I liked being up there, but I never ever thought I'd be a recording artist. Many a time I found myself trying to think back, like, "When did you ever think you'd be a recording artist?" I just never thought that was going to happen.

But I enjoyed being on stage, because we used to play showtime in the area where I lived here in New Orleans—after I came back from the country, we lived on Felicity Street. There were two buildings, they were rooming houses, they had like small apartments that my parents rented out—Felicity between Carondelet and Baronne, right there in the 1700 block—and we used to play showtime, and each one of us would do what we did best: either would sing or dance, you know, make up our own thing, and this was television to us. So I guess it was inevitable for me to be in the business, because I can't remember ever being frightened of being in front of anybody. Even when we did it in the country, we used to do it.

I love the story about when you were stepping out from behind the waitress post and onto the stage—whether the management liked it or not.

Well, they were asking for the singing waitress, and I think that's what pissed my boss off. He wasn't paying me to be a singer, he was paying me to be a waitress. So I must've been a pretty good waitress for him to get mad and fire me, huh? [*Laughs.*] I had to be doing a pretty good job, evidently, because he sure fired me. I mean, the people were asking for the singing waitress, so I couldn't... Well, think of the times: we're talking mid fifties, okay, still segregated times, and still those prejudices and what have you.

Where was the Pimlico Club?

The Pimlico Club was on the corner of South Broad and Eve. The front part of
it was in the middle of the block, and there was a back part that—prior to them
turning it into a totally black club—blacks used to go in the back side of it, and
the whites used to come in on the front side.

And then they decided to turn it into an entirely, what they would call back
then a "colored" club, and then it became the Pimlico Club, and they had live
entertainment there Wednesday through Sunday. I was being paid four dollars
a night, plus whatever tips I could hustle. Five dollars could go a long way back
then. That's what I made, and when you had good invention skills, you could
stretch it. I had survival skills, so I could stretch it. Did a pretty good job.

Are you working a lot now?

Average. I'm not runnin' and rippin' like I used to, but I'm maintainin', payin'
the bills and stuff like that. They haven't come to kick me out the house yet. The
band would love to be workin' a lot more, and they do with other people, so I
don't hold 'em to the grindstone as much as I'd like to. I make them aware of the
dates that I have, and then they can fill in the gaps.

When you got the Grammy nomination ...

Which one, the first or the second? [*Laughs*]

For the live record, in 1991—did things pick up considerably?

You wanna know something? They didn't. I went from working every weekend
somewhere to working twice a month. It went backwards. It shocked me, too. I
think a lot of the people and powers that be, in terms of booking agents and club
owners, thought that because of the Grammy nomination, my prices would go
up, and the phone just didn't ring. My jobs didn't pick up until 1993, '94, and
then they started to pick up again.

Didn't you win some WC Handy awards?

Yeah, I've won a couple of them, and the irony is, I didn't even know I was
nominated, and then I got this thing in the mail. You know, when you're
considered rhythm & blues, and you get nominated in a strictly blues category,
you kinda wonder if that's where you are, because I don't consider what I'm

doing blues, although it is blues, but if that's the way they feel about it, I don't have any problem with that. "Thank you very much." [*Laughs*] And even when I got the Grammy nominations, it was in "contemporary blues". So I guess, you know, you get a nomination any kinda way you can get one.

You've kept a good band together for a long time.

Yeah, the drummer's been with me twenty three years this year. The rest of 'em, off and on, ten, six, eight, you know—all of 'em have been with me more than a couple of years, except the new trumpet player, he's goin' into the second year. The kind of show that I do, you'd have to be a musician who is open for anything, because I don't do a playlist.

You feel your way through a set?

It's not a matter of feeling my way through. I feel the audience, and I give them those options to ask me to perform whatever songs that they feel like I might know, or remember—because it's getting to that point now—and I try to accommodate, so the band has to be very flexible when it comes to that kind of a show.

I usually start off with something either from my latest CD, or something else recent, and then I work my way back to the older things—I call them "my standards"—and in between I open up and give the audience the opportunity to make requests or what have you, and I try to accommodate them.

It's easier that way, I think. I mean, when they spend their money, I feel they're entitled to hear what it is they want to hear. I do it even in concerts, when I'm doing the larger venues—I still do it. I bring my cheat-sheet tablet on stage with me, put it on the music stand, and, you know, even if I only have, say, forty minutes to kill, I'll kind of guess at what they might want to hear. But if they give me an hour's time out there on that stage, I'll open it up for suggestions, and I'll run right on through them.

I mean, I think the audience walk away with a much more fulfilled feeling that way, rather than have to sit there and listen at what I choose to sing for them, and it may not necessarily be what they want to hear. This way I'm giving them their money's worth—I'm hoping I am, anyway. That's what I'm shooting to do—give them their money's worth. I don't assume that I can please everybody, but I sure try.

What are you working on now?

I have a CD coming out this spring. I finished it up yesterday with David Farrell, who's been my engineer ever since I've been with Rounder. He and I spent about two and a half hours in the studio yesterday going over some things I wanted to redo, some vocals that I wanted to redo, that I wasn't happy with. The company was pretty much satisfied, but I felt that I could do a better shot at them. And now I'm satisfied.

These are some songs that are written and co-written by Dan Penn and several other people, so part of the title of the album will have the name of Dan Penn involved. They haven't come up with the exact title as of yet, but it'll have his name in it somehow. Over the years I've done quite a few of his pieces, so this time we did the entire CD with him writing or co-writing on all thirteen songs. I co-wrote two of them myself—one is called Irma's Song, and the other one is Keep It Simple.

Did you co-produce this album with Scott Billington?

I didn't take the co-production attitude with this particular CD. I let him and Dan more or less direct and produce what they were comfortable with doing. We were going in a different direction this time, and I wanted to leave it up to them in terms of what they were looking for—and then afterwards I'll go back and do it my way. [*Laughs*] So this time I didn't take the producer's—I mean, he may give me credit for some things, but I didn't have a lot to do production-wise on this one.

I would think that Scott's probably pretty easy to work with.

Scott Billington is an excellent producer. He learns his artist, he gets to know the artist's personality, he tries to work with their talent and keep it as close to natural as possible, he allows them some freedoms to be who they are in the studio as well as any other venue, and that makes a difference in the way that a record comes across—a lot, to me anyway.

He's worked with me ever since I've been with Rounder, about fifteen years now, and what's good about it, we haven't always had the greatest of material sent our way, and so up until the Grammy nomination in 1991, it was like trying to pull teeth that didn't need pullin', you know, to find a good song, or to get the writers to even send anything in my direction.

That's when we went on and did the live album, because we really couldn't get anything going, and then all of a sudden, pop, it's nominated for a Grammy. It's still my biggest selling album, next to *Sing It!* Now *Sing It!* is really doing well, with the other two ladies and myself. We've even got royalties! So that's inspiring, very inspiring. We did the p.r. tour, and we played some venues that I'd never played before.

It was a mutual feeling there: we enjoyed each other's company, we enjoyed each other's talents, we respected each other's talents, we gave each other their space onstage and offstage, and it's rare to find females working under those conditions and not having any scoop or crap to talk about. We all traveled on the same bus, and we knew—we enhanced each other's weaknesses, and we held each other up, you know, in our strong points, and that's the way it should be when you've got three veteran entertainers out there.

It wouldn't be right for the three of us to be out there and be in competition with each other, when there is no competition to be in. We all have our own levels in this business, we all do our own type and style of music in this business, we just happen to fit so well together when we come together as singers until … we just didn't expect it to be so great.

It came off very well in the studio. We discovered that we had natural harmony—we didn't have to look for our parts or anything, it just fell together. Just sing, and it all fell together. I mean, how often can that happen? You just don't get that to happen too often. So we were really hoping, once we got nominated, that we would have gotten the Grammy, but the powers that be said otherwise. So be it. At least somebody was out there listening to us.

I've talked with Scott about the process you use to select the material for your albums.

Oh, yeah. He sends me a tape and says, "Okay, Irma, here's some things I think you might find something among." He knows I'm a person who prefers songs with storylines. I don't think I've cut a gimmick record since I've been with Rounder—it's always been a storyline.

So he always sends me these songs that have storylines, and they'll either be up-tempo, or they'll be ballads, or they'll be outright blues. And usually, among them I'll find something that we agree on. Let's say he sends me a tape with, maybe, twelve songs on it. And I may choose, out of the twelve, I may choose half of them. And then we'll sit down and we'll listen to that and pick out the best ones out of that segment, and then we'll decide on two. Then he'll send me another batch, and then we'll eliminate them though that process.

I noticed you've been soliciting more material in the last few productions. I thought that was a great thing, because I could see guys out there saying, "Oh, man, I'd love to write something for Irma Thomas—she'll sing the hell out of this."

Right. But, oftentimes, what somebody thinks I might sing the hell out of is something that I probably don't care for at all, you know, because—maybe they hear this voice connected with this song, but if this song is not telling a good story, then, no, I don't think so. It has to have a combination of things: a good storyline, a good music line as well, not sound a lot like something else—although most music sounds like something else at one point or another—but usually we come up with some pretty decent things.

It's kind of unusual for a woman artist, who's a singer and not a musician per se, to direct her own recordings.

Well, I've been at it a long time. You gotta realize, this is my what? My forty second year, somewhere in there, and you do learn some things over the years about music if you're in tune to what's going on around you, if you have a good ear for what it is you're doing, and this is the way I go with it.

I mean, I'm not totally unaware of how music should be—I don't play proficiently, but I can run the scale on the piano, and that's about as far as my piano dexterity goes. But when my band is playing, I can tell when somebody's out of key, and I know what keys I sing in. I do have a pretty decent ear.

So when I'm in the studio, I'll come up with an idea and hum it to them and say, "Okay, I want this to sound like this," or "I want this to go like that." But usually, especially when you're blessed with the musicians that you have in New Orleans, you sing it, and they can come up with these fantastic arrangements that everybody can hear at the same time, and it kinda comes together, so you don't have to really do a whole lot to steer them in a different direction. You may have a certain little passage that you want played a certain way, but other than that, usually it works out.

The only other place where I've recorded in recent years that comes up with the same caliber of musicians that I work with here locally was in Memphis, where we did the tracks for my new CD. Those guys are another bunch of guys who, when you play the raw stuff, they can come up with all these fantastic arrangements and things. So it kinda makes my work easy.

But you take a pretty active role, don't you?

I do—not really direct, but we have rehearsals, and the only thing that I may tell them: let's do the bridge twice, or we may shorten it here or lengthen it there, but that's basically all it is, because I'm working with professional guys who are music majors, or they may have had music as their second major when they were in school. I have teachers in my band, principals in my band, so I don't really have a lot to do, other than bring it there and play it, and they go for it, you know.

I've been blessed by being surrounded with some pretty easy musicians to work with. I mean, I pass my opinions on things, and I can always tell when somebody hasn't done their homework, and I will voice my opinion about it, but other than that, I give them the respect that I expect from them, and it works out. I don't have to play mother hen all the time. It's just a matter of how important is it to you to be a professional person, to play the stuff and have it ready at the time I need it, and beyond that point, I don't have to say any more, because if they want to work with me, this is what I expect, and I usually get it.

I don't have time to re-raise somebody's son—or daughter, if it's a female. I haven't had the pleasure of having a female in my band as yet, but it's not an impossibility. But this is how I treat them—they're adults, and I don't have time for egos to be flying, because we all have our own egos, so we leave them at home. Because when it's a job, egos get left at home.

I'm the front person, I'm the, as they put it, quote, "the star", but I don't go that way. But I'm the one who gets paid to put on a performance, and I pay you to help me, to back me up to do this performance. So we're gonna have to have a mutual understanding, and I lay the groundwork: there's no drinking on stage, no smoking on stage. The only time I allow any kind of drinking is water, and it's when it's extremely hot and all of us need some water. But the alcohol stuff—that's when you're on your time, you can get as drunk as you want, but not on my time!

And the other side of that, you want your musicians to be professional, because whenever something happens, you're representing me, and I'm not a drinker. I don't indulge in any kind of things that's gonna make me not be clear-headed when I'm doing my performances. So I tell them: I don't drink, I don't smoke, I don't do any kind of drugs of any kind, and these are the kind of musicians I want. Now, if you do this, I don't want it done on my gig, and I don't wanna be aware that you are doing them, because I don't need that kind of a musician.

If you have to depend on a drug to get you to do your job, then you're not the musician I'm looking for. Okay? I want you to have a natural adrenaline from what you're doing, a love for what you're doing, because if you don't love it, then I don't need you. Because I love what I do, and I'll go as far as to do it *a capella* if it comes to that.

So I make them aware of how I feel about what I'm doing, and find out if that's where their head and heart is, then fine—we'll get along great. I've so far been blessed to have the kind of musicians who love what they do. They love music, and they enjoy playing—they wanna sound good.

I think the last time I saw the band in action was at the Tommy Ridgley memorial show at Tipitina's, where you all came over from another gig and went right up and put on a helluva show.

Yeah. Well, Tommy's gone. Quite a musician. He goes back to my beginning [as an entertainer], and I really feel good in that I was able to express my gratitude. It wasn't a thing that, "Oh, I wished I shoulda, coulda, woulda", I didn't have to do that. I had enough time in my career to show my appreciation in ways that most people wouldn't even bother, so I don't have any regrets in terms of not being able to say or do the things that I should've done for him when he was living.

I would want to do that with any person who has been a part of my career in such a way. Because, even though I had the talent, if he hadn't brought me to the places where the talent could have been heard, I could still probably be washing somebody's dishes or waiting somebody's table.

Well, I woulda gone back to school, which I've done—in fact, I have to go register for my last two classes. I plan to graduate this spring. I'm looking at—I can see the light at the end of the tunnel!

All right! How long have you been pursuing this?

Oh, God, since I was forty five. [*Laughs*] I started when I was forty five, and then I took some time off, because when I got the [Grammy] nomination, I had to back away. I couldn't go to school regularly, and I stayed out maybe a year and a half to two years. I coulda been through, but work was more important, you know. And I was pursuing this as a self fulfillment—it wasn't for any job market, whatever, or nothin'.

What's your degree gonna be in?

Business. [*Laughs*] I changed my major, because I talked with a lot of ladies who are social workers, and even though I have that natural ability to be able to comfort and counsel and all that kinda good stuff, she said, "No, Irma, I don't think you wanna be in this, not after what you've been in. The kinda business you're in," she said, "this is not for you." So I said, "Okay, well, I'll change my major and do business."

And it has helped, believe it or not. It has helped so much. I've learned a lot that I wasn't aware of. Because in business, it's a never-ending learning process. And, you know, being a teenage parent, not getting my high school diploma—I did go back and get my GED, got that out of the way, and I said, you know, "I've

never really actually graduated from anything. That's got to be an experience."
So I wanted to experience that. And then after seeing several senior citizens—as
we are called—graduating... [*Laughs*]

I don't know if I'd be happy in retirement. I was off six weeks for surgery, and
I thought I'd go nuts. In fact, I didn't even take the whole six weeks—I came
back to work after four weeks, against my doctor's wishes. But I promised him I
would sit down, I wouldn't dance around.

Performing has its rewards, though.

Oh God, it made me heal so much faster. There's nothing like it—nothing.

I really enjoyed your gospel album.

Thank you. I take my religious beliefs very seriously, and I don't down anybody
for what they do. To each his own, when it comes to religion, but I take mine
very seriously. I'm heavy into participating in my church, and I don't feel that
that's going to get me into heaven, but it's for my own feelings. I get out of
church what benefits Irma personally—you can't buy your way into heaven, you
know—so I go there to get my own buckets refilled, my own soul replenished,
and that's what it's for.

I invite people, when they ask me when I'm doing shows to sing something
gospel, I say, "Well, if you come to 2216 Third Street on Sundays, I'm in the
choir, second row in the alto section, and you'll hear me there." Because I don't
mix the two. It's bad enough they have, you know, people out there drinking,
and you don't wanna be singing Amazing Grace to some drunkards. What do
they know? They might be thinking about something totally different. You're
singing Amazing Grace and thinking about the Almighty, and they might be
thinking about Grace at the end of the bar.

I've always maintained some groundedness, because I've had a family since I've
been in the business, and I didn't wanna do anything as an artist that my family
had to hold their head down about. Even in the business aspect of it, if I didn't
like what they were presenting to me financially—the cut that they wanted of
my talent—I just said, "No, that's too much, and you're not guaranteeing me
anything." So they'd say, "No, we'll let her go." And they sure did. I'm not sorry.
I always figured: what was for me, I was gonna get it, one way or the other, and
I believe it was meant for me to be still in the business, doing what I'm doing,
the way I'm doing it.

A lot of times these people have these preconceived ideas, you know. Back
then they used to 'make' stars, and they would want you to wear certain kinds

of clothing, and you'd have to carry yourself in a certain kind of way, and …
I could not be that phony person. Because I'm not phony—I'm just Irma, and
you either like what you see, or you won't like what you see, you know, but the
human side of me is me—that's the total me.

And they were looking for this other … whatever they had in mind, and I
wasn't it. I wasn't gonna be it, put it that way.

But we still have an audience out there, thank God! The younger people are
realizing what it's supposed to sound like.

I'm finding that I have to explain myself less and less now—who I am, and
what was, and what is—they're becoming more aware. And thank goodness for
the internet: I think that has made a lot of the youngsters aware of who did what
first.

You're kind of active on the web, aren't you?

Yeah, I'm doing it. [*Laughs*] I'm learning now that a lot of the youngsters were
not aware that a lot of the sampling that they've heard with these rap artists is
stuff that was done when their parents were children, and they think it's new—
they think it's something fresh and new. So I'm getting a whole new generation
of youngsters.

I had a young man—I'll never forget, this was Mother's Day at Audubon Zoo,
and I thought it was so precious. He walked up to me and says, "You sing good."
And I said, "Well, thank you." He must've been about fifteen. [*Laughs*] And all I
said was, "Thank you". I guess coming from him, that was quite a compliment,
and I took it as such.

It's like you're getting this younger generation of people who are becoming
aware of what music is really supposed to sound like, and so they find that this is
really cool, as they would say—cool, or the bomb, or whatever the new word is
these days. By the time I've learned the new word, they've changed it.

New Orleans
January 11 > January 30–31, 2000

202

#84

"rhythm-a-ning" [28]

for paul lichter & the great ernie harwell

it's the top
of the 5th, two men
on & monk

on the mound
to face the meat
of the defending champion

new york tenors
batting order—it's the
rhythm

inning, time now
to get something
going—& at the plate

for the tenors,
digging in deep now,
center fielder sonny rollins

    (also known as 'newk'
    for his remarkable resemblance
    to the great don newcombe)

is taking his cuts. rollins
checks the sign from arnett cobb at 3rd
& takes a called first strike

right down the middle. on the basepaths,
the leadoff batter,
johnny griffin, dances off 2nd

& james moody takes a short lead
off of 1st. on deck,
the clean-up hitter,

fellow native of north carolina,
veteran of many hard seasons
in the minor leagues,

john coltrane picks up his bat,
weights it,
& pounds the air without mercy.

monk
checks the runners,
shakes off the sign

from art blakey
behind the plate, nods,
stretches & delivers

a most wicked curve
& newk strikes air. the fans know
if monk can get past rollins

there'll be one down,
coltrane up & coleman hawkins
waiting on deck. so monk

looks in,
puts that rocky mount grip
on the ball, & sends newk back

to the bench
with a deadly screwball. trane fans,
& bean dribbles one down

to john birks gillespie at 1st. diz
steps on the bag & monk
puts another inning away

toward an eventual shut-out
of the defending champs. in the bottom
of the 8th, miles davis is hit

by a pitch,
steals 2nd,
bud powell draws an in-

tentional pass, & bird
puts the game away
with a 3-run homer. the series

goes to the challengers,
the bebop all-stars,
4 games to 3

& monk is voted most
valuable player
over dizzy gillespie

in the closest of votes. the year
is 1954, the legendary "subway series"
is now history,

& baseball,
dear friends,
will never be the same

detroit
may 1, 1985

after jack kerouac,
"memory babe"

special thanks to
peter klaver & martin gross

WADE IN THE WATER

Dr John Weathers the Flood

THERE IS NO NATIVE SON of New Orleans more fiercely native than Mac Rebennack, known professionally now for almost forty years as Dr John. Born in November 1940, Mac grew up in the golden age of New Orleans rhythm & blues and has spent a long and exceptionally productive lifetime in uninterrupted service to the music and the community that nurtured it.

From his first album, *Gris Gris Gumbo Ya Ya* (Atco, 1968), through classic early Atlantic/Atco LPs like *Babylon, Sun Moon & Herbs, Remedies, Gumbo, Desitively Bonnaroo* and *In the Right Place*, and into the modern era with productions like his Grammy-winning *Going Back to New Orleans* (Warner Bros, 1992) and last fall's Hurricane Katrina benefit disc, *Sippiana Hericane* (Blue Note, 2005), the Doctor has proclaimed his love for the music and culture of New Orleans and helped turn the world on to the many joys of the Crescent City.

So when the high winds blew and the levees broke and eighty per cent of the city was underwater, Mac's mental landscape was as bleak and desolate as the gruesome geography of greater New Orleans. Although he's been based in New York City and its environs for many years, he's got hundreds of life-long friends and family members going back to his childhood in the Third Ward sixty years ago, and he's remained a particularly active member of the Crescent City music community since returning home to cut *Going Back to New Orleans* in the early 1990s.

Mac has recorded countless albums under his own name and remains a ubiquitous participant in the music and recording activities of others way too numerous to list here. In New Orleans alone he's collaborated with everybody from Pete Fountain and Al Hirt to Donald Harrison Jr and James Andrews, and he's played a key role in several historic Mardi Gras Indian recordings by the Wild Magnolias, Golden Eagles and Guardians of the Flame.

The Doctor's hometown practice is both wide and deep. He's tight with everyone from Eddie Bo and Dave Bartholomew to Lillian Boutte and the Dirty Dozen Brass Band. He came up under Professor Longhair and Prince La-La and Roy Montrell and Harold Batiste, Jessie "Ooh Poo Pah Doo" Hill and Joe "Mr Google Eyes" August, and he's an exact contemporary of James Booker, Allen Toussaint, Art and Aaron Neville, Irma "Soul Queen of New Orleans" Thomas and Oliver "Who Shot the La La" Morgan (whom he still calls "Nookie Boy")—and he's influenced at least two entire generations of hip musicians of

206

the Caucasian persuasion who have followed in his wake.

More than anything else, though, Mac Rebennack is a leading exponent of that small but potent fraternity of white Americans who have fully embraced African American life and culture in all its glory and completely immersed themselves in the musical and daily life of the black world within the United States that remains hidden to all but the very few white people who want nothing more than to be a part of it.

That said, it's easy to understand Mac's consternation at the ugly unfolding fate of the City That Care Once Forgot. From the days immediately after the flood when he was trying to locate a lot of the people he cares about, through the series of benefit concerts and recordings and important national appearances he's made in the months since, to his continuing participation in every sort of relief effort in the present, he's stayed in constant touch with the situation and done everything he knows how to do to make things better.

"You know," Mac confides in a trans-Atlantic telephone conversation between my base in Amsterdam and his Long Island home, "I ain't never got un-angry since the hurricane. Every night on the gig, no matter where we at, I give the audience an earful about my thoughts about it, you know?

"Every night on the gig I get on my robe and—you know I'm crazy, so I don't give a damn what I tell 'em. And the only time we ever had any complaints about it—actually, I got one in Seattle that was a complaint that I didn't say enough.

"In Miami, the only negative thing I got was a Mayor, I think it was Hollywood, Florida, she come up and said, 'We don't use the "C" word in Florida'. I said, 'Well, look, Lady Mayor, I'm a coon-ass. I think we had dibs on possibly inventin' corruption, so if you don't like the "C" word here, what do you call it? What you call corruption?'"

When I replied, "I think they call it 'business as usual,'" Mac said, "Well, we know all of what they might call it, but their business ain't cuttin' it for me. I don't know who it's cuttin' it for, but their portion of the pie looks kinda cock-eyed to me. So I'm very glad to see some of 'em fall, it makes me feel a tinge—as Jelly Roll Morton would say—a tinge better.

"But if I was to look at these lames and try to say, hey, well, I feel good about anything, wow, I'd be really jivin' myself."

I reminded the Doctor that I'd heard him preaching at the Jazz Festival in Detroit last Labor Day weekend, right after the flood. "I heard you all the way down on the other end of Woodward Avenue from the stage, sayin' 'President Bush don't like black people'. Man, I heard it three blocks away!"

"Hey," Mac laughed, "I got it from some hip hop kid. I was talkin' to Bobby Charles, and I told him that, and Bobby says, 'Well, Mac, it's kinda obvious, daddy,' he says. 'Look on the TV. If ya look at the Convention Center and the

Super Dome, you ain't gonna see no white faces—maybe one or maybe two, but you ain't gonna see 'em.' And Bobby was pissed."

Mac and Bobby go back a long way. Mac was a fifteen year old guitarist and band leader in New Orleans when Bobby Charles came in from the sticks and cut Later Alligator, Take It Easy Greasy and his other mid fifties hits for Chess Records under the direction of Paul Gayten. They've been friends ever since, and Mac's cut a number of Bobby's hip compositions over the years.

For his hurricane relief album, *Sippiana Hericane*, Mac framed his four-part *Wade: Hurricane Suite* with the Bobby Charles anthem Clean Water. But Bobby had a new tune, written after the flood, called The Road To The White House Is Paved With Gold...And The Truth Will Set You Free.

"I wish we coulda got the words and all," Mac laments, mentioning a garbled phone conversation where Bobby played and sang the song for him, "and the music for it—I woulda cut that sucker. But I didn't get the words from Bobby until like a month after we had done cut the record.

"I was wantin' to cut Clean Water anyway, but I wanted to put that other one on too. Man, he had did it on the phone, but I couldn't hear it good enough, you know. Man, I was gonna roust up somebody to do some little hip hop thing on there—that was my plot for that, but I couldn't get the words.

"Man, look, we was scufflin' just talkin', you know. Bobby had lost his pad—I mean, everything where he lives at was gone. I mean, the whole town don't exist no more, amongst a whole lotta other places.

"We was comin' back through southwest Louisiana from Austin to work in Lafayette," the Doctor remembers, "and man, it was like—all of a sudden you could tell when you was outta the state of Texas and hit the Louisiana border. It was like—Lake Charles looked like a volcano flowed over it and alla that.

"We know we definitely Third World country material now," Mac says. "You know, everybody I know in New Orleans is elsewhere. You know, look, I run into people—I talked to little Tracy the other night, he said he just got his FEMA lights on...and he's lucky. And he's callin' it like it is. It's just pathetic crap, you know?"

Trying to get to a little brighter place, I brought up the subject of his new album, *Mercernary*, a full-scale tribute to the compositions of the great tunesmith Johnny Mercer in which classic pop numbers like Blues In The Night, You Must Have Been A Beautiful Baby, I'm An Old Cow Hand, Lazy Bones, That Old Black Magic and Moon River are dragged through the Ninth Ward mud by Mac's Lower 911 wrecking gang and turned entirely to the Doctor's own twisted purposes.

"Yeah," Mac says, "You know what was the song that got me to do that Mercer record? My daughter was singin' that song about 'Personality' from a buncha

years ago—she listens to all kinda shit, and she said, "I got a song for you to do."
Now it ain't by him, right, but he recorded it when he was first runnin' Capitol
Records."

I allowed that I'd found the album pretty entertaining but thought maybe
the liberties he'd taken with the composer's works might find Johnny Mercer
perhaps pinwheeling in his grave.

"Yeah, thanks. I thought there was a couple of pimientos in there. But you
know what? I know when I messed up Hoagy Carmichael's song and called it The
Nearness Of Love, instead of The Nearness Of You, and the publisher wanted
me to yank it. And I was thinkin', 'Oh God, I'm whacked.' And he said—Hoagy
personally called and said, 'Hey, listen, I did real good with that doo-wop record
of Blue Moon,' and he told the publisher, right there on the phone, he told the
guy, 'Leave it. I think it's funny.'"

I mentioned Mac's sole original composition on the album, I Ain't No Johnny
Mercer, where he pokes fun at his own deficiencies as a songwriter with the
refrain: "It just gets worser and worser / I ain't no Johnny Mercer." Mac replied
that he had always been taken by Mercer's slick and sophisticated manipulation
of the English language, even though Johnny worked at the other end of the
funk ladder from where the Doctor does his business.

"I read his book, you know? So I was readin' about all the stuff he did, and
the lines he used, and I took a lot outta that. But there was one line he wrote,
it was like somethin' way back in the game, but he said, "You're so sexy / You
give me apoplexy." And I had to look it up to make sure I knew what the word
'apoplexy' meant.

"You know, I took a buncha stuff he wrote, like 'Pardon my southern drawl,'
and said somethin' else, like 'Pardon my southern accident,' you know—like I
do? I tried to do stuff that he woulda dug in today's parlance. Because they don't
have nothin' like what he did now in terms of intelligence and language.

"He was comin' from this thing where he was tryin' to write stuff to get him
in—he always wanted to be—see, I didn't know all this, but he always wanted
to be like one o' them Tin Pan Alley, Broadway guys, but he was from out in the
sticks somewhere and they just didn't let him in.

"So he was like—him and Hoagy Carmichael and certain guys, when they
wrote together, you could buy it. These guys had like another thing, you know.
It's like, Lazy Bones got a certain thing, and I always liked that song, but I didn't
even know they had writ it together.

"But then, a lot of that stuff... you know, I brought in Tangerine as a tribute
to [the late New Orleans saxophonist] Red Tyler, and Save The Bones for [the
late New Orleans guitarist, author and raconteur] Danny Barker—Danny wrote
that with him.

"I've got an *Austin City Limits* video that I took the words off—I didn't take 'em out the song book version, I took 'em right out the *Austin City Limits* video with Danny singin' it with my band. And it was hilarious! The only line I changed, insteada takin' 'vegetarian' and whatever he rhymed it with, I said 'He was a vege-terrible.'"

Me, I've always loved Danny Barker's version of Save The Bones on his classic Orleans Records album of the same name, but I thought Mac had added his own little touch as well and took old Henry Jones all the way outta the Seventh Ward and down into the Lower Ninth, where Mac's rhythm section hails from and the Doctor himself received crucial early musical and life training.

"Well, you know," he concedes, "Listen, all of it has connections." Then his mind connects to the version he made of Mercer's old warhorse, I'm An Old Cowhand: "Listen, you know, I always liked it from when Sonny Rollins cut it, and Sonny was the one that made me actually think maybe I could do something different with this sucker other than what he done, but keep it in a thing that's kicks.

"So I was determined to do something different than Sonny but make it an instrumental, but I was thinking, 'maybe we'll put some background parts...' So we cut the thing and, I couldn't help it, I was so shot—when we came into New Orleans to cut the record I forget we was supposed to do a tribute to Ray Charles, and I had told Sonny [Schneidau] at the House of Blues that we was gonna do a 'Tribute to Ray' set. I figured we'd have the charts for that, and we could roll with it.

"But all of a sudden I'm writin' up a tribute to Ray, and so it turned into a whole other set of petunias. I was up for like two or three days tryin' to hustle up and write the charts for that gig. I was so shot by the time we got in to cut the record, I never finished all the stuff I was gonna write for the horn parts for the record. What the hell, I figured, listen, we'd just do somethin' different instead, somethin' like an extra keyboard, or some other strangeness."

I had thought it was nice with the horns coming in to accentuate Mac's eccentric arrangements every couple of tunes instead of always being there. They stood out more sharply and seemed to come in right on time.

"Two of the things I did" to make up for the missing horn parts, Mac said, "was to get Herbert [Hardesty] to just him play on a couple of tunes, and I wanted to get somebody in there like—and it worked out really good, because I was able to get James Rivers for Save The Bones. You know, James has got that little cross between like Fathead, and Donald Wilkerson and James Clay and alla them cats from kind of a freaky school of that Texas sound, you know."

I remarked that his reading of Mercer's Come Rain Or Come Shine reminded me of the beautiful version that Johnny Adams cut for Rounder Records late

A John Sinclair Reader

in his life. Mac hadn't heard it but testified, "You know me, I love Johnny, I don't care what he done. Johnny coulda belched in the mike and made it sound good."

"Alright, man," I concluded, "I'm gonna write this up for a little magazine outta Oxford, Mississippi called *Honest Tune*, and they gonna put you on the cover."

"Yeah, that's cool," the Doctor chuckles. "Hey, listen, you just do whatever the hell you regulationally do, and it'll work. You know, I'm just tryin' to agitate the people." And speaking of the kind of connections we were talking about, he blew my mind with his last crack:

"You know what, it's a funny thing, but—where the hell did I just put it? I got one of your—wait a minute, I just put the sucker somewhere—a CD that you gave me with some guy that I don't even know who this guy is.... Here it is. I can't even read it—looks like, is it Wayne Kramer? Where you did Doctor Blues…?"

"Yeah," I shouted into the phone, "you know what's on there? I'm An Old Cowhand. Give it a spin, you'll enjoy it. We used the Sonny Rollins arrangement…"

Amsterdam
April 14–17, 2006

DR JOHN COMES CLEAN
Kicking Dope & Taking Names

JOHN SINCLAIR: *First things first: everybody wants to know who did your hair for the record cover of* Television?

DR JOHN: Oh yeah? You think I look like Bobby Marchan? Do I have that real Esquerita look? [*Laughs*]

On the real side, I'm enjoyin' your new record immensely. This is all new stuff, huh?

Well, there's Sly's thing, Thank You Falettin Me Be Mice Elf Again, and Barrett Strong's Money, but all the rest is original new stuff, yeah. Actually, one song I had already wrote for another thing—U Lie 2 Much—but other than that, the rest is for this record.

That rap number, Shut The Funk Up, put me in mind of that record you did with Duke Bootee a few years back called Jet Set.

211

Yeah, I like that we done that, man. That kid Anthony Keidis is cool, you know? I gave him a tape with me talkin' about Otis Redding and whoever I thought about as my inspiration for funk, and he did what I told him. I said, write about what inspired you, and he used his own cats that inspired him—and a lot of 'em inspired me too.

I see he got his man George Clinton in there...

Yeah, P-Funk, and Defunkt, too. Man, I remember Defunkt, but I had forgot about 'em 'til he brought 'em up. He snuck in Maze on the deal and, you know, I'd never have thought about Maze necessarily as a funk group. I like the way he put George Clinton in there, and a lot of cats that maybe I might not have considered in there, but I like that. That's what the world is about today—gettin' it all in.

How'd you come on the Television *thing for the theme of this?*

You know, it's like it's partly my way of lookin' at, like, the world condition á la me—like how I add to the problems of this planet by the very nature of not watchin' television. But it's also about like how my boy always shoots that rib at me—"What, you don't watch television?" I'm pretty quick to snatch up somethin' that makes sense and run with it.

What's funny to me is that so many people who heard it, what they saw from it—from this side of it—like, oh, it's a statement on birth control, it's a statement on overpopulation, it's a statement on this and that—from their point of view. And that's cool—it's all of that to me, too. I just like hearing from other people's side.

Or maybe television as a form of birth control...

Yeah, you know, television is definitely the opiate of the masses, so in that way you can also consider that opiates can control that situation by null and voidin' out the sex drive. [*Laughs*] So, on the other side of this, as television bein' the opiate of the masses, therein lies somethin' that Mr Trotsky or Mr Lenin said back in the game about religion, but it still holds true.

Or maybe opiates is the television of the masses...

It still holds true—it's true that way too.

The thing I like is this goes back to that old Dr John sound...

Well, you know what that's like—you take some funky shit and have some fun with it. The most fun was taking all the new technology and, instead of using it like all the cats was using the thing, we used it the opposite way—we took all the modern things we had access to in the studio and played with them like an instrument. We used all of these electronic devices and played them by hand instead of how they were meant to be used. Just having some fun with this shit, just doing how we like to—just playing something and makin' it fun to do.

I hope somebody starts doing some of this stuff—maybe some of these young rascals will just take this shit and start doing what they feel like. It's sorta like the Big Youth version of record production: get up there and run with it, whatever it is. Push this one way, and if you feel like taking everything out, do it. It goes back to the idea that old theories is cool and new technology is cool, but if you can reverse the two—make up some new theories and look at the technology like we been here a little bit, that's whereof we cometh.

So what are you looking for with this record?

Well, I'm hoping we got a record out there that will get some people to just straight out dance and have some fun—and getting back to doing some gigs that we like to do. We ain't trying to get into no hysterical areas of music or nothing, just doing some funny stuff, making some sociable commentaries, and just looking at stuff the way it is from a distorted viewpoint—playin' some undistorted music with a distorted viewpoint and see where that leadeth...

Is GRP—your new record company—happy with this ?

Oh yeah, they been cool from day one. The GRP people, they said, like, hey, what do you want to do? And out of all the labels we spoke to, they were the only ones that said anything like that. Everybody else was telling me who to use, and they didn't even know what I wanted to do.

Just the fact that that happened—well, I was interested. In fact, I think one of the hip things about GRP was that the cats that run the label is musicians, and the next thing that was hip was that they wasn't trying to put me in no one particular jazz thing or some particular bag—they just said, do whatever you feel like doing.

They just said, make the record and we'll sell it?

They was cool about that—it wasn't no got to do this or got to do that. I been there, you know, I been there for thirty-something years, and I had one option to do something I felt like doing totally and I took it, and that's cool. I was happy doing something, and especially doing some funk, and I think we did some other kind of little things in the set.

This is the first record I ever put some rainforest jungle sounds on—I mean we got the real McGillicuddy. It wasn't no piped in from California stuff, it was the real deal. I ain't trying to be ecological or nothing, but I figured in the area where music is stepping I like to keep something on the level of nature and the environment—something hipper.

Plus you got the other environment surrounding this—the spiritual environment.

Yeah, we dealing with some kind of apocalyptical thinking—it's kind of some leftover Babylonian thinking—and I always liked apocalyptical thinking, especially if you could put a little smirk or a grin with it. The music keeps it on an upbeat level, so it don't feel too preachy or nothing—hey, that's just the way we singing it.

It's funny, I seen a flick from a George Clinton video the other night, man, and we was talking about some of this stuff. There is a concept George had run with and we was running maybe parallel in different directions and didn't know it. Maybe we was running the opposite direction, but the point is it's a very connectable realm of thinking, you know, the stuff we do.

It's that line of the funk, and different cats along the way, from the Meters on, you see connecting links that went other ways within the thing and hopefully we might talk…maybe some of them cats that go out for record scratching might want to take a band on the road, something like that, you know what I mean? We got to get some more musicians on the gig so we can see actual human beings instead of somebody programming something or another.

One of the things I think is important today, too, is that people is getting locked into certain things. Like, last night I watched one of those video reels like they put out every month with all the new videos what's coming out on different labels? I guess somebody use them for a video jukebox. And in watching it I realized almost every record on there had programmed drums, sampled sounds, very little real musicians—maybe one or two per tune. I knew it was like that on a lot of rap things, but now it's like that on pop things, R&B things, everything. So hopefully maybe we can revamp somebody's thinking with that.

You used all the cats from your band on this record throughout?

Yeah, under the auspices of Alvin Tyler. He kept it all together for us, and it was a gas working with Hughie McCracken, because we go way back in the game together.

I like these tunes, man. Witchey Red, that's back in the Jump Sturdy kind of pocket.

Oh yeah, that's out that gris-gris satchel. I feel like that one and another one me and Doc Pomus wrote, about only the shadows know, that's kind of out of that gris-gris thang.

I like what you did with Sly's thing too.

Oh yeah, I been wanting to do one of Sly's tunes, and that's the one I like the best—just that message I like to use as an affirmation for me, I Like To Thank You Fallein Me Be Mice Elf Again. We was going to cut that way back in the game, you know, on the *City Lights* or *Tango Palace* records, but we winded up takin' the bass line from it and cut it to keep the music simple.

But it was always in the back of my head, and this time it just seemed like a good time to do it. I ain't never knew the words of it, and if we wouldn't have gotten a lead sheet for it, I still wouldn't know the words, but I had messed them up a little bit because that's what I do the best...

Changin' the charts around...

That's right. You know this is your modus operandi, Sinclair, you know: we just change the beat around, which we done that too. We did that Spaceship Relationship—we just turned the beat sideways and upside down and messed with it. But that's what pocket they into out there today, you know, people don't have no relationship today, they have spaceship relationships.

That's popular—it's like having Captain Kirk fall in love with Dr Spock, that's what's happening. It ain't nothing about no real deal stuff, you know—just some chump-change stuff and feel-left-out stuff and outer-limits-galaxy stuff. Maybe somebody will think about what's happened to families and just relate it for the people. It don't have to be no deep issue, just what happened to all of those little things.

I see that you got a new publishing deal on all this material, too—'SNews Music.

215

It's funny because we had a song we didn't use on the album called If You Snooze You Lose. Well, you know, it's a popular saying and all of that stuff, it was one of the three tracks or four tracks we dumped off the record, but that's where the new publishing name come out of.

It's news...

Yeah! Well, it's gospel—gospel according to the psychotic reformation. Life has its ways, and they say nothing lasts forever.

Amen. And sometimes it's a good thing.

It's like that old Guitar Slim song, I'm So Glad Trouble Don't Last Always—and you know all the rest of the songs that had that theme in mind, I Done Got Over It and all of that stuff is important music. You appreciate 'em, I appreciate 'em, it's like we listen to them and we know where the truth is at in the song.

That's another thing with me—I like to put some songs out there that I feel like this is my little thing, whether it's...whatever it is, it's me, and you can't always do that with somebody else's song. And then it's some songs I totally like, like Thank You (Falletin Me Be Mice Elf Again)—I'm totally in agreement with that.

How about that Barrett Strong tune, Money (That's What I Want)?

That's getting ready to be my main example! Hey, look, I done made everybody else some money, it's about time I made a dollar three eighty out the deal for myself, you know? It's a funny thing, John, you know this—sometimes you get so caught up in trying to do so much for everybody else and can't do nothing for ourselves in the middle of it.

Sometimes you try to do something for yourself and everybody else get salty because they're used to you not doing nothing for yourself. So, you know, you live and you learn and you learn and you live and all of that, and if you don't make no move on it what you gonna do, collect spider webs? I got a few, but I don't need to keep my brains full of them though. You know I can do something better with the brain cells than that today.

Are they going to send you out on tour behind this record?

Well, we working out behind this—we getting a video, we getting the whole *schmeir*. We did a video on the tune Television—we did it on the television, in the television, with the television, without the television [*Laughs*]. Well, you know, that's kind of the nightclub of today.

I wish people will look at that album cover with me clicking off where the TV ain't and with the TV on, and there is a message in there whether you want to look at it surrealistically or any other way, but people is looking one way and thinking they is looking somewheres else.

And they got to get they coattails pulled on some of this, 'cause you ain't gonna find no real life on TV. You ain't gonna find no whole deal on no TV. You look at them all day long, but you got to be somewhere around people, real deal stuff. You in the Treme, right? Well, you know whereofeth you liveth. [*Laughs*]

Yeah, they haven't got none of this on TV.

It ain't even close! If they tried to figure out how to put that on there, they would have a rough time. You can take any area of the Treme and try to figure out how to apply to what you see anywhere. You can take the Florida and the Desire projects and maybe apply it to Bosnia and Herzegovinia and Serbians and all of that, but you ain't going to apply it to too much you see on TV. And even then that don't even apply that strong, but in one sense you can always apply something to something...

They got a whole different reality that don't even come close to TV.

TV is like, today, besides being the opiate of the masses, it's kind of like the baby pacifier, and it's kind of like the hot water bottle. I mean from the baby to the great-grandmama, they got everything covered unless you watching the news, and even then you might do better reading the newspaper, you might do better talking to somebody down the block—at least you get something real even if it's wrong.

*Talking about reading, I see they got this tied in with your book too [*Under a Hoodoo Moon*].*

I did this book hoping somebody might realize from my mistakes that you ain't got to mess up totally to play music, and maybe they will learn from my mistakes to have a better crop of musicians that ain't so lamed out as a lot of cats that came up in my time.

It ain't necessary to be a lame to be in the game, and it ain't necessary to be a jerk to see if it work. I hope that some of the youngsters will flounce through some of that.

You know, this book is as unaccurate with dates, times and places as it could get, but what the hell do they expect from some old ex-dope fiend? They expect to get a, well, at 6:30 on December 29 or I think was Juneteenth or whenever the hell that was...?

It was some pretty raw data in there though.

Well, what do you expect from a guy that just came out of a psych ward? You want something that come out sounding like a *Beowulf*? I was kicking it raw, man, coming out of rehab. What do you talk about in rehab? You talk about stuff that's raw, and I was kicking it as raw as it gets.

Yeah, it put me in mind of Art Pepper's book, Straight Life.

Oh, yeah. You read his book?

Sure!

Well, you read everything—you are a dedicated reader of stuff. You probably read Miles's book...

Oh yeah! I read it three times!

Well, if you read Miles's book three times, you could stomach my book. You are a part of the connected link, and I hope this whole two-way package serves the connected link.

To me the other side is this: I'm a professional musician, I ain't no professional book writer. I'm a professional musician and I'm an amateur in this area, and if someone learns something from my mistakes out of that book, it will have served a purpose.

Who was that guy that did the book with you?

Jack Rummel—you know, he was a cat that wanted to write a book. And I give him credit for weaving through the New Orleansese, the musicianese, the Chinese and any other-ese.

One of the things, even though he took out some chunks of stuff that probably could have got more people salty than we already got salty, I think in some ways he tried to keep the raw flavor of it all, and he probably done the best he could with it.

He not only kept the raw flavor of it, but he made it so you could understand it.

That was the problem of doing the thing, you know—a lot of the stuff come from conversations from me and [Joe] Google Eyes [August], different cats—me and Red [Tyler]—whoever we was sitting around in a thing with at that minute. It was like, wow, maybe you can see that this is what cats talk about—not what you think musicians talk about, but this might be a little picture of something of that particular reality.

I thought it gave a pretty well rounded picture of that—I mean as far as the cats talking about some real far-out stuff. I know I really enjoyed all the southern California parts, Dave Dixon and the rest of those characters...

The land of fruits and nuts! Well, you know, you could write a whole thing on Dave Dixon alone. All you got to do is turn the tape recorder on and mention his name to Earl King and you got two or three novels.

Red told me the other night that Big Time Crip was by the gig, and there is another one of them kind of cats, you know what I mean—it's so many characters in this world, all by they self they is an epic saga. Whoever wrote the epic for the Norwegians and the Vikings, they could have gotten some more different opinions on that from just talkin' to any one of them characters.

I wanted to ask you about that Rhino anthology, Mos'Scocious. *Did you have anything to do with putting it together?*

Well, they asked me about some of the titles, and they sent me a copy. I think it was pretty cool. The only thing that bothered me was, I think Johnny Vincent burnt them on that version of Roland Stone on Down The Road, because that wasn't the one they actually played in New Orleans. That version sounded like it was cut in a studio, or something close to a studio, but we did it first at a radio station and it had a real primitive sound. It was real raw, and that's what I think people liked about it.

But man, they reached back for that stuff—Bad Neighborhood and those things from the late fifties.

I was talking to some GRP people and they finding in their catalogs some stuff I cut with Leonard James in 1959—an old Decca record with Leonard James—they found it and they gonna send me a copy of it.

Who produced that stuff, Danny Kessler?

Danny Kessler would come in there and have me and Allen [Toussaint] audition twenty million people and then cut four of them, you know.

So that's how you got Leonard James out?

Well, actually, at the time I had cut some stuff for Capitol—I don't know whatever happened to that stuff—and we was cutting a record with [James] Booker for Eddie Messner [at Aladdin Records], but I don't know what happened to that either. Danny Kessler had something to do with all of it—it was all pre-being-in-the-union and all, pre-everything else…

One thing I found out about reading your book was your hook-up with Mercury Records.

I tell you, man, one thing about it, I really grew to love working with Irving Green over the years. But at the time I was working for him, I didn't know what was what and where was where and how was how and nothing else. But looking back on it, I learned one thing: Irving Green knew a lot. I mean, when you consider the records he done in them days—Quincy Jones and Clifford Brown and Max Roach and Dinah Washington and all them people.

Mercury made some great records that everybody forgets about.

I mean, you name it, they did it. That old record on Baldhead that they did on Byrd [Professor Longhair], that was classic.

Right, Roy Byrd & His Blues Jumpers. And Hadacol Bounce—"like a fish in the ocean, I just wanna flounce…"

Yeah, "Got me doing the Hadacol Bounce". Yeah, they sold some hellified product, I tell you that—that Hadacol was a growing concern in them days. Probably when they took it off the market they had sold as much as Dr Tichenor's Tonic. [*Laughs*]

But Irving was an original. I really look back with a lot of fondness toward Irving Green. I can't say that of some of the people that worked for him, but Irving was special.

Was that before the stuff with Harold Battiste?

Well, all around in there, me and Harold did some stuff, and then later Harold sort of iced me out of it and brought Melvin [Lastie] in. But we did different stuff for Mercury like King Floyd, Wayne Talbert, we did a record with [Alvin] Shine [Robinson], stuff with Poops [Jessie Hill], just all kinds of people. Irving was looking for guys like Joe Barry and Jivin' Gene, who had cut on Mercury before, and I knew where to find them.

We had a pretty good time. It was funny—when they was looking for some of them cats, some of them cats probably would have re-signed with Mercury. It was at a strange time for me, but then on the other side of it I had that attitude of I ain't giving up my friends. Whatever it was, it wasn't about being straight up, and that's how life was in those days.

You get a helluva picture of that in the book—scandalous dope fiend behavior. I thought, boy, Mac is really kicking it to bring all of this shit out into the light of day…

Yeah. What the hell, you know? I think they got a lot of youngsters out there today, they think that smoking them rocks and stuff enhances their playing, when in fact they ain't enhancing nothing but their illusions, and it's good for them to get a little picture of that.

You know what I'm saying—that whole syndrome of guys thinking that they got to get outside of themselves to try to get to something. Whatever it is, it's inside, and it's coming from the spirit, and if they ain't getting it from the spirit kingdom, it ain't there.

You carried that burden for a long time.

Well, some people hit a brick wall and try to remove it a brick at a time, and some people dig it. Some people are into S&M and don't know it. And, you know, it's a lot of people that do some sick things in life and think, hey, it's cool, I ain't hurting nobody but me.

But thinking that I ain't hurting nobody but me was a cop out and I didn't know it. When I look at all the pain my family endured and all the people I hurt over the years, I realized, hey, I wasn't jivin' nobody but moi. It's a typical syndrome.

That's one of the reasons I hope when someone gets to the end of all of that, that they will see one thing. Four years and four months and change later, I'm getting' to sanitize my brain and feel good spiritually, emotionally, physically and living like a human being, and my music is even maybe gettin' better— that's the idea of it, you know.

Life after drugs is life after insanity, it is life and it's a lot more to it than just living. It's like it ain't just surviving today—I'm enjoying things that the regulation people enjoy—whether it's sex or just smelling the coffee, it's just looking at the sky, you know, they got one up there!

It might be a flower growing—wow! They still exist! There are still ducks in the park, there's still a swan swimming in the park somewhere. You can feed them ducks some popcorn, you can feed them flowers, some fertilizer, you know, you can sprinkle some water on some of them flowers—these are things that a lot of people actually knew about. Wow! Where in the world have I been? You know, and the world went on.

There's a lot of those cats that I still see today—the ones that are still alive, that ain't in Angola or Texarkana or one of them dungeons—and they're just as much a trip today as they was back in the game, but you just got a different perspective on the thing.

It ain't too easy to look forward when you're looking over your shoulder—it ain't too easy to feel comfortable when deep down inside you're in a state of panic. And it's hard to feel psychologically fit when you're in a state of schizophrenia, or maybe just a stage of—what do you call those people that don't move?

Catatonic?

Yeah, catatonic. It's hard to feel like participating in a relay race when you are catatonic...

When you're carrying somebody around on your back...

When your complexes have complexes and your flexes have flexes, it's hard to appreciate anything coming up—with your nexus, sexes, anything else—you develop inside phobias and fears that ain't got nothing to do with nothing that has the word reality connected to it.

Oh, it's beautiful! Life is like a... I listen to the worst news today and I just be laughing. We have a lot of beautiful things out there, and I ain't just referring to nothing in particular, but I mean some of the scientific things we done here lately, some of the medical things we done did in the latelys. We done sit down there and done philosophised it, and the main thing we was discussing was the world policy, and none of us had a clue on what our own policy was. We're all in the same boat, so we all better try and figure out how to do it together a little better.

Amen.

The truth is the truth and a fact is a fact and opinions come and go like the wind, but them few truths that's important—the rest of this stuff we will put on the back burner until we figure it out.

If it's music, we know we can turn it to magic; if it's magic, we know we can turn it to music. That's straight from the creator to the creation—that's straight through the meat. It hits your ear drums, it hits your soul, your brain cells, wherever it hits you, it keeps going.

I feel good about this music. I feel like it gives me a chance to do something that I feel like doing, when I feel like doing it. Wow! That impression has got nothing to do with Curtis Mayfield, but I relate to him from that: People Get Ready, we got a train coming, you want to jump on board, cool!

Yeah, well, I'm jumping on board.

Hey, you been on, John, you been on.

I'm re-upping, though.

Well, that's what they say: old characters never die, they just tell another lie!

Are you going to do any special promotion on the book? Are you going on the talk show circuit?

Sure, I'm gonna sign a few books, I'm gonna check every circuit, and I'm gonna check my circuitries. Maybe you'll see me on *Geraldo*. I want to do the whole thing. If this is what the package is, you know what? It's cool with me!

It's *Television Under a Hoodoo Moon*. If you want to watch *Television Under a Hoodoo Moon*, you are in the right place, and it's desitively mos'scocious. We can tie them all up. I think I'm Roy Rogers today, I like Trigger, we gonna ride them a long way and see if we can catch up with the Cisco Kid and Pancho.

New Orleans
March 28, 1994

#24

"my melancholy baby" [30]

for stevenson palfi

in the awful aftermath
of hurricane katrina,
amid the wreckage
of his city,

his neighborhood,
his home,
his painstaking work
& his life itself,

looking forward to nothing
but increasing pain
& suffering beyond measure
as far as he could see,

the relentless public indifference
to the fruits of his labors,
the bitter impossibility
of completing his allen toussaint film

already 15 years in the making,
songwriter: unknown,
pieced together in fits
& starts, when he could wheedle

enough bread for a shoot
or get a print made
or edit something together
so he could see it—money

he had to beg for
from people at arts agencies
who couldn't stand him
& tried to ruin his life,

or people who dug his work
but never gave him enough cash
to make it all happen
the way it was supposed to,

this beautiful cat
with a big heart
& huge imagination, & a mind
that never stopped working,

the creator of "piano players
rarely ever play together"
starring professor longhair
& tuts washington

& the great toussaint,
documenter of emmanuel sayles
& papa john creach
& jabbo "junebug" jones,

employer of my daughter celia
& treasured friend & accomplice
ever since that day in 1982
when me & harry duncans

banged on his front door
on banks street
& begged him
to let us see "piano players"

& he showed it to us—
& that's the way i'll re-
member him, a guy who gave
& gave of what he had,

smiling through the pain
that wracked his body
& his heart, in love
with his work

& his daughter nell
& the music we all love—
always & forever,
brother stevenson palfi,

always in love with the music

st. philip street, new orleans
december 30, 2005 > february 22, 2006 /
rochester ny
january 19, 2007

THEY CALL US WILD

The Mardi Gras Indians of New Orleans

"There is never a dull moment
in the streets
where the Zulus

& the Indians
& the Baby Dolls
live & play,

in the streets
where every night
is Saturday night"

—Robert Tallant,
Gumbo Ya-Ya *(1945)*

URBAN AMERICAN CULTURE begins and ends in the streets, where wave after wave of ethnic immigrants has crested, broken, and, largely, dispersed into the vast suburban landscape of metro America.

Life in the streets of the cities of America is now by and large a thing of the past. Except for New York City, Chicago, Miami and New Orleans, say, the vitality of street life, the teeming masses of pedestrian citizens, the portable marketplaces, the corner stores crammed with customers inside and loiterers lined up outdoors, the bars and pool rooms and record stores and barber shops where people met and gathered for their fun and necessities—all of this is gone from the lives of all but the most recent immigrants and the most destitute sectors of the African American community, where good times in the face of impending doom have been replaced by the doom itself, and fear stalks the streets wearing a gun.

Everywhere else the streets have been abandoned and boarded up, or rolled up and moved to the suburban dreamland where life is contained in the home and moves from workplace to shopping mall to school and back in tightly locked automobiles.

But it is the culture of the street that has made America great, and where life remains in the streets there will always be great music, great poetry, great painting, great art of all sorts, at once reflecting and feeding back the brilliance and energy of the people in the streets.

In the streets our cultural heritage will live and grow, our music will swing with vigor and intelligence, our imagery will be ripe with oranges, hot tamales, cans of soda, yellow trousers, a sea of faces, legs and shoulders—brimming with humanity and pulsing to the many vigorous heartbeats of our citizenry.

Take the streets of New Orleans, where life exists in almost boundless measure even today, and where modern life is incredibly rooted in the rich dark soil of the city's long and continuous cultural history.

> *"New Orleans*
> *is the most receptive place in the world*
> *to the artist,*
>
> *this music spirit*
> *that flies around in the air*
> *all the time,*
>
> *waiting*
> *to be reborn*
> *& reborn"*
>
> —*Bahamian band leader Exuma,*
> *in* Wavelength #4

On the same streets where jazz emerged out of the brass bands by way of Congo Square, where rhythm & blues merged the sound of the piano professors with the emotionalism of the spiritualist churches, where Buddy Bolden, Jelly Roll Morton, Louis Armstrong, Professor Longhair and Sweet Emma Barrett once walked home from the gig every night—these streets today carry their music in the very air, and what is most incredible is the continuing presence of the original, the prototypical music of the street in its original form—the Mardi Gras Indians of New Orleans.

IT'S MARDI GRAS DAY, early in the afternoon, and five tribes of Wild Indians are heading into a big showdown at the intersection of Washington and Derbigny, just above the Magnolia projects in uptown New Orleans.

The Wild Magnolias, led by Big Chief Bo Dollis, and the Golden Eagles, with Big Chief Monk Boudreaux, banded together with their immense second line, have been dancing and chanting all the way up Washington from Dryades. The Golden Stars and the Young Sons of Geronimo, backed by a huge gang of supporters from their own neighborhood, are prancing down Washington from the opposite direction. And the Black Eagles, with twenty or thirty of their own pals behind them, are heading up Derbigny, hell-bent for a showdown.

All around them, in every direction, packing the streets from sidewalk to sidewalk, hundreds of neighborhood citizens mill about, trying to get a clear shot at the action. "Ooh, them Indians is pretty today," people who can see the brilliantly costumed warriors bubble to their friends.

Before the final push got underway, Bo Dollis had paused at the corner of Washington and Magnolia to pull his forces together. His Spy Boy had raced ahead, searching for traces of other tribes on their turf, and came running back with shouts of "Golden Stars! Geronimos! Headin' down Washington!"

The Flag Boy of the Wild Magnolias adjusted his magnificent war bonnet and lifted high the huge, hand-beaded and brightly feathered standard of his tribe, ready to lead his gang into battle.

Other tribal officials, all wearing their indescribably beautiful hand-sewn Indian costumes—the Council Chief, Second Chief, the Trail Chief, the Wild Man—stationed themselves along the line of march, about twenty feet apart and separated by members of the Wild Magnolias second line with their beat-up old drums, cowbells, tambourines, whistles, wine bottles and sticks ready to pound out the hundred year old beat of the street.

The trusted inner-circle members of the second line—that mass of non-costumed followers who march behind the Wild Indians in the streets, wielding their raggedy rhythm instruments and shouting back the appropriate responses to the wild calls and boasts of their Big Chiefs—were getting their marching orders now, and the spectators on the sidewalks started moving into position to witness the big push through stopped traffic across Claiborne (a major thoroughfare) and up to Derbigny, where all five tribes would meet up at last.

Now the Wild Magnolias and the Golden Eagles resume their forward motion, their cries and shouts growing louder and stronger by the minute. "Let 'em come, let 'em come," a Flag Boy hollers impatiently, and as the second line hammers out a steady chorus of Two Way Pak E Way ("Tuez pas qu ou'est", or "Kill anyone who gets in the way"), Big Chief Bo Dollis begins to carry on for real:

> *What I say now?*
> Two Way Pak E Way
> *Oh y'all, is you ready?*
> Two Way Pak E Way
> *Oh now, what I know now!*
> Two Way Pak E Way
> *Injuns is ready, y'all!*
> Two Way Pak E Way
> *Hey people, is ya ready?*
> Hey Pak E Way

Let's all have fun now!
Hey Pak E Way
Wild Magnolias comin'!
Hey Pak E Way
Let's do what we wanna!
Hey Pak E Way

Headed across busy Claiborne Avenue now, stopped motorists gawk through their car windows, point and stare as the Mardi Gras Indians dance through the intersection in full tribal regalia, pushed on by the surging second-liners and their relentless beat. Spy Boys and Flag Boys gesture fiercely, brazenly stopping traffic to let the Big Chiefs and their legions through.

Then it's straight ahead up Washington, the Big Chiefs dancing and hollering like Wild Indians, the second-liners strutting and shouting that endless "Hey Pak E Way", the Flag Boys running ahead crying "Make way for the Wild Magnolia! Make no houm-bah! Make cha-wah! Wild Magnolia make kill-o-way!"

> *"They used to carry hatchets,*
> *razor sharp, and real shotguns. Now*
>
> *it's all changed. They fight*
> *with their costumes.*
>
> *We used to fight*
> *with knives and guns.*
>
> *Now we compete*
> *by the beauty of our costumes."*
> —Tootie Montana,
> Big Chief of the Yellow Pocahontas

The Mardi Gras Indians—also called Wild Indians, or Black Indians—have been enacting their frenzied street rituals in the funkiest, neediest, most ancient districts of New Orleans since at least the late 1870s.

Today's active Wild Indian tribes—the Yellow Pocahontas, Wild Magnolias, Creole Wild West, Golden Arrows, White Eagles, Wild Tchoupitoulas, Golden Eagles, Ninth Ward Warriors, Black Eagles, Golden Stars, Yellow Jackets, Young Sons of Geronimo, Yellow Cloud Hunters and several others—carry on the tradition of black men and women masking in elaborate costumes on Mardi Gras to honor the spirits of the native peoples (Choctaws, Cherokees, Natchez, Seminoles) who greeted their ancestors with respect and helped inspire their ultimately successful resistance to the slave masters.

The Wild Indian chants, dances, costumes and street activities at Mardi Gras are only the most visible manifestations of a comprehensive system of secret societies dedicated to keeping alive the West African, Caribbean, Choctaw, and Black Creole heritage of African Americans in New Orleans. Deeply rooted in poverty-stricken, laboring-class uptown and downtown neighborhoods, these societies (or tribes) hark back to the ceremonial societies of West African village life while they continue to adapt the ancestral forms to changing realities in the new world.

"When Blacks dressed
as American Indians

they were assuming the composite identity
of a spiritual people

who fought & died
for their way of life & beliefs.

Masking Indian
was & is

a rite or ritual
for spiritual guidance."

—*Michael P. Smith,*
Spirit World

The first Mardi Gras Indians are alleged to have appeared on the streets of the Sixth Ward downtown on Mardi Gras Day ten or fifteen years after the Civil War. Their astounding presence was first noted by Elise Kirsch in her account of the Mardi Gras festivities for 1883, when she spotted a band or tribe of sixty or so men masked as Indians with turkey feathers in their hair on Robertson Street near St. Bernard Avenue—just blocks from the childhood home of Ferdinand "Jelly Roll" Morton, inventor of the jazz idiom, born in 1885.

The first reported tribe was the original Creole Wild West, founded around 1880 at 1313 St. Anthony Street by Becate Batiste, a Sixth Ward Creole of African American, French and Choctaw heritage. The Yellow Pocahontas, headed since 1945 or so by Big Chief Allison "Tootie" Montana (grand-nephew of Big Chief Becate Batiste), followed in the late 1890s with Henri Marigny as Big Chief and a full-blooded, 7'2" Choctaw, Eugene Honore, as Second Chief and musical arranger.

An old-time Black Indian, Vincent Trepagnier, recalls Eugene Honore as "a real Indian who came with his mama from up in the country, somewhere the other side of Baton Rouge. They lived in tents. And when they come in the city they moved on Burgundy and Toulouse." Another old-timer, Arthur "Creole" Williams, claims that Honore "mapped all them songs out", establishing the form and essential content of Wild Indian music for the next hundred years.

> *"The (Wild) Indians' songs*
> *articulate a lineage*
>
> *of past tribes*
> *and great leaders*
>
> *whose collective memory*
> *lives*
>
> *in the chants of bravery*
> *and spiritual solidarity*
>
> *as passed on through generations*
> *of the oral traditon."*
> —Jason Berry, Jonathan Foose & Tad Jones,
> Up From the Cradle of Jazz

Michael P. Smith adds, in *Spirit World*, that the "songs and impromptu 'calls' testify to Black street experience, past and present, recount slave days, ancient or famous 'blood' battles, call up images of prison or ghetto life...all to an intense polyrhythmic beat."

> *"Everything we do in this city,*
> *regardless of what we play,*
>
> *whether they call it 'jazz'*
> *or 'soul', or 'gospel', or whatever*
>
> *you call it, it all has*
> *Two Way Pak E Way in it.*
>
> *It's something about our music,*
> *they all have that 1-2-3-4,*
>
> *Dun-Ta-Dun-Dunt,*
> *you know, that's always in there."*
> —Abe Sturgis,
> Tribal Hawk of The White Eagles

For the student of contemporary popular music and its African American underpinnings, Wild Indian music provides the missing link which connected the West African perambulating chants, the ring shouts and sankeys of the slaves on the Eastern seaboard, the brass band marches of the post-Civil War period, the piano ragtime of Missouri, the earliest Mississippi blues, and the musical remnants of European court dances brought over by the French and Spanish to the first strains of American jazz as played by King Buddy Bolden and his ratty New Orleans ensemble at dances, outings, picnics and parades starting around 1894–95.

Wild Indian music—basically a new world fusion of the ritual musics for religious ceremonies by Dahomean, Carib and Choctaw peoples with lyrics drawn from Choctaw and Black Creole sources and taken straight to the street— stuck the second-line shuffle into the traditional marches and spirituals played by the pre-jazz black brass bands of New Orleans at funerals (a centuries-old West African tradition) and parades before the turn of the century.

Wild Indian music brought the Spanish tinge—actually the Afro-Caribbean tinge—into North American popular music. It moved Jelly Roll Morton and Buddy Bolden (who resided just three blocks from where the Wild Magnolias practice today) to change the shape of American music once and for all. It put the drive in the blues and the roll in the left hand of the piano professors. And following World War II, it put the rhythm in the new rhythm & blues idiom that provided the basis for rock & roll and all popular music today.

> *"The (Wild Indian) songs*
> *in addition to recounting*
>
> *a Black history*
> *few have heard*
>
> *outside the ghetto,*
> *express masculine codes of conduct*
>
> *and other social lessons*
> *and knowledge that are*
>
> *necessary to survival*
> *in a brutal street world."*
>
> —*Michael P. Smith,*
> Spirit World

While the musical impact of the Wild Indians has had worldwide effect, the broader cultural concerns of the Black Indians continue to be focused in the neighborhood and on the preservation and regeneration of the ancestral heritage. "Certainly the most significant aspects of the Black Indian tradition," photographer/journalist Michael P. Smith points out, "are the tribal organizations and friendships, which continue all year long, and the 'practices' on Sunday evenings during the fall and winter leading up to Mardi Gras, where the dancing, drumming, and communal traditions of the tribes are continued...these meetings, which now occur in neighborhood bars, are a natural continuation of the dancing and drumming celebrations in Congo Square on Sunday afternoons and evenings during slave days."

The Wild Indians provide a heady contrast to the gaudy decadence of the official Mardi Gras celebration on that day when they take over the streets of their neighborhoods and 'have their fun' all over town. But their public ritual, like the Mardi Gras spectacle enacted annually by the city's ruling class, serves to reinforce and strengthen the cultural basis of daily life by pointing up its historical foundation, its class struggles and triumphs through the stages of its development.

For African Americans in New Orleans, who are just beginning to gain some measure of control over the political life of their city after almost 300 years of residency, modern life is rooted in active resistance to the slave-holding class by West African slaves and freedmen acting in concert with—and genuinely inspired by—the natives of this land whose communal life and culture were all but exterminated by their common oppressor.

The dances, chants, costumes and rituals of the Mardi Gras Indians pay constant homage to the fierce fighting spirit of the Natchez and Choctaws, the rebelliousness of the West African slaves, the spirituality and creativity of both Old World and New World cultures, and the centuries-old oral tradition by means of which the historic accomplishments, trials and tribulations of the ancestors are codified and passed on in songs, stories and ceremonies from generation to generation.

"The Mardi Gras Indians
give light to the memory

of an African past,
but in a ritual fashion

that embraced the Indian
as an adopted spirit figure...

The Indian
followed the procession

of rebellious slaves,
voodoo cultists, and Congo Square dancers

as a spirit figure
in the historical memory"
—Jason Berry, Jonathan Foose & Tad Jones,
Up From the Cradle of Jazz

What is most remarkable is that in New Orleans, at Claiborne and Orleans as at Washington and LaSalle, on Mardi Gras Day and all year round, the Wild Indians persist even today, when everywhere else the communal memory of the native peoples, the ex-slaves, the waves of immigrants from Europe and Latin America and Asia is being obliterated by the modern weapons of cultural genocide wielded by the owners of America—radio, television, newspapers, magazines, movies, pop music, fast food, and the rancid cornucopia of consumer products they shill for.

Even more incredibly, the Wild Indians continue to hold forth on the exact same streets into which they emerged from literal slavery in the years following the Civil War, during the last stages of native American resistance to the genocidal forces of the federal government. Their tribal lore, handed down for over 100 years from one generation of 'hawks' (oral historians) to the next, is based in the freshest contemporary accounts of the bravery of the Indians in battle, their pride, intelligence, and deep spirituality, their relentless resistance to cultural and physical annihilation by an enemy vastly superior in numbers and weaponry.

These images survive today, vivid and alive, in the rites and rituals of the Mardi Gras Indians of New Orleans. They flood the streets, pouring out of the neighborhood repositories of African American culture. The irresistible thrust of their street-driven rhythms has penetrated and regenerated American popular music for an entire century, offering spiritual sustenance to the down-pressed citizens of several generations, and it continues today as ever—strong as a thousand heartbeats, deep as ancestral memory, powerful with the invoked spirits of the ancestors, straight and direct from the streets which gave it life and continue to sustain it.

"We're the Indians of the Nation,
The wide, wild creation,

We won't kneel down,
Not on the ground,

Oh, how I love to hear them call
My Indian Race"

SOURCES

The quoted material in the text was taken from the following sources, listed in the order of their appearance:

Robert Tallant, ed., **Gumbo Ya-Ya: A Collection of Louisiana Folk Tales** (NY: Bonanza Books, 1945), pp. 1–26 ('Kings, Baby Dolls, Zulus, and Queens').

J. Davis, 'Exuma—The Obeahman,' *Wavelength* no. 4 (Feb. 1981), pp. 17–19.

Lyric Sheet, *The Wild Magnolias* (Polydor Records PD-6026), Two Way Pak E Way (Cosmic Q Publishing Co, 1974).

Jason Berry, Jonathan Foose and Tad Jones, **Up From the Cradle of Jazz** (Athens: University of Georgia Press, 1986), pp. 203–219 ('In Search of the Mardi Gras Indians'), 220–226 ('Willie Tee and the Wild Magnolias') and 227–39 ('Big Chief Jolly and The Neville Brothers').

Michael P. Smith, **Spirit World: Pattern in the Expressive Folk Culture of Afro-American New Orleans** (New Orleans: Louisiana State Museum, 1984), pp. 81–106.

Maurice M. Martinez, 'Delight in Repetition: The Black Indians,' in *Wavelength* no. 16 (Feb. 1982), pp. 21–26.

Lyric Sheet, *The Wild Tchoupitoulas* (Island Records ILPS 9360), Indian Red (Rhinelander Music, Inc., 1976). Also recorded in 1956 by members of the Yellow Pocahontas, 2nd Ward Hunters, 3rd Ward Terrors and White Eagles as The Indian Race on *The Music of New Orleans: The Music of Mardi Gras* (Folkways Records FA-2461, 1959).

Quotations taken from the sources listed above were cast into verse by the present author. The account of the Wild Indians meeting at Washington and Derbigny Streets was adapted from 'Mardi Gras in New Orleans' © 1976 by John Sinclair, first published in the Detroit Sun circa February 1976.

Detroit
Fall 1987

"spiritual"

for linda jones

[32]

what is jazz, but spirituals
played thru saxophones
& trombones,

spirit voices
thru metal tubings
& the terrible repetition

of the formal premise, *viz.*
trance-like
at its best, or boring

when the spirit doth not move,
oh what is blues
but spirituals with a line

removed,
that is structurally,
& in content just a prayer

to the gods of daily life,
 to ask the blessing
that the body of another

may lay warm in the bed
beside you at night, & the rent
be paid, & a meal

on the table, with the sheriff
far away
from the scene of the crime, oh

what is jazz but the registration
of the human personality
in relation to the spiritual,

stripped of literal meaning
but full of sound & portent,
direct as the voice of the gods

detroit
september 15, 1985

236

INVITATION TO A GHOST DANCE

The White Buffalo Prophecy

FOR MANY First Nations people, the birth of a female white buffalo calf named Miracle on a farm in Janesville, Wisconsin in August 1994 fulfilled a key Lakota prophecy and signaled the beginning of a new era in human relations.

According to this prophecy, White Buffalo Calf Woman materialized long ago in a Lakota village in the guise of a beautiful maiden. She gave the people the gift of the sacred pipe of peace and taught them how to live respectfully and harmoniously with everyone on earth.

She would leave them now to learn these lessons for themselves, she explained, but upon her return she would lead them into a new social order based on her teachings.

As the woman left the village the people saw her change into a black buffalo calf. The calf rolled on the ground and came up red; rolled again and turned yellow; rolled once more and changed to white, signifying that people of all colors are one.

Then the calf disappeared, and it was prophesied that the woman would return in the form of a white buffalo calf when the people were ready to receive her wisdom.

As keeper of the sacred White Buffalo pipe and interpreter of the Lakota prophecy, Dr Arvol Looking Horse has traveled far from his home on the Green Grass reservation in South Dakota to spread the word of universal peace to world leaders and people from all walks of life.

In January Chief Looking Horse was invited by President Clinton to pray at the Inaugural festivities in Washington DC, where he spoke of the drum as the heart of Mother Earth and of the need for global healing through the power of the drum and the music it brings us.

Chief Looking Horse enjoys a special relationship with the city of New Orleans since his 1996 visit for our annual White Buffalo Day celebration, where the Lakota holy man blessed Congo Square as sacred ground and sanctified the remarkable treaty made between Lakota and Choctaw Ghost Dancers and the Mardi Gras Indians at their long awaited first meeting on August 27, 1994.

On that day a Sacred Circle was formed in Congo Square by Kam Night Chase (Lakota Pipe Carrier) and David Carson (Choctaw) to greet and honor Big Chiefs Tootie Montana (Yellow Pocahontas), Donald Harrison Sr. (Guardians of the Flame), Larry Bannock (Golden Star Hunters), Spy Boy Nat (White Eagles),

237

and other Big Chiefs and representatives of the New Orleans Mardi Gras Indian Council.

There the Mardi Gras Indian Nation were formally accepted as brothers by the Native Americans, gifted with medicine bundles, and invited to share the sacred 1,500 year old Choctaw clan pipe of Mayan origin with the face of an African warrior on the bowl.

The treaty was solemnified by drumming and sacred songs of both peoples, including a Lakota Ghost Dance song and a jubilant Indian Red led by Big Chief Tootie Montana.

Kam Night Chase, a Lakota Pipe Carrier active in the Ghost Dance movement and leader of the historic ceremony in Congo Square, had learned of the Black Indians of New Orleans from his friend Goat Carson, a half-breed harmonica preacher and barbeque specialist, and his wife Sharon Marie Asch, new residents of the Crescent City.

Goat and Sharon had met members of the Carrollton Hunters at Carson's weekly Sunday afternoon cookouts at Snake & Jake's Christmas Club Lounge uptown. When they spied the Wild Indians in the streets at their first Mardi Gras, Goat and Sharon's minds were blown by the many forms of homage paid to Native American culture by these inner-city Americans of African descent.

Carson could hear the echoes of Cherokee and Choctaw ceremonial music in the songs and chants of the Mardi Gras Indians; he wasn't surprised to learn that these distinctive forms had been arranged for the original Creole Wild West tribe more than 100 years before by a full-blooded 7'2" Choctaw named Eugene Honore.

But the Mardi Gras Indians had developed through successive generations without the benefit of actual contact with First Nations peoples, and Goat and Sharon resolved to try to bring the two together.

Night Chase was shown tapes and photos of the Mardi Gras Indians and heard a recording of the Black Indian prayer, Indian Red, which struck a deep, responsive chord.

Soon Night Chase would receive a vision revealing the Mardi Gras Indians as fellow Ghost Dancers, honoring and keeping the spirits of the ancestors alive with song, dance, and elaborate ritual costumery. In keeping with the teachings of White Buffalo Calf Woman, their prayer for recognition as brothers should be answered.

Night Chase extended an "Invitation to a Ghost Dance and Sacred Treaty" to Big Chief Alison "Tootie" Montana of the Yellow Pocahontas on behalf of the Mardi Gras Indian Nation.

Montana asked that a public ceremony be held in Congo Square to celebrate the realization of this deeply cherished "hundred-year dream".

The historic meeting was capped by the participation of City Councilman Troy Carter, who smoked the peace pipe and joined the city of New Orleans to the treaty.

Following the Sacred Circle ceremony Night Chase continued to pray for a sign that he had done the right thing by accepting the Black Indians as brothers of the Lakota Nation.

That night the birth of the white buffalo calf in Wisconsin was announced by Dr Looking Horse as a harbinger of the return of White Buffalo Calf Woman.

Night Chase now felt certain the Sacred Circle had fulfilled the Lakota prophecy that red, yellow, black and white would all come together and pray, each in their own way, for unity, peace and healing. The Sacred Circle should be joined to the birth of the white buffalo calf as a day of celebration in New Orleans each year.

Equally inspired by this amazing turn of events, Goat Carson began to pursue the White Buffalo vision with messianic zeal. Working with Troy Carter, Goat persuaded the city council to designate August 26 as White Buffalo Day in New Orleans and began planning a massive public event for the next summer.

His series of White Buffalo Day reports on this writer's New Orleans Music Show on WWOZ radio reached the ears of many sympathetic citizens, including incoming New Orleans Jazz & Heritage Foundation President Roxy Wright, who invited Goat to sit on the Foundation's Advisory Board.

There, as a member of the Program Committee, Carson worked with Don "Moose" Jamison to secure the inclusion of Native American performers at JazzFest and arrange the appearances of Dr Looking Horse, the Six Nations Women Singers and the SaskNorthern Drummers at this year's Festival.

For the future, JazzFest will establish Native American music as a regular feature at the fairgrounds each year, and the Festival's International Music Committee plans to meet with Dr Looking Horse to explore First Nation's participation in the International Pavilion and on the international music stage.

But the Native American legacy and its crucial role in shaping our cultural heritage will at last be spotlighted at JazzFest this year when the Coushatta Dancers, Six Nations Women Singers, SaksNorthern Drummers, and Dr Arvol Looking Horse, nineteenth generation Keeper of the sacred White Buffalo pipe of the Lakota, take the stage to add their music, prayers, rhythms and wisdom to the riotous mixture of sound and colors swirling about them at the fairgrounds.

Louisiana's Coushatta Dancers perform and the Six Nations Women Singers from the Iroquois Confederacy appear on the first weekend of JazzFest, singing traditional social songs from the Seneca, Onondaga and Cayuga Nations. On the second Saturday a multi-tribal group representing all the First Nations of Louisiana will present its Native American Dance Theatre at the International Heritage stage.

On Sunday, Lakota spiritual leader Dr Arvol Looking Horse will appear at the Lagniappe stage and at the International Heritage stage. His talk will be preceded by the SaskNorthern Drummers led by Chief Ernest Sundown, who will sing the White Buffalo Calf Woman song he learned (at the request of Dr Looking Horse) from the Pipestone Singers, who have kept the song since it was given to the Lakotas nineteen generations ago by White Buffalo Calf Woman herself.

Featuring First Nations performers at the Jazz & Heritage Festival represents an important first step toward mending the long-broken circle of friendship, amity and cultural exchange with our Native American forebears.

In the spirit of White Buffalo Calf Woman, may it help lead us to the ultimate goal of unity for the family, peace for the tribes, and healing for the wounds of all nations.

New Orleans
April 15, 1997

"If I Could Be With You"

for Penny

From the stage
of Detroit's

world-famous
Graystone Ballroom

on Woodward Avenue
just south of Canfield

Ladies &
gentlemen, the fabulous

Victor re-
cording artists: please

join me
in welcoming our v

very special
guests tonight—

the legendary Mc-
Kinney's

Cotton
Pickers!

> *oh if i could*
> *be with you one*
>
> *hour tonight, if i were*
> *free*
>
> *to do*
> *the things*
>
> *i might, i'm*
> *tellin' you*
>
> *true, i'd be*
> *anything*
>
> *but blue,*
> *if i*

IT'S ALL GOOD

could be
with you

They came to Detroit in 1926, up
from Springfield,

Ohio, led by the circus
drummer, William Mc-

Kinney, & boasting
on banjo & oc-

casional vocals, Mr.
Dave Wilborn

On tenor, alto, soprano &
bass saxophones, oboe

& violin, Mr. Wesley
Stuart

On piano & arrangements,
the great Todd Rhodes

Playing the alto & so-
prano saxophones &

bass clarinet, George
"Fathead" Thomas

On trumpet & arrangements,
John Nesbitt

On trombone &
baritone horn, Mr.

Claud
Jones

The orchestra's dance team,
sousaphonist June Cole

& drummer
Cuba Austin

& in the saxophone
section, the band's musical

director, on alto,
soprano & bass

saxophones, oboe & violin,
Mr. Milton Senior—

They called themselves Mc-
Kinney's Syncos

in Springfield,
but when they came to Detroit

to replace the Jean Goldkette Orchestra
at the Graystone Ballroom

in September 1927
their Caucasian employers,

wise in the ways of Detroit,
insisted that they change

their name
to the Cotton Pickers

& without much choice in the matter
so they became—

First at the Arcadia
down the street from the Graystone

for five months
in 1926 the Syncos

stormed Detroit
& were engaged

by the Goldkette
organization

as its first "all-
colored orchestra" for

two weeks at the Graystone
& then in the summer

IT'S ALL GOOD

of 1927 Jean
Goldkette signed Don Redman

as musical director
of McKinney's Cotton Pickers—

direct from the Fletcher
Henderson

Orchestra
in New York City, the

father
of the jazz

arrangement
& a giant of jazz

at just under
five feet tall, Don Redman

beat the band
into shape

with his mighty arrangements
& for the princely sum

of $300.00 per week
Don Redman

led the band
to international stardom,

a Victor recording contract,
a radio wire

out of the Graystone
onto WJR

with its 50,000 watts
of clear channel power,

"the Great Voice
of the Great Lakes,"

McKinney's Cotton Pickers
rose up out of Detroit

to light up the world
with the music of Don Redman—

> *if i could*
> *be with you one*
>
> *hour*
> *tonight*
>
> *if 1927*
> *if the Graystone*
>
> *were still*
> *standing*

Don Redman
stayed with the Cotton Pickers

till 1931
& went out on his own then

with several of the re-
maining members

but George Thomas was already dead
in an auto accident

on the road,
November 1930,

& the driver,
one of the brightest

trumpet stars
of the '20s,

Joe Smith, was quickly
drinking himself crazy

& Milton Senior had left
& would kill himself

before the '30s
were over

IT'S ALL GOOD

& another trumpet man,
John Nesbitt,

who was Fathead's
closest friend

in the band
also lost his wife

& Nesbitt was lost
to the bottle

& on a west coast trip
where the Cotton Pickers

headlined
over the Fletcher

Henderson
& Duke Ellington

Orchestras, when people
in Hollywood

heard their first
orchestral arrangements

in jazz
in 1931

the band fell apart
& never recovered

its former
glory—

> *if i could*
> *be with you one*
>
> *hour to-*
> *night if i*
>
> *could be*
> *with you*

McKinney's Cotton Pickers, 'the
Mississippi Muddies

of Syncopation,' the
'Sensation

of the Automobile
City,'

their entire recorded output
of 56 sides

for Victor
now available

only on five
out-of-print

French
'Black & White'

RCA LPs
& the only man still alive

from the original Pickers
is my man, Dave

Wilborn, who brought this
back to life for me

& who still sings his
own song as

sweet as ever
& says from the stage today,

"Thank you ladies &
gentlemen and

back in 1928
up at the Graystone Ballroom

Woodward & Canfield
while with McKinney's Cotton Pickers

We were the first black band
to broadcast

out of Detroit
over WJR

IT'S ALL GOOD

Our theme was a
beautiful love song

of the '20s
written by Don Redman—

I was there to sing
that song

over the airways
& by the grace of the good Lord

I'm here to sing it for you
tonight,"

January 7,
1979,

at the Paradise Theatre
in Detroit:

> *i'm so blue*
> *i don't know*
>
> *what to do*
> *all day long*
>
> *i sit & dream*
> *of you*
>
> *i did wrong*
> *when i let you*
>
> *go away*
> *now i dream*
>
> *about you*
> *night & day*
>
> *i'd be happy*
> *if i had you*
>
> *by my side*
> *i'd be happy*
>
> *if i knew you*
> *were my bride*

if i could
be with you

one hour tonight
& i was free to do

the things
i might

i want you to know
that you couldn't go

until i showed you honey how i
love you so

if i could be
with you

i'd love you strong
if i could be with you

i'd love you
all night long

i'm tellin' you
true, you'd be

anything
but blue, if i

could be
with you—

for just one hour—
if i

could be
with you

Detroit, March 25 > June 1, 1982 /
New Orleans, January 1994

Music by McKinney's Cotton Pickers

HASTINGS STREET GREASE

Detroit Blues is Alive, Volume Two

EXCEPT FOR a couple of raggedy blocks straggling south from East Grand Boulevard, Detroit's Hastings Street is gone now.

The Motor City's major African American entertainment thoroughfare was gouged out in the late 1950s to make way for the Walter P. Chrysler Freeway, a federally-subsidized fast track laid down to facilitate the flight of the city's white population to the northeastern suburbs of Hazel Park, Warren, Ferndale, Royal Oak, Madison Heights and points north.

But for twenty years before that Hastings Street swung all the way from Paradise Valley downtown for fifty or sixty blocks north.

The legend of Hastings Street was perhaps best told in a 1948 recording by The Detroit Count, a rough barrelhouse pianist who immortalized that pulsating scene by enumerating the many theatres, lounges, bars and rude nightspots which thrived along the length of the stroll in his two-part 78 rpm single on JVB Records titled Hastings Street Opera.

Then there was the man they called the Mayor of Hastings Street, a dapper, diminuitive gentleman named Sunnie Wilson who painted a vivid portrait of Detroit in the 1930s, forties and fifties in his 1997 autobiography, *Toast of the Town*, written with John Cohassey and published by Wayne State University Press.

Wilson was an intimate of the great Joe Louis and the popular proprietor of nightclubs, restaurants, and hotels serving African American citizens in the racially segregated near-east-side neighborhood between Woodard Avenue and Hastings Street. He saw and heard it all, and his account is a valuable addition to the small body of literature which examines the city's history.

In its prime years Hastings Street throbbed with music, from the elemental blues of John Lee Hooker, Eddie Kirkland, Eddie Burns, Boogie Woogie Red, and Washboard Willie & His Super Suds of Rhythm to the swinging jazz of the Teddy Wilson Trio (with drummer J.C. Heard), Maurice King & His Wolverines (with vocalist LaVerne "Bea" Baker), Paul "Hucklebuck" Williams, T.J. Fowler, Todd Rhodes & His Toddlers, and the Matthew Rucker Orchestra.

Jazz stars like Charlie Parker, Billie Holliday, Count Basie, Duke Ellington, Billy Eckstine and Cootie Williams played the Forest Club or the Flame Showbar as well as the Paradise Theatre on Woodward Avenue, sharing the stage with rhythm & blues recording stars like Dinah Washington, Wynonie Harris, Amos Milburn, B.B. King and T-Bone Walker.

A John Sinclair Reader

Sonny Boy Williamson even spent a few months in Detroit in the early 1950s, playing with Calvin Frazier and Baby Boy Warren and providing inspiration to a young Aaron Willis, who gained national recognition some fifteen years later as Little Sonny, "New King of the Blues Harmonica".

As Hastings Street began to disappear, a whole new generation of singers and musicians who grew up in or around the immediate vicinity emerged to extend its influence across the world, from Jackie Wilson, Andre Williams, Little Willie John, and Hank Ballard & The Midnighters in the fifties to the Motown Records stars who put Detroit on the map in the sixties: The Supremes, the Temptations, the Four Tops, Smokey Robinson & the Miracles.

Aretha Franklin's father, the Reverend C.L. Franklin, pastored the New Bethel Baptist Church on Hastings, where his sermons were recorded by Joe Von Battles and leased to Chess Records in Chicago. Aretha's first recordings were made there when she was fourteen years old, and Joe's Hastings Street record store and JVB imprint were also home to bluesmen from One-String Sam, Detroit Count and Will Hairston to fledgling guitarist Johnnie Bassett, one of the leaders of Detroit's blues renaissance of the 1990s.

After Hastings Street disappeared, the Motor City blues scene dwindled to a handful of bars in rough neighborhoods where stalwarts like Little Sonny, Washboard Willie, Boogie Woogie Red and Little Mac Collins & the Partymakers Inc. continued to entertain their friends and patrons well outside the mainstream of modern entertainment.

In the early 1970s Little Sonny had a shot at blues stardom via several fine albums for Stax Records' Enterprise imprint; a wild collection of Motor City blues artists was spotlighted at the 1973 Ann Arbor Blues & Jazz Festival; and bluesman Bobo Jenkins and deejay/entrepreneur Famous Coachman established a series of free Detroit Blues Festivals, a Detroit Blues Society, and a weekly blues radio program on WDET-FM, but these were at best shots in the darkness of American life in the seventies.

More than a decade would elapse before a new crop of Detroit bluesmen would emerge from the gloom of the city's post-industrial landscape. But the advent of the 1990s finally brought to light well-seasoned veterans like Eddie Burns, Louis "Mr Bo" Collins, and Sir Mack Rice, whose music was documented by a fledgling little record label in Toledo called Blue Suit Records.

Another intrepid local label, Blues Factory Records, issued intriguing albums featuring previously unrecorded Motor City bluesmen like the Butler Twins, Willie D. Warren, Harmonica Shah, Uncle Jessie White and Johnny "Yard Dog" Jones (who went on to make an excellent CD, *Ain't Gonna Worry*, for Chicago's Earwig label and won the Motor City's first Handy Award in the process).

Now guitarist Johnnie Bassett, who got his start on Hastings Street, is issuing

251

albums on a variety of labels and touring the world to wide acclaim. Vocalists Alberta Adams and Joe Weaver, fellow Hastings Street survivors, are following closely in Johnnie's footsteps, and blues from Detroit is beginning to be heard wherever music lovers congregate.

One of the most hopeful documents of the turn-of-the-century Motor City blues scene was issued earlier this year by John Rockwood and Bob Seeman of Blue Suit Records, which continues to lead the way in providing an outlet for what's happening today.

Hastings Street Grease: Detroit Blues Is Alive, Volume One presented music by eight vital modern bluesmen with deep roots in the Hastings Street era, including Eddie Kirkland, Piano Fats, Eddie Burns, Willie D. Warren, Harmonica Shah, Emmanuel Young and Leon Horner. On Hastings Street Revisited (Part 1) Detroit Piano Fats shares his memories of the old stomping grounds with Harmonica Shah, and Kirkland looks back in sorrow in I Walk Down Hastings Street.

Yet the raw energy and drive of the Detroit blues remains intact throughout, as fresh and exciting as ever, almost as if the musicians had come straight to the recording studio from their gigs at some of the little joints on Hastings.

There's nothing of nostalgia here, nor the hokey kind of tribute album ambience that's so popular with the big-label blues producers of today. This is the low-down Detroit blues at its most elemental, and it's as precise and effective as a JVB 78.

Now Blue Suit brings forth *Detroit Blues is Alive, Volume Two*, a second generous helping of modern day Motor City sounds gathered from the same relaxed, sympathetic sessions that produced the first *Hastings Street Grease* collection.

Detroit Piano Fats takes Harmonica Shah way back in the day on Hastings Street Revisited (Part Two) and goes Strolling Through Paradise Valley, the downtown entertainment mecca from which the music spread north along Hastings.

Emmanuel Young and Leon Horner pay tribute to Detroit blues giant John Lee Hooker with I'm In The Mood and Boogie Chillen, respectively, while Harmonica Shah salutes Jimmy Reed on Have Mercy, Mr Reed and contributes the chilling Motor City anthem Bring Me My Shotgun.

Willie D. Warren adds a new dimension to the Memphis Slim favorite simply by pointing out that Everyday *We* Have The Blues and then reveals What Goes On In The Dark with a special dedication to Shah.

Eddie Kirkland, the Hastings Street bluesman who began his career fifty years ago backing up John Lee Hooker, continues his contemporary resurgence with a pair of strong tracks in Going Back To The Backwoods and the ominous There's Got To Be Some Changes Made.

Eddie Burns is in typically fine form on a live treatment of When I Get Drunk; the dynamic Griswold brothers, Art and Roman, of Toledo, Ohio, romp and stomp on a great live cut titled Daddy, Daddy; and the venerable Uncle Jessie White's distinctive approach is nicely showcased on the classic Bad Luck Is Falling.

Hastings Street may have been laid to rest low these forty years ago, but its sound and spirit live on in the performances recorded here and in the music of the Detroit bluesmen who have managed to survive the cruel vicissitudes of time and social deterioration to keep on moving forward, all the way into the twenty first century.

That's definitely something Detroit can be proud of, and it's all right here on this compact disc. Put on your bibs and tuckers, ladies and g's, and dig into these musical ham hocks and collard greens cooked to funky perfection with plenty of that old-time *Hastings Street Grease.*

New Orleans
July 2, 1999

#107

"monk's dream" [36]

for tyree & karen guyton & sam mackey

in the middle of the night
on the east side of detroit
off behind mack & gratiot,

on heidelberg street
where a lot of old houses
be burnt out

or just falling apart
& big weeds be growing up
where there used to be houses,

on heidelberg street
in the middle of the night
when the moon is high in the sky

& people be asleep in they beds
dreaming of new refrigerators
full of groceries for they babies

& maybe a new car outside,
or a number they can hit tomorrow,
put it in a box,

drag a bunch of boxes out
in the vacant lot across the street
& pile them up on top one another,

paint 'em all different colors,
hang a pink bicycle
up in a tree painted polka dot,

nail some old plastic doll bodies
& maybe some road signs
up on the front porch next door

where the people been gone so long
& stick in a telephone booth,
put a television on the porch roof

& plug it in,
change the channel once or twice,
a toy airplane in a bird cage

on the top of the house,
some plastic legs
sticking out the front window,

all different colors of paint
& objects of every description
stuck or nailed on somehow

all over the abandoned house,
"sometimes a thing
just needs some stripes"

says grandpop, 91, who can see
the things that maybe we can't
in the middle of the night,

like the doll in the attic window,
"she's reaching out for help,"
& the line of doors in the field

on the other side of the street,
they came from houses
that used to be here,

they came from old refrigerators
& wrecked taxicabs, they standing there
cocked every which way

& down on the corner of ellery
they got 3 big old vacant lots,
one got a raggedy boat in it

filled with junked tires,
one got a pile of oil drums
painted up in bright colors,

IT'S ALL GOOD

the other one got more doors
all lined up in a row
like tyree say,

"there are so many openings
in life, you just have to pick
the right ones"—

the music comes up in the background
out of the little speaker
on the radio by the porch, it's thelonious

with charlie rouse, "monk's dream"
& the peoples indoors sleeping
turn over in they beds,

a smile on they faces,
they know in their dreams
it's just tyree & karen & grandpop out there

on heidelberg street
in the middle of the night
turning their neighborhood inside out

harmonie park
detroit
may 26, 1988

JOHNNIE BASSETT

Cadillac Bluesman from the Motor City

THE BLUES has always been a big part of life in the Motor City, but it's been a long time since Detroit's musically fertile blues community has seen one of its own citizens go on to national and international success. Not since Little Sonny landed a contract with Stax Records and issued a series of excellent albums on the Enterprise label in the early 1970s, in fact, has a Motor City bluesman raised much of a ruckus in the now burgeoning blues industry.

The scene is changing presently with the emergence of veteran Detroit bluesmen like Johnny "Yard Dog" Jones, recently voted a Handy Award for Best New Blues Performer of 1997 on the strength of his debut CD, *Ain't Gonna Worry*, and the Butler Twins, Curtis and Clarence, who made two fine recordings for the British JSP label. Cannonball Records spotlighted the Detroit scene in Ron Levy's *Blues Across America* series and has just issued what is almost incredibly the first album ever by venerable Detroit blueswoman Alberta Adams.

But the biggest noise from the Motor City is being made by sixty three year old Johnnie Bassett, a soulful, jazz-inspired guitarist and singer who has recently commenced a new life as a featured artist after toiling since the early fifties behind virtually every singer and frontman to grace the city's gritty blues bars and nightclubs.

Johnnie Bassett's singing and playing—perfectly backed by his splendid ensemble, the Blues Insurgents, led by drummer R.J. Spangler—have been propeled into the center of the modern blues scene by a series of albums recorded over the past five years and a busy touring schedule which has taken the band from coast to coast and across the Atlantic several times.

'Discovered' by Spangler at a Montreaux-Detroit Jazz Festival performance as a member of organist Ben Baber's band, Johnnie recorded his debut album live on the same spot in 1995 for a small Detroit company, No Cover Records.

An energetic tour de force through a program of blues standards arranged to showcase Bassett's mellow blues recitations and driving jump-blues swingers backed by pianist Bill Heid and a six-piece horn section, this live recording led to the band's first European tour and the opportunity to record for Holland-based Black Magic Records.

By the time the Blues Insurgents entered the studio in May of 1996 to make *I Gave My Life To The Blues*, an album of original material by Bassett, Heid, Martin Gross, organist Chris Codish and his father Bob, the band had gelled into a tight, completely sympathetic blues unit seriously dedicated to realizing the full potential of Bassett's considerable talents.

Johnnie himself had grown fully into an unaccustomed frontman role, displaying new confidence and strength as a guitarist and singing with power and conviction in every setting.

Back in the States, Bill Heid landed Johnnie a one-off recording deal with Fedora Records and contributed an entire program of tailormade originals to *Bassett Hound*, a relaxed excursion with the Bill Heid Trio into the mellower and jazzier sides of Johnnie's musical personality.

R.J. Spangler, acting as manager and agent for the band, parlayed these two excellent releases into gigs around the United States, a return trip to Europe and a recording contract with Cannonball Records.

Introduced by producer Ron Levy with four selections on his *Blues Across America: The Detroit Scene* compilation for Cannonball, the Blues Insurgents thrust themselves into the forefront of the blues world with their current release, *Cadillac Blues*, and have completed a second album with Levy that's scheduled for release this spring. Bassett and the band are also featured in support of Johnnie's old friend Alberta Adams on her new Cannonball release.

Cadillac Blues, recorded at Willie Mitchell's studio in Memphis, demonstrates Johnnie Bassett's utter freshness and vitality as a contemporary bluesman. His own compositions That's Fair Play and the memorable blues ballad Memories Of Your Perfume, share the limelight with original tunes by a bevy of modern-day Detroit songwriters, including Chris and Bob Codish, drummers Leonard King and Ron Pangborn, and organist Tim Brockett.

The Blues Insurgents, by now a well-seasoned musical organization powered by Codish's Hammond B-3 organ (including foot-pedal bass) and highlighted by the horns of saxophonist Keith Kaminiski and trumpeter Dwight Adams, provide the perfect setting for Bassett's tasty guitar and singular vocal stylings.

The title track, a typically tongue-in-cheek Bob Codish composition, nicely sums up Johnnie's current status: "I've still got the blues, but I've got them in my Cadillac." Bassett's come a long way to get behind the wheel of Detroit's classiest vehicle, but he's riding in style now, and the open road is just beginning to stretch out in front of him for the first time in the almost fifty years since his brother bought him a guitar for his sixteenth birthday in 1951.

I had planned to sit down with Johnnie for an elongated interview when I visited Detroit last fall to join the celebration of the Blues Insurgents' fourth anniversary as a featured act at the Music Menu Cafe, the band's home base, but I ended up having so much fun that the assignment completely slipped my mind until I had moved on to Chicago two days later.

But I caught up with Bassett and the Blues Insurgents at the Blues Estafette in Utrecht, Holland, and spent a pleasant Sunday afternoon in late November talking with Johnnie and R.J. Spangler in the comfortable confines of their Dutch hotel.

JOHN SINCLAIR: *Let's go to the basics of where and when you entered the planet Earth.*

JOHNNIE BASSETT: I was born October 9, 1935. That was sixty three years ago now, in a little town down in Florida called Marianna. That's in the panhandle. We had a successful business there: my dad was a bootlegger. Very successful—successful enough for us to open a restaurant and run it.

Was that a dry area? Except for your father?

BASSETT: Yeah, it was then. They knew that he was making corn whiskey, you know, and they enjoyed it because he had the best in the county. So everybody bought from him, including the sheriff, you know. And periodically they would give him chase, to let everybody know that they were on the job. But they never caught him.

R.J. SPANGLER: He was a mechanic, and they had a souped-up car...

BASSETT: ...with a horn that played Mary Had A Little Lamb. Yeah. So we left—my dad left Florida in the late 1940s and moved to Michigan, then sent for the family after he got his job in place. So we moved up to Michigan in '47, and been there ever since. I was eleven at that time.

It was a good time to get to Detroit. It was a fun time, you know. People still left their doors unlocked and stuff. Everybody was workin', and neighbors cared about each other, and everybody looked out for everybody's kids and stuff like that, you know. A lot of old southern traditions was still—because there was a lot of southern families there in the neighborhood that I was living in at the time when I first went to Detroit.

I grew up in Ferndale, and I had both—the good of both worlds, because I lived in Ferndale about two years, and then I moved on the Detroit side. So I had friends on both sides of Eight Mile Road. I grew up there on Bethelon, right off Eight Mile, right there behind Uncle Tom's Cabin.

Oh, man, that was a great place. All the jazz musicians, all the top names in jazz would come to Uncle Tom's, man. We used to sit out in the parking lot, on top of the cars, man, and listen to the music when I was kids. You could hear the music in the summertime, you know, they had the doors open.

I heard people like the Count Basie Band, and so many guys would come through, because they had big names come through there at least once a month. Oh yeah, all the swingin' guys—Billy Eckstine's band, I heard him when I was twelve years old. Al Hibbler, I heard him sing there, you know, when I was twelve.

I remember all those guys, because he used to hire the kids and they would go around and put up the posters on the telephone poles, and I was one of the kids that used to have to go around and put up all the posters up and down Eight Mile Road, you know, to advertise who was the next coming attraction. It was great, man. We'd sit out on the parking lot there and hear all these people sing, and bands play, and it was great.

Did you get to meet the cats?

BASSETT: No, I didn't meet any of 'em when I was a kid, but we were allowed to stay out until 10:30 at night and catch the first show. The guy that owned the club, Doc Washington—I think that was his name, everybody called him Doc—when I moved on the Detroit side, that's where he lived.

He lived on Cherrylawn between Norfolk and Pembroke, I remember, and I was one of the good kids, so he hired me and my buddy—one of my friends who lived across the street from me—he hired us to wash his car, and keep his lawn mowed, and that type of stuff, and clean up around his house, keep his yard clean, and hey—I've been a hustler for a long time, man, made good money, you know.

That was a good gig, man. Because we were good kids. We didn't steal or nothin' like that—good kids around the neighborhood. And the two of us had a little business goin'—we would go around and, once we got that job and everybody knew we did a good job, and then we got other jobs from that, you know? Cutting lawns, and cleaning up garages, and—oh, man, cleanin' up businesses.

Did you have brothers and sisters?

BASSETT: Four sisters and one brother. And it's three of us left out of that: two sisters and my brother and myself. So it's four of us. Mom and Dad has passed away, and my two older sisters. I got a slew of nephews and nieces still left, and I have two kids and four grandkids myself. They live in Seattle, which I did for five years, after my service days—I was stationed out at Fort Lewis, Washington. After I got out in 1960 I just decided to hang around out there, because the money was good, you know, I was making good and playing and I enjoyed it and that's where I stayed.

So when did you start playing?

BASSETT: I started playin' about 1951, but not professionally. I just started foolin' around with the box. Before then I had fiddled around with it, because my older sister played the church songs, and we would sit around and we would sing the church songs. She had an old guitar that she would lay on her lap and fram the chords, and when I was in eighth grade I would come home from school and I'd go get that guitar and fram it and, you know, play around with it.

After we left Florida I went to grade school there in Ferndale. Then I went to Carver, George Washington Carver, and Higginbotham, on the Detroit side. Then I went to Condon, which is on [Grand] Boulevard and Buchanan, on the west side, and I went to Northwestern High School, on the Boulevard and Grand River. That's where I met Joe Weaver. I met Joe before then, but he went to Northwestern too. I got into playing music the more and more I was around it. In school, I started in the ninth grade playing clarinet.

Northwestern had a pretty strong music program then.

BASSETT: Oh, very good, very good music program.

Who came out of there? Roy Brooks...

SPANGLER: He worked with Joe Weaver & the Blue Notes, at the Basin Street over in Delray, for a year.

BASSETT: Okay, well, my sister was a waitress there in Delray—Louise, she was a waitress out there at the West End Hotel for a long time. Those guys used to have that session out there every weekend. It started at 2:00 in the morning and it'd go from 2:00 to 7:00am. Kenny Burrell, Tommy Flanagan, Paul Chambers, Yusef Lateef, all the guys used to come through that was playin' down at the Flame [Show Bar], and the Rouge Lounge, used to come out to the sessions.

You know, I went through that, and I started playin' in high school, I played alto sax and clarinet, and got interested in music. But the guitar was the thing, though. I liked playin' with that, because it was light, easy to carry. At that particular time I had a little Kay guitar that my brother bought me in a pawnshop for my birthday, in 1951.

Would you have to carry your own amplifier?

BASSETT: Yeah, I had a little amplifier with a little 8" speaker in it. I don't know if you ever saw that picture of me in the magazines? That's the one. I heard Joe Weaver playing an old upright piano at his girlfriend's house down the street from where I was living. I was going to Condon Junior High when I first heard Joe, my last year in junior high, matter of fact, when I first heard him in the summer after school was out and everything.

I was going to the cleaners, which was down the street—long blocks, really long blocks between Buchanan and Hancock, long blocks, oh—and I was going to the cleaners and I heard Joe playing. So, you know, all this playing, and stompin' on the floor—boy, he would stomp his feet, you know—so I stood there and listened for a while and then I went on back home. And a couple days later, I was going back to get the clothes from the cleaners, you know, and I heard him again. I said, man, geez, this cat's good. You know? What I heard. So, I didn't meet him, but I heard him.

So about two months later, we moved from off of Buchanan—we bought a house over on Herbert, which was basically the same neighborhood but down near Warren and a couple of blocks over from where we were living. I had been living on Bangor, between Buchanan and Hancock, and we moved on Herbert, which was three streets over and two long blocks down. It was still in the neighborhood, so we still used the cleaners around on Hancock and Bangor.

So I went to that cleaners again—this was sometime after I got my guitar, for my birthday—and I heard Joe playing over there, and I said, let me go see who this is, you know, because there was people all on the porch, and everybody havin' a good time, and he's in there just bangin' away.

So I stood there, and they told me to come up on the porch, you know, and I went up on the porch, and oddly enough, the young lady that lived there, we had met already. Incidentally, Joe and the young lady ended up gettin' married—she was his first wife, Ruth Tyler.

And I went in, and there's Joe. I had seen him around the neighborhood, but I didn't know it was him. I didn't know he played, you know. I saw him practically every day, but it never dawned on me that it was him. But sure enough it was Joe.

I said, man, hey, I said, you play piano, yeah! I said, man, you sure do sound good. You mind if I play with you? He said, what you play? I said, guitar a little bit. He said, where is it? I said, at home. He said, go get it.

Man, I ran back home and got my box, and I come back and plugged it in, and we had the biggest jam session. Man, we had folks comin', you know, dancin' all over the porch and stuff. And that's how I got started.

And we got a drummer out of high school, who played in the band, and we started doin' amateur shows right in high school. Three piece group, without a bass player or anything, just the three of us. Calvin Andrews, a very good drummer. And we won our first amateur show, at the Arcadia Theatre, over on West Warren and Junction.

All of the theatres all over the city was having amateur shows, because this one guy was doing that—Frank Brown—he was a big promoter. He brought in all the big name shows around the city of Detroit, okay?

He was a big promoter of concerts, and he'd bring in all the big names. And he was hooked up with all the theatre owners, and doin' the talent thing. It was a good thing, too, because it gave the kids something to do during the summertime other than, you know, hang out in the parks and whatever.

We would go and do these amateur shows all over the city, and whatever we played, we would win in our category. They had the musical categories— instrumental category, singers, vocal and female singer category, single instrument, whatever. And we would win, and we kept winning, and kept winning, every weekend we went to the theatres all over the city.

We'd go east side to west side, and, you know, down on Hastings, they had a little theatre down there, and we'd win that one. There was a little theatre right there around the corner from where I used to live, on Buchanan and the Boulevard there, the theatre there, they'd turn that into a bowling alley after awhile. But we played there too.

Then we picked up a saxophone player from one of the amateur shows, who was doing a Big Jay McNeely type thing, kickin' up his heels and blowin' this one note. Jesse Ulmer, we called him Jesse "Mad Lad" Ulmer, he got that name from doin' flips and stuff, blowin' his horn. He won that day from being a solo act.

And so we got hold of Jesse and asked him if he wanted to play with the group. He said yeah, man, so we started rehearsin' and playin' with the saxophone.

We'd rehearse over [at] Joe's girlfriend's house, and it was quite funny, you know, because when I met Joe, we didn't know a hell of a lot about music or playin', but I was listening to blues since I was a kid, you know, and I had a lot of knowledge about it.

I could play in about five keys when I met Joe, and Joe could only play in one. Joe played only on the black keys, in E, man, Joe played in E—everything on the black keys. I'd say, whatta you got against the white keys, man? Don't you play those too? He said, no, man. [*Laughs*]

So we rehearsed every weekend, man. When we had some time, I'd get together with him and go over some tunes and stuff like that. And he was interested enough to want to do that, and we would take records and put on the record player and go note for note, man, and play, and pick 'em out. Amos Milburn, and Willie Mabon, and stuff like that, you know.

SPANGLER: Johnnie's dad was friends with Big Bill Broonzy...

BASSETT: Yeah, and Tampa Red. Back when I was a kid, they'd spend a lot of time at my grandmother's house every summer. My grandmother would have this big fish fry, you know, once a year, and all the guys like that would come through. We had a big record collection, and when I was a teenager, goin' to that intermediate school on Eight Mile, we used to pick up, on a good night, in the summer especially, we would hear records being played on the radio all the way from Nashville—WLAC—Gene Nobles, John R. We would order all our records from Randy's Record Shop in Gallatin, Tennessee. When I was twelve and thirteen, fourteen years old, you know, I had paper routes and everything, so I had my own money and I could buy my records, man. When they came out, I'd have my own money to pay for 'em.

So Joe and I hooked up, you know, in high school, and we did the amateur show thing until, after winning so many, we went in one night and the guy told us, said, you guys can't play tonight. He says, if you wanna play, he says, what I'll do, I'll just hire you to back up everybody that don't have their own accompaniment, so you'll make a few more bucks. So we said, okay, that'll work.

SPANGLER: Who were the singers you were backing up?

BASSETT: The first singer we backed up that didn't have accompaniment was winning first place all over in the male vocalist [category], was Little Willie John. He was great, too. Willie would sing anywhere he could get a chance to sing, man—he'd sing on the corners, on the playground, stuff like that.

Willie and me grew up in the same neighborhood. He was just four blocks over. I lived on Northlawn between Chippewa and Pembroke, and he lived on Greenlawn between Chippewa and Pembroke. He lived on the east side later, but they was from the west side—from the Eight Mile Road district. Then they moved over on Canton.

So we backed up all sorts of people—Johnny Mae Matthews had a thing going, and Laura Lee, and—oh man, there was so many. Hank Ballard and those guys—you know, I didn't play with those guys until I was in professional things, some years later. We played professionally in 1953, that's when I first started a nightclub gig. It was a place called Basin Street, right down in Delray, two blocks from the West End. It used to be called the Black & Tan, because that's what it was in that area at that time: the black and tan.

SPANGLER: You and Joe were telling me a wild story last night.

BASSETT: Oh, yeah. Well, there was a crowd of people in the club. We had built up our popularity around town from the amateur shows, and playin' house parties and stuff like that, and we were in this club and it was a line out around the building to get in. The place was already full, and people were waitin' to get in to see us, and there was a young couple that just had gotten married, and this guy was pushin' and shovin' at the door tryin' to get in—it was only $2.00 to get in—and this guy stepped on somebody's shoes, and the guy got in a confrontation with him—they say he apologized and all like that—but he got in a confrontation with the guy, shovin' and pushin' and carryin' on, and the guy stabbed him and he died—right there at the door, man. We were in there playin' and didn't know nothin' about it until the next night. It happened on a Friday, and, you know, we didn't even know it until the next night. Didn't even know it, the place was so crowded.

Lines around! You must've been huge.

BASSETT: Yeah, and it was like that for a long time. Back then, people were goin' to nightclubs, they were supporting live music.

SPANGLER: How many guys in that group, Johnnie? There was Mad Lad and you, and was there a bass player?

BASSETT: No, that's when Joe was using an Organa, with the bass thing. That was before we had the bass player. So Joe bought an Organa for the piano, old upright piano—that was the only thing you could use it on.

SPANGLER: So it was a quartet. You had Roy Brooks on drums?

BASSETT: Yeah, I had Roy playin' drums. We had some good drummers, boy. Paul Humphrey played drums with us, Roy Brooks, and Louis Hayes. These guys went on to bigger and better things. And Paul Williams' son, Earl Williams, played drums with us. Paul "Hucklebuck" Williams. George Davidson was in the studio with us on some of those Fortune things.

We had a good time comin' up through the music thing. I went in the service and left the group in 1958. I played with Joe and the group until I went in the service, and that's when I left. They carried on for a while, but when I got out of the service, I didn't come back to Detroit until 1965. I came back off and on to visit, but I always went back to Seattle because I was playin' out there with several groups.

Between '53 and '58, did you start recording then?

BASSETT: Oh yeah. Before Fortune I was on DeLuxe. We had a tune called 1540 Special and J.B. Boogie. On DeLuxe. We recorded that in Joe's Record Shop on Hastings. That's where I met John Lee Hooker the first time. Yeah, Joe Von Battle's record shop. Because his son and I were in high school together, Joe Battle Jr. Yeah, we had classes together. It was great, you know. He hooked us up with his dad, matter of fact. And Jesse's father knew the old man, Joe Battle Sr. Jesse Ulmer's father knew him, because Jesse's dad owned a restaurant down the street, two blocks away, in Paradise Valley. And that's where we used to go after our rehearsals—we'd always go to the restaurant and eat.

So we recorded that 1540 Special—at a rehearsal. We wasn't planning on recording anything, but he always had the microphones and the tapes going, and that's what happened. When we heard that thing again it was out on the street. What he would do, he would allow us to come in and rehearse. He'd say, well, when the studio's not being used, you guys can come in and rehearse any time you get ready, you know, after school. And fine, we'd go over there, and he'd have the microphones and everything set up, and we didn't know they were on. He'd have the tapes rollin', and he'd splice stuff together, and put stuff together, and 1540 Special was a result of that. Joe Weaver & the Blue Notes.

1540 Brewster Avenue—the address of King Records in Cincinnati.

BASSETT: That's right. That was on DeLuxe, which was a subsidiary of King, and that's what happened. And it was a big seller. 1540 was a big seller, man. And we didn't get nothin' for it. He did, you know, but I think we got $50 out of it—apiece. You know. And we didn't get compensated for the writers' parts—we didn't know anything about all that stuff, so we got ripped off a lot of times.

Then we got with Fortune. Going down the street—we were all over in the area, on Linwood, right across from Central High School. We had been playing ball over there, and we were coming down the street and we heard this quartet singing inside. And Joe said, hey, man, says, somethin' goin' on in here. Let's check it out.

So we go in there and who do we hear but Andre Williams. It's guys in there doowoppin' and singin', and we went in and started listenin', and then they wanted to know who we were and everything, so the introductions were made. We told him we had a band and, what? You guys play? Yeah!

Fortune Records, that was Jack Brown and his wife Devora. Yeah, Jack was somethin', man. They were very nice people, they were very nice, but they didn't know a lot about the business, you know. They were very enthusiastic about—

You guys play? Come on, hey, you can come and play here. You know. You got a group.

So we ended up comin' back there and rehearsin' those guys, you know, no charts or music or nobody had written any music out or anything like that, just words on paper. And they would sing and say, listen to this, man, listen to this. And they'd sing and say, what can you put with this? Put somethin' with this. And we'd put the music to it, and that's the way it came out. You know, creative minds together.

You backed them up on their first recordings? Goin' Down To Tiajuana and Pulling Time?

BASSETT: Yeah, we did practically all of it. And then there was Nathaniel Mayer, he came in and did some things, and Nolan Strong & the Diablos—The Wind, Mind Over Matter—and then there was another group, the Royal Jokers, You Tickle Me Baby. They were great groups, I mean, those guys are, you know, they are the ones that really made Fortune Records—Nolan Strong, Little Eddie Hurt & The Five Dollars, all those guys, they made the label.

It was a great time around the city. Music was all over town, man, everybody was playin' on every corner. We had bars on every corner had live music, you know. I played with John Lee Hooker when I was still in high school. I played with John Lee for about, oh, a little over a month, down in Black Bottom, in a storefront bar. They didn't have anybody but a piano player and a drummer and me and John Lee.

I played with Eddie Burns during that same time, after that, and Eddie Kirkland, I played with Little Sonny, you know, played with Mr Bo—practically everybody that was anybody during that time, that needed a guitar player, heard about me through bein' in Joe Weaver & the Blue Notes, and when I wasn't playin' with the group, somebody would hire me to play, so I was always busy playin' somewhere.

SPANGLER: Johnnie played over at the Good Time Bar with Washboard Willie.

BASSETT: Yeah, on Buchanan and Lawton. Pete McCluskey's, McKinley and Buchanan, Bucket of Blood they used to call that place. Oh, man. Wow.

SPANGLER: You played a couple years with Mr Bo and the Blues Boys.

BASSETT: I played with Bo three years, and a couple of years with Little Sonny, down at the Apex, and the Bamboo Lounge. The Bamboo was on Brush and

Gratiot, and the Calumet was down on 12th Street, and then there was another bar, the Webbwood Inn [at Woodward and Webb], I played with Joe Weaver and everybody else down at the Webbwood—the Four Tops used to play there.

I played at the Angel Bar, over on Linwood and Euclid, and I forget the name of that other club down there where the Temptations used to play before they were the Temptations. I played behind them. They were called The Primes, and matter of fact, I'm the one that told 'em that, hey, you guys oughta be called Temptations, the way those girls are actin' out there. We was in the dressing room at the time, the dressing room was downstairs in the basement, you know, little old dressing room where we always hung out down there, drinkin' wine and talkin' shit.

We had a good time with those guys. Plus we made the Miracles' first four records, in Esther Gordy's living room, in the early sixties, Found A Job and those things. That was on Motown—no, on Tamla, that was Berry Gordy's first label.

But anyway, it was a great time, man. The music scene back then when we was kids was a lot of fun. Wasn't anybody makin' a great deal of money, you know, but it was a lot of fun and everybody enjoyed it. We were all kids, and it was like one big family, man. These guys, when we would get together on the shows, like when Frank Brown hired us to back up—he had a rhythm & blues versus jazz tour type thing, and it came to the Paradise Theatre, and we backed up Joe Turner, Big Maybelle, Arthur Prysock and Red Prysock, and Bobby "Mumbles" Lewis.

SPANGLER: Johnnie recorded with him on Tossin' And Turnin', not the one on Beltone but an earlier version, it might've been on Chess.

BASSETT: Yeah, it might've been Chess. But, you know, the music scene back then, the musicians didn't go behind and undercut somebody to get a job. Everybody was tryin' to work and everybody was one big family, and when you left this club, it was an understanding that they would hire the group that come in behind you at the same money, you know, because we were all local cats tryin' to make it.

It was just a lot of fun, man, jam sessions all the time. I mean, every time you wasn't workin', somebody would be havin' a jam session somewhere. It was a good thing for the guys to keep playin', you know, and keep their interest. Every day it was someplace.

SPANGLER: Johnnie played house parties with, what was his name, Stanstill?

BASSETT: Rudolph Stanfield, yeah. That was before Joe Weaver. Rudolph and

I, we took my old guitar, man, the first weekend my brother bought it for me, and went and played a house party and made, shoot, fifteen bucks, in tips, plus free chicken sandwiches, fish dinners and stuff like that.

When you were with the Blue Notes, did you ever go out on any tours?

BASSETT: We did a couple. We backed Faye Adams when she had Shake A Hand, and we did a little thing with Lowell Fulson in Richmond, Indiana. I used to go every weekend and play down in Columbus, Ohio. That's where I met Roland Kirk, Rahsaan Roland Kirk, down in Columbus, Ohio. He was playin' in one of the bars like we were playin', where you'd go behind the bar and the bandstand was up behind the bar, you know, and, boy, they'd get you up there—a nightmare gig, man. You'd be up there with all these horns.

SPANGLER: Did you ever play that farm down there in Toledo?

BASSETT: Castle Farms! Yeah, we played there. We came from Kentucky to come to Castle Farms. We had played a VFW Hall up in, I think, Richmond, Kentucky, yeah, something like that, and we came back from Kentucky to Castle Farms.

Our big thing at that time, though, was Honky Tonk, our big instrumental thing. Everybody wanted to hear that, and I taught it to Joe, because I heard it on the radio and went home and then picked it out note for note, and then I went to the record store and bought the record when it came out—I had to wait for it to come in—and then played it for him.

I played along with it and he said, man, how you do that? I said, the way you gonna do it. He said, but that's the organ, man! I said, hey, if you do the bass line, the rest is simple.

So I showed him the bass line, and he finally got the bass line with his left hand. And then I had to make Jesse listen to the horn line and, you know, we studied that record, man, for about three days, and after that—that's all people would want to hear.

We'd play Honky Tonk at the beginning of the night, and at the end, you know, in the clubs, and that was it. That was the big thing. Once people found out we could play Honky Tonk, oh, man, we had more jobs than we could handle. [*Laughter*] Because we was the only band that could play it. We were the only band around town that could play Honky Tonk almost like the record, with a piano. Not too many organs around then.

There was a lot of great stuff happened at Fortune Records, man. Mack Rice went through there for a while and helped the guys out, with material and stuff, and helped coordinate the groups. We went to high school together, man. Mack was always a good writer, good lyric writer.

There was a lot of other little groups around that came through that never got any recognition, because the guys wasn't interested enough to stay together. They'd do some stuff and then, you know, their girlfriends would bind 'em up or whatever, and they wouldn't stay in music.

But the leader thing was—I was always a sideman in most all the organizations. When I came back in '65 I had my own organ group, you know, and I played around the city for a long time. Clarence Price was my organ player—he was a blind organist.

Then I had Benny Baber, he was another organist that I used. And I played with Rudy Robinson and the Hungry Five, I played with Sonny Allen—he's another organ player—and Andy Martin. He was just seventeen when I met him, playin' with Mr Bo.

Were you always listening to jazz as well?

BASSETT: Both, yeah. Yeah. From an early age. I always liked the big bands— that was all there was.

SPANGLER: He got to play with Dinah Washington one weekend.

BASSETT: Yeah, at the Frolic Showbar in Detroit, down on John R, down the street from the Flame. I played at the Frolic after it moved over on John Lodge, too. Don Davis used to be over there. Don and I are good friends, too. We go back a ways. We used to play together, off and on. But he just wasn't interested enough in playing—his thing was in the studio.

He tried to sell me his guitar at the Paradise one time—no, at the Graystone Ballroom once. This was in '55, and I just had bought my Gibson and I said, man, I just got a guitar. He had a Guild, with all those buttons on it and everything, and it frustrated him because he couldn't get the sound he wanted out of it.

He said, man, why don't you buy this one? And I said, man, why didn't you see me two weeks ago? Where were you two weeks ago before I bought this one? I just got this, I'm makin' payments on this thing. So he held on to it for a while. I don't know what he ever did with that guitar, but it was a good guitar. Beautiful. It had more buttons than I wanted—I didn't want it either, you know, I didn't know what to do with all those damn things. I never saw one after that, either. Of course he went to Memphis and he got with Stax and everything, and the rest is history.

So you were in Seattle for the early sixties?

BASSETT: Yeah, '60 to '65, with the Gil Ray combo. We hooked up—he was in the service, he was a sergeant and he had a group and he was in special service. I worked with him until I got out of the service. I met him when I first got to Fort Lewis. That's where we met.

I was just in Detroit to help celebrate the fourth anniversary of Johnnie Bassett & the Blues Insurgents at the Music Menu Cafe. How did you guys hook up?

SPANGLER: I saw Johnnie playing one year at the Montreaux-Detroit Jazz Festival, it must've been 1991, and it was with Ben Baber's organ group. Ben was gonna die of cancer that year, and he had one more shot at Montreaux, so a lot of cats who were interested in organ groups came out to see him.

He says, I'm gonna feature the bluesman in my group. And Johnnie gets out of the back row and he comes up and stands there and plays this slow T-Bone Walker kind of thing, B.B. King, funky blues, and I loved it. I knew [Detroit jazz scholar Jim] Gallert was a pretty good friend of Ben Baber's, so I asked him for Ben's number. And that's it.

We hooked up and we made that tape with [keyboardist Bill] Hyde. See, Hyde was a great Fortune-o-phile, being from Pittsburgh, so I used Bill with Johnnie and he was knocked out and said let's do some stuff. The tape came before the band, really, and then Bill left, so [organist Chris] Codish came into the group to play organ with us full time about five years ago.

This group's been together basically about five years in this incarnation, and we had a solid year or two ahead of that with Scott Peterson on sax and Bill [Heid]. But Bill was always taking off to go to Japan for six months at a time, so Chris came in.

We wanted to build this group up to do something, because we thought we had the potential to go somewhere with it. Mike Boulan bought a tape that I'd gotten from the Montreaux-Detroit Jazz Festival, and he put it out on the No Cover label, and that enabled us to tour Europe for the first time in 1996.

That's the part that's remarkable to me—after all these years you guys were the first ones to really emerge out of Detroit and blaze a trail.

SPANGLER: Yeah, since Little Sonny made his records in the sixties, we're the next group to come along—it's been so long since someone came out of Detroit. There was a big dry spell. We still meet people on the road that ask me how Eddie Burns is, you know, or Little Sonny, around the world, because they were really the last people from Detroit to make a dent out here. What's his name, he's been gone for so long—Eddie Kirkland—he's barely a Detroiter, I guess, although I hear he's spending time there again lately.

So we made the record on No Cover, and we came over here, and while we were here, we made a record for the Black Magic label, and with that record we were able to acquire agents over here, and they've really got us going over here now. We come a couple times, two or three times a year now, and...

BASSETT: This is my fourth trip to Europe with the group, and this is building and building. They want us back over here again, and hopefully we can do it equally as well the next time we come over, you know. It's hard work, but it's fun, you know, and it's a living. [*Laughs*]

I'm hoping to play the North Sea Jazz Festival next year, and I haven't played the King Biscuit Blues Festival yet, and when I make those two then I'll be satisfied.

Utrecht, Nederland
November 22, 1998 /
New Orleans
January 25–26, 1999

"my buddy"
for henry normile

Marcus Belgrave
standing outside the church
in that tan trench coat,

snowflakes dropping softly
into the up-turned bell
of his golden horn,

sending up some beautiful music
into the celestial ears
of our beloved pal,

literally blasted away
just days ago, at cass & willis
by shotgun shells

through the neck, but now
surely resting his weary ass
on a cloudly bed

full of gorgeous angels
busily ministering to his every need
according to his personal creed:

   "cocaine,

           pussy,

                   & lobster,

   in that order"

O Henry, you fucking
candy bar of a man,
you sweet motherfucker,

IT'S ALL GOOD

I can see the big grin
that lights up your angelic face,
digging the lovely sounds of marcus

now as always,
in heaven
as it was on earth,

forever & ever,
amen—my man, a-
fucking men`

snug harbor
frenchmen street, new orleans
september 15, 1993 /

french quarter
new orleans
september 15, 1995

after dr. john,
"my buddy"

BOB RUDNICK

Remembering the Righteous One

GOING TO CHICAGO last September to help celebrate the life and times of the late, great Righteous One—Stanley Bob Rudnick of Pottsville PA, Coral Gables FL, New York City, Detroit, Chicago and the West Coast—felt particularly apt for me, because Bob really gave me what I know of the Windy City and made for me a second home there in the poetry bars and gin mills of the modern era, in what Rudnick always referred to as the city of Nelson Algren.

I go back a long way with the Righteous One—all the way back to the Winter of 1967–68, when I was managing the MC5 in Detroit and Rudnick was music columnist for the *East Village Other* in New York City and founding coordinator of the fledgling Underground Press Syndicate. A devout follower of Lenny Bruce, his lifetime idol and role model, Rudnick hustled his music columns and other demented writings to *Cavalier*, *Circus*, and diverse other large-circulation publications.

I was writing an arts column called 'The Coat Puller' for the *Fifth Estate* in the Motor City and sending out inflammatory press releases detailing the daring exploits of the MC5, who were drawing as much attention from the police and other authorities as they were beginning to win the affections of thousands of alienated post-industrial youths.

My modest writings soon captured the already well-inflamed imagination of the Righteous One and his partner in crime, the young Dennis Frawley. Together they penned the weekly 'Kokaine Karma' column in the *Other* and hosted one of the first truly creative "free-form" radio programs at WFMU-FM, the voice of tiny Upsala College in East Orange, New Jersey.

When we released the MC5's 45 rpm single of Looking At You/Borderline on the A-Square label in the Spring of 1968, Rudnick and Frawley immediately slapped it on the WFMU turntables, where it joined the heady mix of music by Jimi Hendrix, Muddy Waters, John Coltrane, Lenny Bruce, Bob Dylan, Jim Pepper, Larry Coryell and Howlin' Wolf that the two scenesters had devised for their listeners.

Big Apple radio exposure for our single—pressed in an edition of only 500 copies—was combined with almost weekly mentions in the *East Village Other* as part of Rudnick and Frawley's personal crusade to ensure that everyone they knew was aware of the MC5. This resulted in much big-label interest in the band and the particular attention of a young A&R man at Elektra Records named

275

Danny Fields, whose opinion at the label had been held in high esteem ever since he had suggested that Light My Fire be lifted from The Doors first album, edited and issued as a single.

Danny Fields also did an air shift at WFMU following the Kokaine Karma Show on Friday evenings, where Rudnick and Frawley's repeated spins of Looking At You had kindled his interest in the MC5. Bob and Dennis introduced me to Danny one night while I was visiting the station during a typically kamikaze venture into New York City in hopes of landing a record deal for the MC5, and we hit it off at once.

Soon Danny convinced his employers to sign the 5 to an Elektra recording contract and gave us the beginning of our national career, serving unselfishly as my principal mentor and guide through the maze of the music business for the next two years. Danny also got Elektra to sign James "Iggy" Osterberg and the Psychedelic Stooges—the 5's close associates—following Rudnick and Frawley's repeated raves and a trip to Ann Arbor to see the bands in action at a Draft Resistance benefit at the Union Ballroom.

I can't recall the exact date when Bob Rudnick and Dennis Frawley came out to Michigan to join our commune, Trans-Love Energies Unlimited, and take paying jobs at Detroit's first 'underground' radio station, WABX-FM, but I know we were together in Chicago for the Festival of Life at the Democratic National Convention in August 1968, where the MC5 was the only one of the many bands committed to playing that actually performed in Lincoln Park, and they were there for the recording of the MC5's first album, cut live at the Grande Ballroom on October 30–31, 1968.

While Rudnick was in Michigan he helped me with national publicity for the MC5 and generally carried out his duties as Minister of Propaganda for the White Panther Party, furthering the cause of "rock & roll, dope, & fucking in the streets" and "every thing free for every body" which was the unholy mission of the only revolutionary organization in American history to be led by a rock & roll band.

A founding member of the WPP, the Righteous One was with me one ugly evening in the early summer of 1969 when the MC5 dropped the bomb on Jesse "Brother J.C." Crawford and myself, relieving us of our respective responsibilities as road manager/emcee and personal manager. They had decided to pursue a more conventional path to popular music glory than the one they had blazed as founders of the White Panther Party, and the three of us were the first to be cut loose.

The Righteous One was always close at hand to provide genius media manipulation support for my court battles in Detroit in the summer of 1969, and Rudnick's is one of the last faces I saw when the Recorder's Court bailiffs dragged me out of the courtroom into a holding cell to begin serving my nine and a half to ten year sentence for possession of two marijuana cigarettes. Righteous had been closely following the proceedings with a microphone up his sleeve and our first-generation cassette machine strapped to his body, providing the defense with an accurate recording of each day's testimony. At night he would champion my cause on the airways, which soon led to the precipitate departure of Kokaine Karma from WABX in the summer of 1969.

The next two and a half years are a blank to me as far as happenings on the streets are concerned. I was incarcerated in Michigan's maximum security prisons without appeal bond while Rudnick and scores of others worked selflessly upon my behalf to get me out.

When our organization, by now known as the Rainbow People's Party, staged a massive rally and benefit concert at Ann Arbor's Crisler Arena on December 10, 1971, drawing 15,000 marijuana advocates to the University of Michigan campus to demand my release from prison, Rudnick was on stage to host the show and bring on people like John Lennon, Stevie Wonder, Bob Seger, Bobby Seale, Jerry Rubin, Archie Shepp, Commander Cody & the Lost Planet Airmen—sort of a live version of a Rudnick radio program.

The Righteous One and I were together again in Ann Arbor during 1972–73, and for a short, glorious period we were both on the air at WNRZ-FM, spinning out hours of freeform, black music-based programming...until Rudnick reported for his shift one Sunday afternoon in 1973 and phoned to save me a trip out to the station: the new owners had locked the doors and changed the format to country and western music.

While I was in prison Rudnick had established a new base for himself in the Windy City, and for the next few years he went back and forth from Detroit or Ann Arbor to Chicago as events dictated. I called him there one night in 1974 to invite him to join us as house emcee and deejay at the Rainbow Room, a nice little joint in the basement of the Shelby Hotel in downtown Detroit where Rainbow Productions was presenting a continuous blues and jazz festival onstage, featuring artists like Howlin' Wolf, Charles Mingus, Hound Dog Taylor & the Houserockers, Albert Collins, Sun Ra & His Arkestra and Sunnyland Slim. A free room at the hotel was included in the deal, you could sign for your food in the coffee shop, and the lounge in the lobby boasted the Motor City's finest jazz ensemble, the Lyman Woodard Organization, six nights a week.

The Shelby Hotel turned out to be a very interesting place indeed, but—as always—the good times had their limits, and soon we were back in Ann Arbor while John Petrie and Lisa Gottleib ran the nightclub (now called the Savoy Room) until the hotel itself folded in 1975. Rudnick split for Chicago, I moved back to Detroit with my family, and I lost touch with the Righteous One for quite a few years.

One Sunday afternoon in 1986 I accompanied three Detroit-area poets—M.L. Liebler, Errol Henderson, and the late Larry Pike—on a trip to Chicago, where Liebler had promised we would do several poetry performances. After fifteen years as a political and cultural activist in Detroit and Ann Arbor, including three long years in prison, I had returned in 1982 to my original calling as a poet and journalist and had resumed reading my works in public, usually enjoying the musical accompaniment of a band of jazz and blues players I titled the Blues Scholars in honor of the late Professor Longhair's splendid ensemble from New Orleans.

This was my first trip to Chicago as a poet in twenty years, ever since I had performed at the University of Chicago and other venues with Joseph Jarman and his band in the mid sixties, and I was eager to make a good showing. Our first night was a Sunday at No Exit, just around the corner from the Heartland Cafe, and we were scheduled to appear at the Monday night set at Butchie's Get Me High Jazz Lounge, one of Mark Smith's early venues.

When I walked through the door at Butchie's the first face I saw belonged to the Righteous One, who had been lying in wait for me along with my old friend John Petrie. It turned out that both were now poets themselves and would read their works there before the night was over. Rudnick had this particularly great piece about the scene at Butchie's in which he remarked on the practice of charging the poets a dollar to enter and wondered if he could read five poems if he paid $5.00.

Another of Rudnick's striking works in verse was called 'Food Fascists of the North', addressed to his former co-workers at the Heartland Cafe, where this old-school, Lenny Bruce-inspired, hardcore dope fiend and meat eater had labored at constant ideological loggerheads with the resident vegetarians under the employ of our old comrade from Rising Up Angry, Michael James.

Everything I heard Rudnick read that night was bright, well-written verse coming from his own uniquely twisted take on the world and rooted in the particulars of daily life, and my first impression remains true today: Bob Rudnick was a very fine poet with magnetic stage presence and a wildly effective delivery.

He was also in considerable trouble as a person: dodging a narcotics warrant from New Jersey, living off General Assistance and the occasional weird job, drinking too much alcohol, hustling for drugs and living just one step ahead of the game at all times. Bob was rich only in friends and in his own creative potential, which he sold as cheaply as the market demanded.

But his many friends cared about the Righteous One very, very much, and time and time again I was blown away by the depth of devotion and the unconditional love and tolerance evidenced by people in Chicago who took care of Bob in the eighties.

Rudnick's sweep was vast: he hooked up a lot of people, relentlessly but quite unobtrusively, and brought friends together with friends in ways and places that enhanced the lives of all concerned. He stayed connected to our old pals from the sixties who remained active and vital in modern Chicago life—people like Warren Leming, Mike James, Abe Peck, Kate Nolan, Marshall Rosenthal, John Petrie and Skip Williamson—and continued to make and share new friends in the postmodern era, a number of whom have become important persons in my life.

After that night at Butchie's Get Me High Jazz Lounge, Rudnick took over my case in Chicago and arranged appearances for me at a great number of establishments during the next five years, including the Heartland Cafe, Estelle's, L&L Lounge, the first Frankie Machine Festival in Wicker Park, the Green Mill, Links Hall, and my favorite nightspot, Weed's—the world's greatest tavern—where the Righteous One, Sergio Mayora and I conspired to bring poetry to the club in a series of group performances Rudnick called "The Nights of the Cookers".

Rudnick was at his finest as a producer of collaborative poetry events, and his several historic series—like the legendary Literary Bouts (the forerunner of Mike Smith's Poetry Slams), the Erotic Poetry Festivals, the Nights of the Cookers, the tribute to William Burroughs at Lower Links—made important contributions to the development of the contemporary literary scene in the Windy City.

These events brought together a great many disparate poets and presented them intelligently, with great humor, in a dynamic setting. Rudnick was not a person to manage a continuing enterprise, but he was a fantastic starter—he got good things going, and then he stepped out of the way, back into the shadow world where he preferred to live, and let his ideas live on in the work of others too numerous to count.

During the eighties I pursued my calling as a poet and performer in the time I could spare from my duties as a Detroit-based artists manager and booking agent. I was personal manager for a horn-led dance band called the Urbations, which was desirous of entering the Chicago nightclub market, and I importuned Rudnick until he got us our first gig in Chicago (I can't remember the name of the place) and supervised our many subsequent bookings in the Windy City, which took us from Weed's and the Heartland Cafe to the Park West, Biddy Mulligan's, Fitzgerald's, and other finer establishments.

Rudnick was such a beautiful street-level cat from the old school: he knew everybody in every joint in town that was worth a visit, and he reveled in amassing weird groupings of people whose only common contact was Rudnick himself—working out vast details of logistics over the phone, wrestling everyone into vehicles and propeling each small mob from place to place, mixing with the inhabitants, regrouping ("All right," he'd whisper in each person's ear, "we'll be leaving in ten minutes and—let's see—it'll take us exactly twenty four minutes to get there from here"), and lurching off into the night, always unbelievably attentive to every social, sexual, recreational drug and musical need of each member of the party.

By the fall of 1987 things had pretty much bottomed out, each in our own way, for Rudnick and myself. My younger daughter had graduated from high school in Detroit and left to attend college in New Orleans. My companion and I had separated, the band I was working with broke up, leaving me in considerable debt, and I was living alone in a loft in downtown Detroit from which I was about to be evicted.

Rudnick had burned out most of his support network in Chicago and had been offered rent-free lodgings by an old friend in the Motor City who had somehow developed into a low-level slum lord with several properties in the Cass Corridor, a desolate post-industrial wasteland that stretched north from the wreckage of downtown to the campus of Wayne State University.

Rudnick immortalized his first night in the Motor City—October 30, 1987—in a brilliant poem called 'For Gavin Whose Night It Was':

Walking down Woodward at 1:57 a.m.
when Detroit bars close
and no one is on the street
but me—

The wind chilling to the bone like the Hawk,
Chicago's Hawk,
welcomes me to the Murder City
on Devil's Night.

A smell of burning wood in the air
Only a hooker and me witness the burning
pausing paranoid to hear if there are any screams

And from abandoned Victorian townhouses
the cries of copulating cats
echo through the Cass Corridor
bouncing off my consciousness
sounding like the helpless pleas of abused hillbilly children

Tonight is Devil's Night
One thousand nine hundred and eighty-seven years
after the Common Error
even the word Detroit feels cold

And Geraldo Rivera missed an exclusive interview with Jesus
and last call by three minutes and a field goal
Murder in the Motor City is up 10%
Think we'll pass Hank Aaron's home run record
by Christmas

As things started to pick up for both of us—Rudnick energized by the companionship and devotion of a young woman from suburban Detroit named Jenny—we hooked up in Detroit on the poetry issue. First at a place called the Mansion, then at the Union Street Bar, Alvin's Detroit Bar, the City Arts Gallery, 1515 Broadway Theatre and other venues we hosted several well received poetry series showcasing the great contemporary bards of the Motor City: Ron Allen, Mick Vranich, Lolita Hernandez, Trinidad Sanchez, Rayfield Waller, Leslie Reese, Jose Garza, Nubia Kai, Melba Boyd, Glenn Mannisto, Dennis Teichman, George and Chris Tysh and others.

In the fall of 1988 I went to work for the Detroit Council of the Arts, an agency of the City of Detroit, as editor of *City Arts Quarterly* magazine and director of the City Arts Gallery. Rudnick was an important collaborator during this period, always coming up with exciting ideas for fresh presentations and helping bring people together in a common artistic purpose.

At the same time he was living a life of utter penury, staying in crash pads or people's basements and scrambling for what he called "turd money"—enough to put something in his belly to hold the beer, wine and spirits which dwelled there in such abundance. His drug use was cut way down—he'd definitely cop every two weeks, though, when his GA check arrived—and by the time I left Detroit to resettle in New Orleans in the summer of 1991, Bob'd started having trouble with his liver.

During the next four years I'd get calls from the Righteous One in the middle of the night. "This is your rabbi," he'd croak, "Why haven't you called me?" And we'd laugh and carry on like we always did, but his report on what everybody was doing would be laced with horror stories about operations, stays in the hospital, doctors' ultimatums, and the vain hope of a liver transplant.

Things were happening to his body that terrified him, but the desperate, degenerate lifestyle to which he'd been committed for so long wouldn't allow any escape. He shuffled back and forth between friends in suburban Detroit and

IT'S ALL GOOD

hospital beds and borrowed pads in Chicago, still hopeful of getting a new liver, but without the resources to guarantee even his next meal.

In the summer of 1995, by now unable to process what food he did eat, Rudnick checked into the hospital to get his bloated stomach drained, but the swelling wouldn't go away. Then they diagnosed cancer in Bob's pancreas, and we all knew the time of his departure from this earthly plane was nigh upon us. Jo Jaffe and John Petrie rescued the Rud from the dreadful hospice to which he'd been condemned and got him comfortably back into the hospital, where another tirade by his friends resulted in a steady flow of morphine into his veins to ease the pain.

By mid July people were flying in from around the country to hold Bob's hand and say goodbye. Richie Stoneman came out from New York one weekend; Skip Williamson arrived from Marietta, Georgia and stayed by Rud's bed around the clock. When I called one night a week before Bob passed, Skip told me how the Righteous One had scrabbled around the room that afternoon looking for his purported stash: "I know I've got some heroin in here somewhere," he cawed, pawing through toilet paper rolls and discarded tissues. "I love heroin."

So, after twenty five years of half expecting nightly to hear of Rudnick's death from an overdose of drugs, the Righteous One finally passed away, a week short of his fifty third birthday, in the hospital, surrounded by friends, of more or less natural causes—or at least the natural results of his dedicated lifetime of beatnik degeneracy. He lived every minute exactly the way he wanted to until the illness took over his life, and he died as happy a death as anyone could ever have wanted for him.

Now the long night of pain and suffering is over, and the Righteous One is safe in the spirit world. His poems and his many key contributions to the cultural life of our nation in the second half of the twentieth century will live here with us as long as we have breath.

Goodbye, dear friend. We miss you like crazy.

New Orleans
October 21, 1995

"Hold Your Horn High"
("Big Red")

for Ron Redman Gulyas

early sunday afternoon
taking coffee at The Dolphins
& the spring training reports
from the Detroit News on-line,

all of a sudden
I'm at the batting cage
in Royal Oak 20 years ago
with Big Red,

a great big character then in his late 20s
who weighed about 390
& played the tenor saxophone
with the sound of yore

like Coleman Hawkins
& Ben Webster were whispering
in his ear
while he fingered his horn,

Big Red
was a great big crazy motherfucker
who could tell you
the high school & college stats

for all the players
coming up on the Tigers in the spring,
& he still played baseball himself,
semi-pro for a Lansing team,

not the popular Lansing Lug-Nuts
but some obscure outfit
that would pay him a few bucks
to suit up & power a couple of balls

283

IT'S ALL GOOD

out of the park,
& he claimed to be a gypsy
or either related to the little giant
of jazz, Don Redman

& he played anything he wanted
on the tenor saxophone, with a round
warm sound
that was always good to hear

but his weight would go up &
down the scale
from 390 to 210
& then back up again—

Big Red,
my man,
he backed me up so many times
& played with so much feeling

& in the early '90s
he fled the United States
& roosted in Budapest
for a few years

& had a ball playing his horn
& digging his gypsy roots,
calling himself "Ron Goulash"
like the Hungarian stew

& why he ever came back
will never be known
but he passed in East Lansing
just before Christmas of 2005—

Big Red,
hold your horn high,
let us hear your raspy breath,
my brother, just one more time

the dolphins, amsterdam
march 19, 2006 /
rochester ny ,
january 18, 2007

MASTERS OF WAR

WAR IS never something to be proud of, but an unprovoked war of brutal aggression to seize and control the resources of a small, defenseless nation halfway around the world from the United States is particularly shameful.

While it was extremely painful to witness the merciless bombing of Afghanistan to drive out of power our former allies, the Taliban government (remember the "heroic Islamic freedom fighters" of the 1980s?), our nation's blitzkrieg assault on Iraq heralds a new era of American imperial atrocities of frightening proportions.

But of course our populace doesn't remember the heroic Islamic freedom fighters of Afghanistan. Allen Ginsberg said, "the name of yesterday's newspaper is amnesia," and the war in Iraq revealed that nearly three of every four Americans had come to believe that Saddam Hussein had ordered the airstrikes on the World Trade Center and the Pentagon just a short year and a half ago.

Forgotten also has been the fact that our military establishment supported and helped arm Iraq in its eight-year war against Iran not so long ago.

This is madness, for sure, but it is also a precise measurement of the degree to which our citizenry has been successfully dummied down by the relentless, decades-long attack of the wholly compromised news media and the mass entertainment corporations that own them.

Now it's "America At War", "Operation Iraqi Freedom", "Homeland Security", "Shock and Awe", page after page and hour after hour of disgusting pro-war propaganda building public support for the bully boy adventures of our illegitimate president.

With its ducks all lined up in a row following the Bush *putsch* of November 2000 and the Republican Party takeover of the House and Senate in the disgraceful 2002 elections, the ugly cabal of unbridled greedheads who rule our social order is now determined to install its long anticipated New World Order.

The regime change in the United States engineered by Karl Rove, Richard Cheney, Donald Rumsfeld, Condoleeza Rice, Paul Wolfowitz, Chief Justice William Renquist and their henchmen proceeded so smoothly and with so little protest from the electorate that foreign conquest by their smash-and-grab tactics seems easy—and they're going for it in a big way.

So pay close attention, ladies and g's, because the nightmare has only started. The meanness and unmitigated greed which for so many people around the world have for so long characterized the American spirit are now unleashed and will soon be functioning at full force.

It's time to stand up and be counted in opposition or stand by and watch the imperial juggernaut steamroller everything we hold sacred.

Chicago
April 20, 2003

285

"Fat Boy"

for Charles Moore

There is something
about the American
mind

set on de-
struction, re-
lent-

less, un-
penitent,
eager to bomb.

There is the hatred
that fuels the A-
merican mind,

the shriveled-up
heart
the heartless

always ready
to kill
& maim

brutal
with the urge
to crush & destroy—

This is where
they built Fat Man, Mr. U-
235

& they sent
Fat Man
& Little Boy

to Japan
to level Hiroshima
& Nagasaki—

They love Fat Boy
They feed him the sweets
of their hearts

singing their filthy songs
into Fat Boy's u-
ranium ears

& let the rest of us
eat the shit
of their hatred

of anything
or anyone
that is *not them*—

Ah! Fat Boy
so round & ugly
so full of hate

stuffed
with the dead spirits
of the Americans

blinded
& lost
in the deserts of Iraq

Detroit
April 9 > June 1, 1982 /

Flint
April 4, 2003 /

Detroit
June 9, 2003

Music by Fats Navarro

MOVING TOGETHER

TO EFFECT a change of direction in the perilous course upon which our sorry nation is now embarked may seem a difficult—even hopeless—task, and the problem is so vast that it's hard to know just where to begin.

But mass movements sprout from the efforts of singular individuals or isolated handfuls of people who come together to make social change when they can no longer stand the way things are.

When disgusted Americans rose up in the 1960s to demand an end to the war in Vietnam and the institution of racial, sexual and economic equality for all citizens, we were driven by deep feelings of revulsion for what our country had become and the conviction that it was our personal responsibility to change the way things were.

Then as now, the radical right and its corporate superstructure had established what they believed would be a changeless system of exploitation and control that would allow them to loot and plunder the populace without effective opposition.

But this social fabric began slowly to unravel as small oppositional groups started to cohere and take concerted action in support of their needs and beliefs.

The civil rights struggle was touched off when a singular individual in Montgomery, Alabama named Rosa Parks—inspired by the teachings of Rev. Martin Luther King—refused to move to the colored section in the back of the bus, and it grew into a massive movement that won the support of millions of Americans.

When the military-industrial complex decided to wage war on a tiny nation of rice farmers called the Democratic Republic of Vietnam, they were severely shocked when one, then two, then dozens, scores, hundreds and thousands of young Americans refused to serve in the armed forces. And they were ultimately defeated after public opposition to the war spread from tiny collectives of students and intellectuals to the very mainstream of American society.

On the cultural front, who could have known what would follow when Little Richard screamed out Tutti Frutti, Chuck Berry hit with Maybellene and Bo Diddley proclaimed I'm A Man? When Allen Ginsberg howled "I saw the best minds of my generation destroyed by madness" and Jack Kerouac celebrated the ecstasies and adventures to be discovered *On The Road*? When Bob Dylan sang The Times They Are A-Changing and the Beatles urged us to "turn off your minds, relax and float downstream"?

America was humming along on whiskey, beer and prescription narcotics when young people began to discover by ones and twos the mental benefits and sensual joys of smoking marijuana and turned on the populace one person at a time. Then Tim Leary and Richard Alpert revealed the amazing results of their early experiments with LSD and blew the minds of millions.

The truth is that we can move as far as our imaginations will take us. We can turn our backs on popular entertainment, shut off our television sets and make and enjoy art and creative activity of the highest order.

In fact, we can insist upon and institute in our own lives a culture of humanism and creative intelligence. We can inspire others by example and spread the word through astute use of the communications media available to us in our homes, studios and workplaces.

What follows are a few pointers from back in the glorious days of cultural upheaval and political protest that you may find useful:

❑ Live your life according to your own principles and beliefs. Refuse to be a working part of the imperialist paradigm and, in the immortal words of the late Dr Timothy Leary, "Turn on…Tune in…Drop Out". Once you take the vow of poverty, you'll be free to engage in any sort of creative activity you may imagine and make it the central force in your life.

❑ Develop organic affinity groups among friends and co-workers who share your outlook. Pool your human resources, rent a big house, share the economic burden and live and work together collectively.

❑ Choose your work and your targets with great care. Be clear in your heart and mind and clear in your slogans and pronouncements so that your fellow citizens may be able to understand and support you.

❑ Never forget, as Che Guevara taught us, that the true revolutionary is guided by great feelings of love and shape your activity accordingly. Never allow yourself to be reduced to the base moral level of your oppressors.

❑ Always remember that "a revolution is not a dinner party", as Chairman Mao pointed out. Serious consequences beyond your control— beatings, arrest, jail, felony prosecution, prison time—may result from oppositional political activities. The more extreme your actions, or the more successful your efforts at organizing resistance, the more vicious the official reaction is likely to be.

❑   In political action as in life itself, we must always remain flexible and we must retain our sense of humor. There's nothing wrong with having our fun in whatever circumstances we may find ourselves, and if you can't enjoy yourself in the pursuit of your goals, you've probably chosen the wrong path.

❑   Finally, whatever you do to express your beliefs in the months before the presidential election, be sure to get yourself and everyone you know to the polls on November 2 and cast your votes against George W. Bush. This is where democracy begins.

Detroit
May 17–20, 2004

IT'S ALL GOOD

for Michael Veling & the 420 Café

When you go to the Cannabis Cup
in Amsterdam
They got people coming there
from all over the world
to check out the finest marijuana
grown by the seed companies of Holland

for us to smoke
& get high
& enjoy the wonderful atmosphere
of a society
where people just don't care
if you wanna get high—

Hey,
that's just fine,
c'mon over here to the coffeeshop
& order up whatever kind of weed
or hash you might wanna smoke
because it's all good—

       It's All Good
       It's All Good
       It's All Good
       It's All Good

And by the end of the week
they gonna pick the finest marijuana
that's been submitted
for the testing
of the exalted panel of judges
here at the Cannabis Cup

& guess what? While we're smoking
all those different kinds of weed
& trying to figure out
which one is gonna win the Cup,
every different brand we try
is gonna be the BOMB
because it's all good—

       It's All Good
       It's All Good
       It's All Good
       It's All Good

But when we get back to the United States
it ain't gonna be nothing like this.
In the United States
it ain't nothing nice
because they got a war on people like us—
They call it the War on Drugs

But they don't give a fuck about drugs,
'cuz if you got a prescription
you can get just as loaded
as any human being
has ever been
on the planet Earth—

They just don't like us getting high
on marijuana
or cocaine
or whatever we might want to use
to effect a certain change
in our consciousness.

Now, I like to get high.
I'm not gonna make any bones about it.
I like to get high, & you know
whatever I like to get high on,
I believe I have a right to do this—
& you too,

& everybody in our society.
Because people want drugs.
They want to get high.
People have been getting high
ever since there's been people.
They've been fucking,

they've been getting high
& they've been buying some pussy,
you know. These things
have been going on
& they will continue to go on
because that's all good.

So to keep us
from getting high
like we are today
here in Amsterdam
at the Cannabis Cup
They got police—

They got so many police
you couldn't even believe it.
They got electronical equipment,
They got helicopters,
They got exotic chemicals
killing the shit off in the fields,

They got people going out
all over South America
& Asia
& all over the world
trying to keep this shit from getting
to the United States,

& when it finally does get here,
you got to pay so much money for it
that it's about to drive you crazy—
& that's another thing,
they ain't got nothing for people like us
in terms of money—

if you're an artist
or a poet
or an authentical musician
they ain't got a motherfucking thing for you
except the War on Drugs
& a whole bunch of police,

undercover agents,
rat bastards & snitches,
narco terrorists,
they got motherfuckers coming through your front window
with guns in their hands
& they wrong for that—

Because the war on drugs
is about building a police state.
The war on drugs
is about building prisons
& filling them up
with more & more people like us

& employing more guards,
employing more cops,
more special agents,
more narcotics police,
more wire-tappers,
more snitches,

more prosecutors,
more judges,
more wardens,
more jailers—
the worst elements
of our society.

Now they got 2,000,000 people
locked up in penitentiaries
in the United States
& 8 out of every 10 of them
are prisoners
of the War on Drugs.

But then there's the way
they've inflated the cost of things:
What you could buy for 10 dollars in 1973,
now you got to pay $100. You got to hustle
10 times as hard today
than you did 30 years ago

& you're a lot older now,
& they won't let you have a job
without a motherfucking drug test
& you're living by your wits
& you're still trying to figure out
how to get some money

without *having* a job, but everything costs
10 times as much. That's severe.
And that's one more reason why
we wanna have some drugs—
we're out here living by our wits,
& our heads are sore. We want to get home at night

& put something in our heads, or get up in the morning
& put something in our heads. We don't know
what we're going to have to face
out in these streets that day,
& we need a little something
to help us get high—

Like everybody here
at the Cannabis Cup
in Amsterdam
smoking that reefer
& having a good time.
because it's all good—

        It's All Good
        It's All Good
        It's All Good
        It's All Good

So we gonna forget about America
& enjoy ourselves here
at the Cannabis Cup
all week long
& on Thanksgiving Day
when they announce

who grew the best pot
for us to smoke
& get high on
Let's give thanks
for every strain of weed
that's made its way here to us

IT'S ALL GOOD

With special appreciation
for all the growers of marijuana
all over the world
& our intrepid comrades
who risk life & limb to supply us
with the substances we require

& all the warriors doing time
in the vast penitentiaries of America
as prisoners of the War on Drugs—
We salute you all
& thank you once again
for all the good you have done

   Because it's all good—
   It's All Good
   It's All Good
   It's All Good
   It's All Good
   It's All Good

New Orleans
November 8–15, 1998 /
Detroit
May 29, 2003 /
Detroit
October 20, 2008

IT'S ALL GOOD
A John Sinclair Reader

CD PROGRAM

[01] **friday the 13th** (John Sinclair/Wayne Kramer) with Wayne Kramer (3:39)

[02] **Consequences > Blues to You** (John Sinclair/Wayne Kramer–arr. Charles Moore) with Wayne Kramer & the Blues Scholars (8:17)

[03] **Ain't Nobody's Bizness** (John Sinclair/Wayne Kramer) with Wayne Kramer & the Blues Scholars (3:57)

[04] **everything happens to me** (John Sinclair/Jeff Grand) with Jeff Grand & the Motor City Blues Scholars (4:29)

[05] **in walked bud** (John Sinclair) (5:34)

[06] **brilliant corners** (John Sinclair/Mark Ritsema) with Mark Ritsema (11:00)

[07] **Fattening Frogs For Snakes** (John Sinclair/arr. Bill Lynn) with the New Orleans Blues Scholars (7:17)

[08] **We Just Change the Beat** (John Sinclair/Bill Lynn) with the New Orleans Blues Scholars (2:27)

[09] **Spiritual** (John Sinclair/arr. Marion Brown) with Marion Brown (2:27)

[10] **monk's dream** (John Sinclair/Thelonious Monk–Thelonious Music, BMI) with Luis Resto (4:08)

[11] **My Buddy** (John Sinclair/Jeff Grand) with Jeff Grand & the Blues Scholars (6:10)

[12] **Fat Boy** (John Sinclair/Johnny Evans) with the Motor City Blues Scholars (6:12)

[13] **It's All Good (Radio Mix)** (John Sinclair/Langefrans-Baas B) with Langefrans & Baas B (4:39)

PRODUCED BY JOHN SINCLAIR

All selections published by Pretty Big Chief Music (ASCAP) unless otherwise noted.

IT'S ALL GOOD

John Sinclair, voice with:

[01]   Wayne Kramer, guitar, with bass and drums (1994). Produced by Wayne Kramer and John Sinclair. From the Alive Records 10" LP *Friday the 13th*.

[02]   Wayne Kramer, guitar; Paul Ill, bass; Michael Voelker, drums; Charles Moore, trumpet; Ralph "Buzzy" Jones, tenor saxophone; Craig Stewart, alto saxophone. Recorded live at KXLU-FM, Los Angeles, August 1987. From the SpyBoy Records album *Underground Issues*.

[03]   Wayne Kramer, guitar; Paul Ill, bass; Michael Voelker, drums; Charles Moore, trumpet; Ralph "Buzzy" Jones, tenor saxophone; Craig Stewart, alto saxophone; Phil Ranelin, trombone. Recorded in Los Angeles, August 1996. Produced by Wayne Kramer and John Sinclair. From the Alive Records CD *Full Circle*.

[04]   Jeff Grand, guitar; Chris Rumel, bass; Martin "Tino" Gross, drums; Vickie Alexander, baritone saxophone; Phil Hale, keyboards. Recorded live at the Detroit International Jazz Festival, September 2006. Previously unissued.

[05]   Recorded at Chez Flames, New Orleans (1994). From the New Alliance Records CD *thelonious: a book of monk—volume one*.

[06]   Mark Ritsema, guitar and percussions. Recorded with Clay Windham at Easter Hill Studios, Amsterdam Zuidoost, January 2005. From the Big Chief Records CD *criss cross*.

[07]   Bill Lynn, guitar; Kirk Joseph, Sousaphone; Michael Voelker, drums; Rockin' Jake, harmonica. Recorded live at Howlin' Wolf, New Orleans, March 2000. From the SpyBoy Records CD *Underground Issues*.

[08]   Jeff Grand, Everette Eglin, Bill Lynn, guitars; Mark Bingham, bass; Michael Voelker, drums; ELS, backing vocals. Produced by Andre Williams. Recorded in New Orleans in February 2001. From the Okra-Tone Records CD *The Delta Sound*.

[09]   Marion Brown, alto saxophone. Recorded live at the Louisiana Music Factory, New Orleans, February 1992. From the WWOZ CD *Smokin': The Sounds of New Orleans, Volume Two*.

[10]   Luis Resto, piano; Paul Nowinski, bass. Recorded in Ferndale MI, October 2007. Produced by Don Was for the Wasmopolitan website at www.mydamnchannel.com

[11]   Jeff Grand, Everette Eglin, guitars; Michael Voelker, drums. Recorded live at the Louisiana Music Factory, New Orleans, February 2001. Previously unissued.

[12]   Johnny Evans, tenor saxophone; Chris Rumel, bass; Martin "Tino" Gross, drums. Recorded live at WDET-FM, Detroit, July 31, 2005. Previously unissued.

[13]   Langefrans & Baas B, vocals, music tracks, production. Recorded at D-Men Studio, Diemen, Nederland, November 2002. From the 420 Café CD *Knockout!*

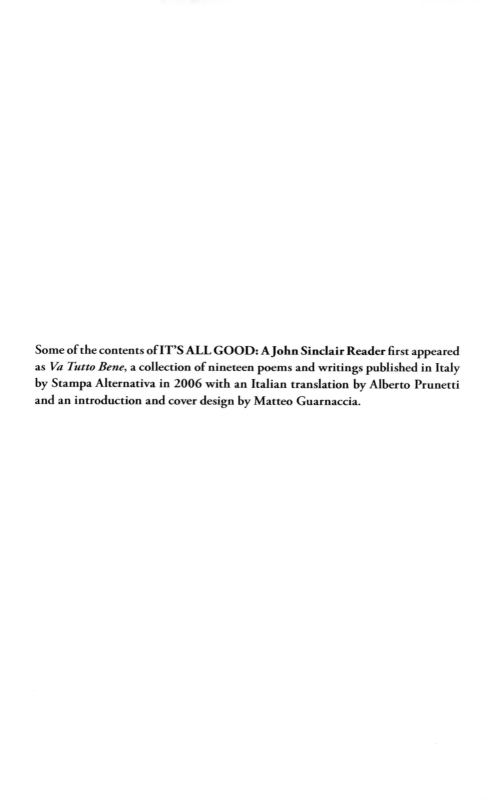

Some of the contents of IT'S ALL GOOD: A John Sinclair Reader first appeared as *Va Tutto Bene*, a collection of nineteen poems and writings published in Italy by Stampa Alternativa in 2006 with an Italian translation by Alberto Prunetti and an introduction and cover design by Matteo Guarnaccia.

HEADPRESS PRODUCT

Headpress28

*Mardi Gras John Sinclair Guanajuato, Mexico
Bangkok Diamanda Galás Third World War
the gospel according to unpopular culture an anthology*

HEADPRESS 28
The Gospel according to Unpopular Culture: *an anthology*

Edited by John Sinclair, HEADPRESS 28 marks the fortieth anniversary of the original White Panthers movement and heralds the launch of the "HEADPRESS PANTHERS," which celebrates the union with historical counterculture figure, social reformer and living legend, John Sinclair, to spread "THE GOSPEL ACCORDING TO UNPOPULAR CULTURE," thus promoting free speech through independent writing and art without boundaries.

"Particularly bizarre, disturbing and sometimes delightful" **Time Out**

"Pushing all the right buttons on the wrong people" **Dazed and Confused**

144 pages + 16 colour plates // UK £10.99

CHELSEA HOTEL MANHATTAN

BY JOE AMBROSE. Every room tells its own story:
Andy Warhol shot Chelsea Girls there, Sid Vicious
stabbed Nancy Spungeon there, and welsh poet
Dylan Thomas died there, having reputedly inspired
the young Zimmerman to change his name to
Bob Dylan, before falling into a fatal coma having
downed eighteen whiskies in a row in room 100.
This is the first factual book on the building. It
has conversations with William Burroughs, Paul
Bowles, Gerard Malanga and Victor Bockris, and
contributions from Gary Panter, Barry Miles, Ira
Cohen and Herbert Huncke.

"Let me assure you, as someone who knows about
these things, that if you took half the 'shits' and
'fucks' out of that book, you'd sell twice as many
copies" **Joe's mother, Mai Ambrose**

192 pages, fully illustrated // £11.99

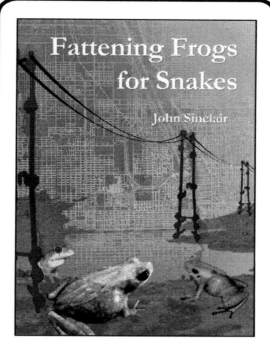

www.headpress.com

A Headpress Book
First published in 2008

Headpress
Suite 306, The Colourworks
2a Abbot Street
London, E8 3DP, United Kingdom

Tel: 0845 330 1844
Email: office@headpress.com
Web: www.headpress.com

IT'S ALL GOOD: A John Sinclair Reader

Text copyright © **Mr John Sinclair**
This volume copyright © 2008 Headpress
Design and layout: **stevewillard.co.uk**
Cover art: **Mr Cian O'Neill** / Cover design: **Mr Joe Scott Wilson**
Marketing & sales: **Ms Bianca Nicholls** & **Ms Shelley Lang**
All photos © **Ms Leni Sinclair**
Proofing: **Ms Jennifer Wallis**
Operations: **Mr Caleb Selah** & **Mr Dylan Harding**
John Sinclair lyric © John Lennon Northern Songs Ltd., 1971

British Library Cataloguing in Publication Data
A catalogue record for this book is
available from the British Library

ISBN 9781900486682